Management
for the 1980s

WILLIAM F. CHRISTOPHER

A SPECTRUM BOOK

Prentice-Hall, Inc., *Englewood Cliffs, New Jersey 07632*

59085

Library of Congress Cataloging in Publication Data

Christopher, William F
  Management for the 1980s.

  (A Spectrum Book)
  Edition of 1974 published under title: The achieving
enterprise.
  Includes index.
  1. Industrial management.   I. Title.
HD31.C525 1980   658.4   79-19536
ISBN 0-13-549154-1

*To John, Lani Lynne, and Justin; to Kent and Janet; and to June
with all my best wishes
as they continue to find their ways toward tomorrow*

Revised edition: 1980
©1980, 1974 AMACOM, a division of American Management Associations, New York. All
rights reserved.

This new Spectrum edition is published in arrangement with AMACOM and is a complete
and revised edition of the hardcover edition entitled *The Achieving Enterprise.*

Clothbound editions of this book are available from AMACOM, 135 West 50th Street,
York City, NY 10020.

A SPECTRUM BOOK

10 9 8 7 6 5 4 3 2 1

Printed in the United States of America

Editorial/production supervision by Betty Neville
Cover design by Tony Ferrara Studio Inc.
Manufacturing buyer: Cathie Lenard

PRENTICE-HALL INTERNATIONAL, INC., *London*
PRENTICE-HALL OF AUSTRALIA PTY. LIMITED, *Sydney*
PRENTICE-HALL OF CANADA, LTD., *Toronto*
PRENTICE-HALL OF INDIA PRIVATE LIMITED, *New Delhi*
PRENTICE-HALL OF JAPAN, INC., *Tokyo*
PRENTICE-HALL OF SOUTHEAST ASIA PTE. LTD., *Singapore*
WHITEHALL BOOKS LIMITED, *Wellington, New Zealand*

Contents

iii

Preface

High levels of achievement and exciting success for business enterprises in many countries have been attained through the concepts and the methods described in this book. They have been used by business people of many nationalities and differing cultures to resolve tough business problems, and to identify and develop opportunities. So this book is neither American nor European, Western nor Eastern. Its origins lie in many countries and many experiences. It is not so much a "how to" recipe book that lays out steps 1, 2, 3, 4 on a road to success as it is a conceptual book that lays out an approach we can use for finding and developing our future. Although it is based on past experience and learning, it is not so much *from* the past as it is *for* the future. It is contemporary rather than traditional, innovational rather than conventional. It is an immensely practical approach to the world of today and tomorrow, well validated by the successes it has created.

The concepts and methods described are not my original ideas or those of the companies I have worked with in developing and applying them, but their totality may be quite original. For this book synthesizes many contemporary concepts and approaches into a new systems concept of business management. It replaces scrutiny of the past with perception of the future. It helps each unit and each enterprise to understand not only what it is today but to determine what it will become tomorrow. It focuses on individual and organizational achievement as the motive force of enterprise. The technology of business science combines with the humanism of achievement to create the achieving enterprise.

The conceptual approach reported is not simply an account of the evolutionary development of business management; it is a restructuring of past experience and learning into new patterns of management for today's world. Learning is not a one-shot affair. My own formal education was interrupted by

v

five years of military service, and has been followed by more than thirty years of business experience. Today I still use some of the economics, some of the history, some of the science, some of the mathematics from college and university days. But most of what I use today comes from experience and continued learning. The professional in business as in other fields must continue to learn—each year more than the year before. He has, really, three full-time jobs—he must learn, he must teach, and he must do. But all three interrelate and interact as we find our way toward tomorrow.

Of my years of business management experience, thirteen were with the General Electric Company, seventeen with Hooker Chemical Corporation, which since 1968 has been a subsidiary of Occidental Petroleum Corporation, and currently I head my own consulting firm counseling managements on the concepts and methods described in this book. In all this professional experience I have worked with more than fifty businesses, in fifteen countries. The overseas examples cited in this book are from my experience with Hooker subsidiaries, joint ventures, and licensee companies. In all the businesses I have worked with we have resolved many problems, achieved many successes. We have made mistakes, too, and experienced failures. We have learned from both failure and success. What we have found to be most productive has gone into this book. We have experienced the motivation that can come from missions participatively developed and carried forward in a supportive way, with high expectations for performance. We have found that objectives in the key performance areas that determine business success can provide direction and a feedback reporting system far more effective than financial budgets and control reports. The organization improves, and so do the financial results.

Many outstanding professionals have worked with us and contributed to the idea system described in the following pages. I would like especially to acknowledge:

For business strategy: Bruce Henderson and Alan Zakon of the Boston Consulting Group; Stafford Beer, writer and consultant; Paul Rubinyi, partner, Ernst & Whinney; H. Igor Ansoff, Vanderbilt University; E. B. Reynolds, consultant; George Kozmetsky, The University of Texas Graduate School of Business.

For marketing concepts: Theodore Levitt, Graduate School of Business Administration, Harvard University; Howard Berrian, consultant.

For motivation and organization development: Saul Gellerman, consultant; John Drake, Drake-Beam & Associates; Gordon Lippitt, George Washington University.

For managerial economics: Douglas P. Gould and Robert Trundle of Trundle Consultants Inc.; Jules Backman, New York University College of Business and Public Administration; Albert J. Bergfeld, Case and Company Inc. Management Consultants; Joel Dean, Columbia University Graduate School of Business; John W. Kendrick, George Washington University.

For futures studies: James R. Bright, President, Industrial Management Center; John Platt, Mental Health Research Institute, The University of Michigan; Ian H. Wilson, General Electric Company; W. W. Simmons, planning consultant; Jay S. Mendell, Florida Atlantic University; Robert Theobald, writer, lecturer.

The ideas in this book flow from all of these, from the creative pioneers whose work is cited throughout the text, and from the work of many achieving individuals in the companies I have worked with. I cannot list them all. They include such leaders as René Rochat, Marius Danemark, and Antoine Savary in Geneva; Dennis Weimer and John Carder in the United Kingdom; Pablo Weinberg in Buenos Aires; João Marcos Simões, Gabor Hevesi, and Aziz Elias in Brazil; Victor Eraña in Mexico; Yukichi Nanjo in Tokyo; and Jack Coey, Bill Wetzel, Frank Hendricks, and John Lenahan in the United States. All have contributed to the concepts described in this book and have supported the development of them in the groups they lead. Many others in company operations have contributed to, developed, and applied the concepts described and the specific techniques illustrated. And once these were down on paper, Diana Faighes efficiently got them into final manuscript form.

So this book, like the conceptual approach described in it, is the work of many. It is an integration of many disciplines, many talents, many achievements. What it all adds up to I have seen bring remarkable achievement to business enterprise. I hope it may be of value to others. And I hope the book will encourage further creative strides toward a normative, human, achieving future for business enterprise.

1
What's New?

A new world comes to us each morning when the alarm rings. True, it looks very much like the old one we lived in yesterday, but the similarity lies more in the way we see things than in the way things really are. From our experiences we invent the world we see and understand, and our creativity in making our invention fit the world around us is an artistic marvel. Of course, we do have to make slight changes in our invention from time to time when the actual world becomes so different from the way we "see" it that we just can't make the two conform to each other. So we make changes when we must, usually while deploring the deterioration from "the way things used to be."

For many of us, our security in the midst of change has rested on our invention of the past—our image of the world as we wish it to be. Then when we say, "Good morning, World," we're greeting the same old friend who was with us yesterday and the day before and will be with us tomorrow also.

This book is not for inventors of the past, but for inventors of the future. More specifically it is for inventors of the future for their business enterprises, or for the parts of the business enterprises in which they work. Many of the ideas will apply to other kinds of institutions as well and to other areas of human effort. We will not be backing into the future with our eyes searching the past for that which we wish to see there. We will be striding into the future openly searching for reality and relating that reality to our goals.

The question "What's new?" will be a constant question to help us see and understand the change around us. We will also ask "What can be new?" to help us read the future and help us establish goals. For the future of our business enterprise will depend on achievement, and that will depend on how we select our goals and set our course to achieve them. All must relate to the world as it really is. We cannot build tomorrow's success on an invention of yesterday.

1

So what's new? We can begin with:

Values. Values determine needs, and needs determine goals. That's where our business enterprise operates—at the level of needs and goals. We serve needs, and our organizational goals will necessarily relate to human goals—all flowing from a common value system.

Technology. Technology extends our competence to serve needs. It may not do so, but it can. And in today's complex world significant new technology may be essential for coping with our problems, even continuing our existence.

Human nature. Many anthropologists contend that our traits are little changed from those of the Paleolithic hunter of 50,000 years ago or the Neolithic farmer of 10,000 years ago. But human natures by the dozen can be very different from human natures by the million. And how human nature behaves in its now and future environment will have an impact on how we work in our business enterprises.

Environment. One crisis replaces another on the stage of popular attention. Since the early sixties ecology has moved front and center, and it promises to remain among our crisis problems. Maintaining rather than exploiting our natural environment has become an objective of business enterprise in cooperation with government and other organizations.

Business. Amid change, business enterprise itself changes, but only with pain and difficulty. We carry with us for too long the wisdom of history. Old solutions may not be applicable to the complex problems we now face; new ways too are known and tested. From all that is now available to us, and with that which can help us learn as we go along, we can create an exciting future of achievement for our business enterprises.

Values

Among students of change there is growing consensus that the world may be in the midst of one of the resocializing upheavals that have shaped the epochs of man's history. Certainly we are now seeing more changes in a given time than ever before. Whether that represents a continuing process of evolutionary development proceeding at an exponential rate or a sudden restructuring in a short time is yet to be known. If the former is true, the extrapolist of present trends finds man's near future to be one of chaos and catastrophe. If a restructuring is taking place, a new order will appear. In either case a humanist philosopher would see an opportunity for man: if living in the extrapolated world, realized only with the greatest of difficulty; if living in a time of societal restructuring, realized almost certainly. In either case, however, values just won't stay the same. Values determine needs; needs determine goals; needs and goals together determine the function and the future of our business enterprises.

An extrapolated future of overpopulation, resource depletion, failure of energy supplies, lethal pollution, and insufficient food production appears all too possible unless trends developed over decades can be checked quickly. However, enough work has been done by futurists in normative forecasting and scenario construction to validate the probability that the future can and probably will be different from the extrapolated one.

Then what of a restructuring, a discontinuous and rapid change from the past? That concept has been explored by Teilhard de Chardin, Kenneth Boulding, John McHale, Robert Theobald, Elisabeth Mann Borgese, René Dubos, and John Platt. In the concept of hierarchical growth as described by John Platt physical and social structures are not discrete things or particular events but are flow patterns.[1] The fundamental patterns are assembled in a hierarchy of larger but less stable ones—particles, chemical molecules, living cells, fauna, social networks, nations. All are more or less self-repeating even though energy, matter, and information continually flow through them. Such flow patterns, if we can think of familiar physical and social structures in those terms, can move through rather sudden transitions to new arrangements. Such changes reorder predecessor systems into new and viable systems. Hierarchical growth occurs in small systems as well as large. It can occur within a family, a community, a nation, or the world; within a unit, a company, or an industry. Within the flow system of business enterprise we can identify many examples of restructuring: pyramidal organization structure, scientific management, human relations, budgetary control, automation, decentralization, multinationalization, management science, motivation theory and organization development, and free-form organization.

The preceding list, arranged in approximate chronological order, includes hierarchical change with which we are familiar from the past, and contemporary change which may be occurring and is not fully known or understood. Evolutionary change continues always. Intermittent, hierarchical change happens with an accumulation of circumstances. We are comfortable with evolutionary change, for we are improving something with which we are already familiar. We are usually quite uncomfortable with the possibility of hierarchical change because we don't know what the new order will be. Hierarchical change in the past, however, seems quite all right. That we know and understand. The point is that we can have an open, friendly attitude toward hierarchical change—as we have learned to have toward evolutionary change—if we recognize the process. We may not only learn to tolerate such change but also learn to use it and encourage it. Not only can we develop; we can also change.

Platt identifies five common features of hierarchical growth, wherever and whenever it occurs, whatever the scale or degree of change:[2]

1. *Increasing dissonance, incongruity, friction within the existing structure.* This is easily seen in science, where increasing dissonance always precedes scientific revolution. Data that do not fit the existing system will be observed. They may be explained away as random or as errors of measurement, but new and

---

[1]"Hierarchical Growth," *Bulletin of the Atomic Scientists*, November 1970.
[2]Ibid., p. 4.

still more divergent data appear. Unresolved problems accumulate. The old system increasingly becomes a turmoil of incongruity. Reconciliation is attempted; new proposals are brought forward. Finally, from a whole new point of view a new integrating theory that restructures all past knowledge and information into a new system is formulated. Everything fits. It is all reordered into something different from what it was.

A similar process is seen in hierarchical change in personality (as from a psychotic state to mental health), in social systems (as when, in the American revolution, deteriorating institutions were replaced by a young, vital republic), and in our business enterprises (as when applied motivation theory and organization development revitalize and redirect a large company).

2. *Broad effect.* A second characteristic of hierarchical jumps is the broad, all-encompassing nature of the accumulating dissonance and the resulting structural change. Dissonance appears in a diversity that has no ready explanation; then all is swept together and reintegrated in the transformation. In our business affairs we may miss opportunity for growth by an unawareness of that concept. Dissonance in the shape of problems appears, and we solve the problems one by one. But often the solutions don't really work, or they conflict with one another. Perhaps if we could identify a system of problems, we could effect a hierarchical restructuring that would eliminate all the problems. For example, the diverse problems of management control might be restructured into a new system created by applying management science and motivation theory.

3. *Suddenness.* Evolution takes time. And in the long run it may be fatal—for a principle of evolution is that the evolving organism or system becomes more and more specialized until finally it becomes extinct in favor of better-adapting successors. Hierarchical change interrupts evolution and starts the process anew from a less specialized starting point. When it happens, it can be very swift; it has been prepared for by the broadly developing dissonance. When a restructuring to a new system is found, the subsystems are ready for it, want it, need it.

4. *Simplification.* Scientific revolutions create simpler and more general explanations. $E = mc^2$ explains more and predicts more than all the accumulated literature of classical mechanics. Money was a vast simplification over barter, computers a vast simplification over manual data processing. Civilization as well as science can be seen as a competition between accumulating complexity (dissonance) and its simplification through hierarchical change.

5. *Experimental subsystem interaction.* As the new supersystem is being formed, there may be interactions of subsystems with potential system patterns. For example, to resolve the increasing dissonance of national interests, international cooperation and forms of world government may be encouraged by subsystem interactions at the international level such as tourism, student exchanges, the multinational corporation, world aviation, international professional organizations, international trade, codes of common practice, and satellite TV. In a business organization, increasing dissonance may impel managers and profes-

sionals to go over the boss's head or outside company policy to seek solutions until all is brought together again in a hierarchical jump to a new order of organization, function, and purpose acceptable to the enterprise. The new system may be largely the result of the experimental interactions impelled by the dissonance, or, of course, the dissonance could accumulate unresolved until the demise of the business enterprise.

Hierarchical growth is not preordained; it has to be achieved. The concept of hierarchical change can by itself be very useful. It can help us see relationships instead of absolutes. It can help us think of problems in systems concepts. It can help us see change in a way that makes normative planning for our business enterprises possible. It can suggest that the future is indeed to be invented.

Future shock can be future transformation if we can invent the integrating concepts. John Platt and other observers of the great dissonance throughout our contemporary world see this period of world history as a time of sudden transition to a new integrating, simplifying level. Such a hierarchical jump on a world scale could avert the collapse of civilization extrapolated from current trends.

The hierarchical jump is a concept we can use within our business organizations to effect constructive change as well as to monitor our environment and relate to it. Like many of the concepts most important to our businesses, however, it cannot be measured accurately and processed by a computer. But then, many of the so-called exact data that we use in business management are really pretty rubbery and not very close to reality. On the other hand, thinking in relationships, approximations, and systems at a conceptual level can be a very practical matter. We need both concepts and numbers. Concepts are improved by quantification. Numerical data require a conceptual framework to be meaningful.

Hierarchical change becomes a restructuring of values, so the concept gives us a framework for understanding values and their changes. Much of the study of values relates to absolutes, so that a value system amounts to a selection from the shopping list of absolutes. Another approach is to think less of absolutes and more of evolutionary change, an idea less popular when applied to values than to biological forms. But neither approach seems to resolve our problems. We are still searching for the kind of simplifying restructuring produced by hierarchical change.

Several values relate especially to our business system and its operations. General Electric Co. studied 18 of those values, stated them as paired opposites, and measured the predominance of each as of 1970. It then developed possible measures for 1985 by studying the "forerunner group" of change leaders. The result of that work, which is described as only a generalized approximation, is shown in Figure 1-1. Whether the scoring is reasonably accurate or not, there is indication here of significant shifts of the kind that our business organizations will be affected by or, on the positive side, can make use of.

The General Electric study sees value changes resulting from societal trends

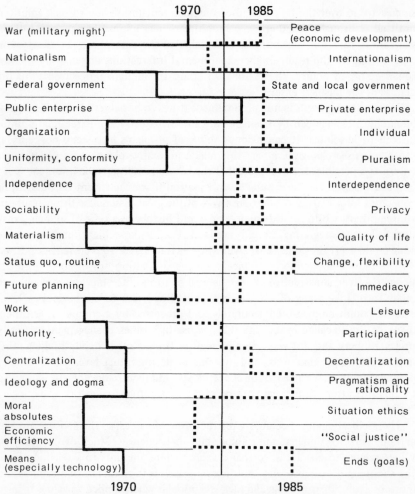

NOTE: The center line represents the midpoint between two extremes.

Figure 1. Profile of significant value system changes, 1970 to 1985 (adapted from a GE chart).

which are acting as forcing functions:

1. Increasing affluence.
2. Rising tide of education.
3. Holistic view of man as a part of nature.
4. Rapidly advancing technology and its broad, systemic impacts.
5. Economic management by governments.
6. Growing interdependence of institutions.
7. Emergence of a postindustrial society.
8. Demographic changes.

Such lists may not strike the businessman as related to his business, or at least to the problems he encounters when he answers his telephone or reads his mail. But many of those undoubtedly real problems may result from a failure to integrate their solutions, or prevent their occurrence, at the level of fundamentals. And we may get close to the fundamentals with such lists as the preceding one. If the workforce shows high absenteeism on Mondays or Fridays, if productivity is down, if there are morale problems, and if quality standards are not being met, those are real problems that can be solved one by one. That's the practical approach, but it doesn't always work. Maybe there's a fundamental that can prevent those problems. In Figure 1-1 there appears a probable shift from the value of work toward the value of leisure. But although leisure is shown as the paired opposite of work, that is not the only possibility. Different forms of work and different structurings of work are other alternatives. The shift in values from work toward leisure may be due to the unattractiveness of jobs rather than the attractiveness of leisure. Now if we can think in terms of hierarchical change, maybe we can find in motivation theory ways to restructure work that will, at a new and different level, resolve our present practical problems that have become unmanageable on a one-at-a-time basis. Perhaps we can learn new ways to be practical.

Technology

Of all change, the kind that is uppermost in the collective consciousness is technological. And the cast of that awareness appears to have changed from the purpurposive pride in progress of the early 1900s to the apprehension, or even fear, of today. After two great wars, a great depression, and many unresolved great problems there are few who believe that all change is purposive and that increasing knowledge will produce still better technology that will better the human condition. Quite to the contrary; to many it appears that technology, instead of being the answer, has become the problem.

But how could that be? Technology is our accumulated competence to provide goods and services for people. If our competence has accumulated to catastrophe, is it fair to fault technology? Technology follows no course, seeks no ends, holds to no values. It is quite neutral and quite natural. If it were not natural, it could not exist. It is a part of nature given substance, shape, and function by man. So it would hardly seem valid to think of technology itself as the problem. The problem was more clearly summarized by Pogo: "We have met the enemy, and he is us."

Us, being what we are, will almost certainly continue to expand our technology. Us, being what we hope to become, may learn to use our growing technical competence to solve problems rather than create new ones. In a sense, that is what we have done. Our present technology did solve many of the problems, *as they were perceived*, of some years past. Technology has profoundly affected survival, sustenance, and security, as Table 1-1 testifies. Technology has, in fact, performed very well in meeting the perceived needs of man. But values and needs change. Satisfying one need or set of needs may create new and even more demanding needs. Perhaps, therefore, our perception of needs has not been future-oriented enough to guide the development of technology. Needs have developed faster than technical competence to serve them. That was true a half century ago also, and technology responded. Perhaps it will continue to do so. At least there seems to be a growing awareness of the problem. Futurism is becoming a science for the guidance of technology, and it increasingly functions in industry, government, universities and other institutions, and the professions to give normative, humanistic dimension to technological change. That is something new. We have laid aside our unquestioning faith that new knowledge and new technology will ipso facto be good for humanity. In place of that faith we are assuming a responsibility to develop new knowledge and new technology for the good of humanity.

Table 1-1. Growth in technology applied to personal needs in the United States.

Technology Indicator	1920	1970
Per 100 of Population		
Installed electrical generating capacity, kilowatts	18.0	177.2
Passenger cars	7.7	43.9
Paved roads, miles	0.35	1.19
Owner-occupied housing units	10.5	19.6
Professional and managerial workers	4.8	9.6
Farm workers	10.6	1.5
Land in farms, acres	904.4	551.7
Telephones	12.4	58.6
Passenger miles flown	–	51,253
University degrees conferred	0.05	0.53
GNP in current dollars	$84,100	$479,400
GNP in constant dollars, 1958 = 100	$129,700	$354,300
Percent of Homes with:		
Electricity	35	97
Telephones	35	92
Radios	–	97
Air conditioners	–	39
Dishwashers	–	26
Refrigerators	–	97
Television	–	96

Source: Compiled from data appearing in Statistical Abstract of the United States, 1972, U.S. Department of Commerce, Historical Statistics of the United States, Colonial Times to 1957, U.S. Department of Commerce, and data and estimates from industry associations and other government agencies.

Technological change will certainly not diminish; but if the preceding observations are valid, it will become more purposive. The pursuit of knowledge at all
its frontiers will proceed with greater vigor than ever, but a synoptic comprehension will apply the accumulating knowledge more beneficiently to the present
and future needs of man.

Peter F. Drucker notes that three great industries—agriculture, steel, and automobiles—have powered the growth of our Western World. He further notes that
those key industries were based on technological innovations from the nineteenth century. And although they have largely built the world we know, they
will not be central to the world we seek to create. According to Drucker, the
industries that will serve the future needs of society will be information, oceans,
materials, and the megalopolis. Just as the great industries of today emerged in
the last century,

> Now, a hundred years later, we are in the early stages of a similar and equally drastic
> shift to industries based not only on new and different technologies but also on different
> science, different logic, and different perception. They are also different in their work
> force, for they demand knowledge workers rather than manual workers.
>
> These industries are capable of providing rapid economic growth in jobs, opportunities,
> income, standards of living, and aspirations for many decades, if not for another century.
> And they are very unlikely to emerge except in countries that have a solid industrial and
> educational foundation—that is, in the developed countries.[3]

Scientific American is one of the leaders in reporting and interpreting technological innovation; each September issue is devoted to a topic of major current
significance. A list of the special-issue topics in reverse order from 1978 to 1960
is instructive: evolution, microelectronics, food and agriculture, the solar system,
the human population, health and medicine, communications, energy and power,
the biosphere, the ocean, light, materials, information, cities, mathematics in the
modern world, technology and economic development, the Antarctic, the living
cell, and the human species. In these topics we see evidence of substantive technological change in the biological sciences, energy, knowledge and communications, and the use and preservation of man's natural environment.

The selections of the editors of *Scientific American* seem consistent with the
expectations of Peter Drucker. They also seem rather consistent with the technological forecasts of the Hudson Institute as reported by Herman Kahn and
Anthony J. Wiener.[4] The authors list 100 technical innovations that are very
likely during the last third of the twentieth century, 25 that are less likely but
possible, and 10 that are far out possibilities. Of those 135 prospective technical
innovations, 48 are in general biology, 22 are in knowledge and communication,
and 17 are in energy. The rest are in construction, transportation, ecology, materials, services, military, and production. Among the innovations that Kahn and

---

[3] *The Age of Discontinuity* (New York: Harper & Row, 1969), pp. 12-41.
[4] *The Year 2000* (New York: Macmillan, 1967), pp. 51-75.

Wiener consider very likely before the end of the century are a flexible penology dependent on surveillance rather than prisons; extensive genetic control of plants and animals; direct electronic communication with the human brain; inexpensive communication of both news and educational materials to home and business; extensive use of lasers and masers in measuring and fabricating; new sources of power for fixed installations; widespread use of fluid amplifiers; longer-range weather forecasting; worldwide application of high-altitude cameras to mapping, prospecting, and the like; and novel structural materials of high strength and thermal tolerance.

Human Nature

Voters, workers, students, women, children, drivers, teachers, teenagers—everyone seems somehow different. "People just aren't like they used to be" is a common observation, and the person who makes it implies that the "change in human nature" has created special problems for him. He, of course, is a politician, an employer, a teacher, a man, a parent, a driver, a school administrator, or just an adult.

People really *have* changed in behavior; whether they have changed as people is open to question. Shakespeare's people of three centuries ago are certainly very contemporary human beings, and so are the people Plato put into his dialogs two thousand years before Shakespeare wrote his plays. In fact, over all the four and a half thousand years of history people have apparently talked, acted, thought, and felt much as they do today. "Flatter a young man," advised a Sumerian proverb of thousands of years B.C., "and he'll give you anything you want; throw a scrap to a puppy, and he'll wag his tail at you."

So has human nature changed? Probably not very much. From the Paleolithic hunter to the modern citizen of megalopolis, man (both Mr. and Ms.) has probably confronted his world with pretty much the same set of human attributes. The change has been not so much in man as in man's world. And although the change may have little effect on man's nature, it can have a great effect on man's behavior. Evolutionary changes in man's nature can occur only slowly, but the response of that nature to different environments can be quite different. Man one at a time is not the same as man in groups; man in megalopolis is not the same as man on the land; educated man is not the same as illiterate man; organization man is not the same as family or individual man. Rather, although each of these men may be quite the same homo sapiens so far as human nature goes, in each of the different situations he will behave quite differently.

People seem not to be the same anymore because the world is not the same anymore. The major areas of change—values, technology, environment, and institutions—account for the apparent changes in people. For people *are* the same anymore. And as we learn to understand ourselves better, we may learn to engineer the areas of change to serve our human nature better than we have in the past.

Much of this book is devoted to motivation and organization development. For business as a major institution of our modern world offers great opportunity for engineering change to the benefit of man. Perhaps in business we can better adjust the contemporary world to human nature and in so doing find a new congruence between the goals of business enterprise and the needs of man. If we can do that, we may find that man is pretty much the same anymore after all. And we may also find that our business enterprises can achieve new and greater levels of success.

Environment

Our environment expands faster than our perception of it. In a simpler day, not long ago, we had not even synthesized the concept of environment. There were family, home, work, people, church, land, politics—all the discrete elements of human life. All acted—and increasingly interacted—but all were separate. With rapid population growth and still more rapid industrialization, the web of inter-relations strengthened. Systems concepts were developed to deal with an increasingly complex world. Political systems, educational systems, economic systems helped to explain the growing complexity. But in a shrinking world, even such macrosystems as those become discrete elements in more encompassing systems. And then we discovered that human systems are a part of and are constrained by the natural systems of our human habitat, our planet Earth. Everything is related to everything else.

A system is a piece of reality that we can identify and do something about. A valid system contains subsystems and itself is part of more encompassing systems. Actions within a system can affect many systems. We no longer live in a world of simple cause and effect. We live in a complex world of system interactions. Action A does not merely cause result B; it effects a whole range of system changes.

In systems terms, then, what is the business environment? The enterprise itself is a system comprising many subsystems, and it is a part of and related to many other systems. Those others include economic, political, social, and ecological systems. The successful business enterprise will have a keen awareness of all of the systems relations, and the awareness will be more than academic. The business enterprise is created for action. Again, action A effects a range of system changes. Therefore, the enterprise must program its actions so that the system effects will be constructive. Its budget plans must become systems plans. Increasingly important in its systems planning will be the impact of its actions on the thin and fragile blanket of earth, air, and water that surrounds our globe and supports all forms of life including its—and our—own. It has become more than evident—it has become legally mandated—that business enterprise actions that have a significantly adverse effect on our biosphere cannot continue.

Ecology is the word. John McHale describes the need to redesign our major social, industrial, and agricultural undertakings toward their more efficient and systematic functioning as *ecologically operating systems* rather than as piecemeal aggregates of unrelated processes.[5] He lists the following among the most urgent of the ecological redesign directions:

1. Recycling the metals and other materials in the system by their use and reuse or their reabsorption within ecological processes.
2. Increasingly using the earth's income energies of solar, water, wind, tidal, and nuclear power in place of the depletive fossil fuels.
3. Changing our food cycle to make greater use of the most efficient natural means of food conversion through the plant-animal chains and the possibilities inherent in microbiological, biosynthetic, and other processes.
4. Setting up global overview and alerting centers to act as early warning systems on the positive and negative ecological implications of our large-scale scientific and technological activities.
5. Establishing networks of integrative planning and study to cope with major transnational problems.

The production of the energy, materials, and equipment needed by the world's population is an immense task, and the restoration of a sizable portion of such energy, materials, and equipment to the natural cycles of our biosphere will be an equally immense task. Recycling on the scale that will be required has a barrier in the considerable commitment of energy, materials, equipment, and manpower necessary to accomplish the recycling. New knowledge will have to be learned and new technology developed to prevent environmental disorder from overwhelming us before we find out how to maintain our biosphere. We may have to retrain our vision to see the significance of the total environment in which business must now operate. But the assumption of an ecological responsibility need not be unbearable. It can be creative of new opportunities.

Business

Throughout our industrial history, our business organizations have been leaders in change. Our expectation is that they will continue to be and that solutions to old problems will be found and new benefits for society will be achieved. But now there are new kinds of difficulties. We have looked briefly at the change around us. What about the change within?

Business organizations are 100, 50, or 25 years old. They have been founded; they have grown and prospered as they provided goods or services for their customers and employment for their people. The organizations have survived, but the people have not. The innovational change responsible for the success was

[5]*The Ecological Context* (New York: Braziller, 1970), p. 18.

the contribution of an earlier time, the creative achievement of leaders now passed from the scene. Today's great industries—steel, automobiles, machine tools, food processing, chemicals, and aircraft—were forged over the years from 1870 to 1920. The management achievements that made those industries possible also were created then and are largely with us still: double-entry bookkeeping and accounting systems, pyramidal organization structure, scientific management, and bureaucracy. They too were great achievements for the predecessor systems they replaced.

Now we confront a new world, but we are equipped to cope with it pretty much as our predecessors were to cope with theirs. More will be needed. A new change must come from within. The past half century has not, of course, been without change. But we must separate in our thinking evolutionary change from hierarchical change—that is, improvement from restructuring. Scientific management, early in this century, restructured the way work was done by standardizing discrete elements of work. Later developments that may appear to be more dramatic have really been evolutionary changes: the assembly line, mechanization, automation, numerical control. Similarly, from double-entry bookkeeping accounting systems, budgetary control, and electronic data systems have evolved. We have indeed had spectacular evolution from the starting points created for us by others, but we have not yet found comparably creative restructuring to better ways.

We are beginning to see some possibilities. The shape of new industries can be discerned, and to some extent these new industries have already emerged. They will be characterized more by services than by goods to provide for human needs in learning and the dissemination of knowledge, communications, urban life-support systems, entertainment and leisure, maintenance of health as well as cure of illness, and the husbandry of our biosphere. We also see the beginnings of possible restructuring in the way our business organizations work. Budgetary control and data processing have so specialized the measurement and control systems of industry that a restructuring becomes possible. It will be at a new level of simplification, and it will depend on performance and achievement reporting concepts. If that restructuring is actually accomplished, the subsystems of automated equipment and data processing will still be used, but in different ways.

Great industrial achievement was built on a number of major contributions of five to ten decades ago: the income statement as a measure of performance, the balance sheet as a measure of assets and liabilities, budgetary control systems, performance appraisal, organization charts, line and staff organization, span of control, hierarchy of supervision and authority, mobility of labor, and separation of public and private sectors. All those concepts may be quite serviceable today for many of our companies. But amid the dissonance about us we can discern possible new patterns based on quite different principles. The remaining chapters of this book will describe some of those principles and how they have been applied by business organizations. Our concern is not with evolutionary change to improve what we are doing now. It is with restructing to new levels of simplicity so that we can cope with our problems more effectively, make a greater contribution to our world, and achieve new successes in our business enterprises.

2

A Conceptual Approach

No people are so addicted to numbers as are businessmen. And the addiction demands incessant effort to generate still more numbers, all to be spewed out by computerized management information centers at 2,000 lines per minute and flooded through the company management levels. Every action and transaction is recorded and compared with a previously set budget model objective or standard, and then the variances are analyzed. Summaries go to executive offices for review, evaluation, and management decision. Numbers create a feeling of security. Like votes to the politician, syllabi to the teacher, and doctrine to the cleric, numbers are to the businessman the key to control.

Or are they? It all depends. We can run very hard but not be in the race. Whether numbers clarify or obscure depends on the conceptual thinking behind them. In many business organizations the conceptual thinking is largely lacking. Numbers are collected, recorded, and reported in vast quantity, but they convey no clear message. Everything can be operating, even at an exhausting pace, while forward motion—real achievement—is almost nil. Transaction problems are many, and their solutions are largely unrelated. Data for each are available, and all are worked on—one by one. Everything is known in its detail but largely unknown in its totality. We have the dimensions of every brick, but we don't see the cathedral. Work is being done, but the conceptual framework for that work has not been built.

The Need for a Conceptual Approach

The organizational symptoms of a need for conceptual thinking include the following:

1. Emphasis on responsibility assignment more than performance achievement, on procedures more than output.

2. Voluminous, statistical control reports—all in financial terms.
3. We-they attitude in different management levels or parts of the organization.
4. Everyone talking but no one listening.
5. Few people thinking of the company as us.
6. Many meetings to review the work or proposals of others; few meetings to confront and resolve problems.
7. The boss making all the decisions
8. Readily apparent personal status differences.
9. Voluminous budgets and long-range plans.
10. Broad use of allocations and transfer prices.
11. Clear job functions but unclear job objectives.
12. Unclear organization values.
13. Operations related to a dominant personality rather than a dominant philosophy.
14. Politics evidently more important than performance as a route to promotion.
15. Difficulty in attracting high-caliber employees.
16. Unsatisfactory company performance.

Relatively few business organizations operate from a sound base of conceptual thought. It's hard to do. It requires an orientation that is not ordinarily required of business managers. Yet we now have more people capable of conceptual thinking than ever before. We must use that resource in our business organizations if we are to cope with the problems and opportunities of our times.

Business is not unaware of a need for conceptual underpinning. Many companies have a president to manage operations and a chairman who concentrates on the future. There are corporate-level planning departments and ventures groups. There are reorganizations motivated by a need for improvement in company performance. But the conceptual thinking behind those observable manifestations may be either significant and valid or almost nonexistent. Many organizations are copying symbols and remaining quite unaware of the realities behind them. There is today a great need in many enterprises to think through to fundamental concepts.

And there is no right approach or right answer. There are many approaches and answers, and some are more right than others. Good answers can be bought from consultants or provided by the top executive, but the best answers can come from people throughout the organization. Although the conceptual talent within most organizations is enormous and the desire to employ it is strong, little of it is used. Two problems are involved: (1) a recognition of the need and (2) a way to make use of the talent.

As for the need, it is made apparent by a comparison of successful business organizations with less successful ones. On whatever basis of comparison, those that excel in that respect far excel over their peers. If profit performance is the measure, the top 25 percent of firms within a given industry will typically exceed the bottom 25 percent by a factor of three or more (see Table 2-1). If the industry is analyzed by size, profit ratios of the top 25 percent within each segment are typically two or three times better than those of the bottom 25 percent and the greatest spread is to be found among the smaller companies. If the measure is market share, innovation, public responsibility, or employee development, similar differences are probably typical. The best are not only better than those toward the bottom of the range, they are three or more times better.

Table 2-1. 1976 net profits on net sales, in percent.

Category	Upper Quartile	Median	Lower Quartile
Manufacturing			
Agricultural chemicals	5.97%	3.53%	1.78%
Broad woven fabrics, cotton	4.48	2.85	1.90
Drugs	10.54	6.62	2.84
Electrical industrial apparatus	6.12	4.03	1.77
Concrete, gypsum, and plaster products	5.94	2.40	0.86
Footwear	4.36	2.70	1.44
Farm machinery and equipment	6.16	3.34	1.73
Industrial chemicals	8.28	5.62	3.21
Metal-working machinery and equipment	4.90	3.07	1.14
Millwork	3.77	2.12	1.38
Motor vehicle parts and accessories	5.66	4.14	2.77
Paper mills, except building paper	6.90	3.59	1.54
Petroleum refining	5.76	3.13	1.65
Plastics materials and synthetics	4.28	3.25	1.69
Wholesaling			
Automotive parts and supplies	4.37	2.50	1.09
Chemicals and allied products	4.95	3.08	1.93
Electrical appliances, TV, and radio sets	2.71	1.45	0.75
Electrical apparatus and equipment	3.00	1.52	0.74
Footwear	3.63	1.05	0.26
Paper and paper products	3.01	1.55	0.58
Retailing			
Department stores	3.38	1.59	0.02
Discount stores	2.86	1.40	0.47
Hardware stores	6.25	3.23	1.67
Variety stores	5.00	2.41	1.15

Source: Dun & Bradstreet, Inc., "Key Business Ratios, 1976 Statistics from 125 Lines of Retailing, Wholesaling and Manufacturing & Construction."

Superiority like that is not an accident. What are some of the characteristics often found in superior organizations? Here are a few:

1. A strong sense of identity felt throughout the organization.
2. Openness to change.
3. Authority diffused broadly throughout the organization.
4. Ideas evaluated more on their merit than on their origin.
5. A strong sense of support of the employees for their company, of the company for its employees, and of the employees for each other.
6. Flexible organization forms.
7. Orientation to achievement more than to procedures or to ritual.
8. Open communications throughout the organization—up, down, and across.
9. Commonly held understanding of company values and objectives.
10. Emphasis on and programs for the development of people.
11. Meetings oriented primarily to problem solving, not to win-lose decisions.
12. Broad content in individual jobs.
13. High performance standards.

An input of conceptual thinking will not yield an immediate output of the listed characteristics. But the conceptual thinking through of the business to agreed-upon fundamentals can create an organization and climate having those characteristics. Through such conceptual thinking a long stride toward achievement and excellence can be taken.

The Nature of the Conceptual Approach

The approach will not be easy. Conceptual thinking is different from the familiar operational thinking, and it will force us to abandon some of our practices. It will reopen matters that have been sealed shut by past policy or past decision. It will reveal areas not yet confronted or dealt with. In short, it will make us and our organization different than we were—maybe a little, maybe a lot.

So let's get specific. What is meant by a conceptual approach? How do we go about it?

The conceptual approach is an organized search for the fundamentals, expressed as ideas, on which the success of the enterprise will be built.

The fundamentals are different from and much more complex than "I'm in business to make money." All three nouns and pronouns in that stereotype are conceptually off target. The very first word, the personal pronoun "I'm," may satisfy an ego but it won't satisfy an organization. The successful enterprise today must be more "we" than "I." Second, neither I nor we are "in business." We are a social-economic institution or enterprise with skills to perform certain functions and a capacity to produce certain outputs. Third, "to make money" can hardly be the fundamental objective. For a business enterprise, profit is the food for survival. The enterprise must have profit to renew and upgrade its resources and to grow. Business profit for the aggrandizement of individuals is a legitimate subject for political debate, but business profit for the perpetuation and growth of the enterprise in the service of human needs is nonpolitical. That can be seen from the fact that the wealth-producing enterprises in all nations with all forms of government operate at an economic profit. Interestingly, in the Communist and Socialist countries the rate of profit as measured by capital formation is as high as in capitalist countries (see Table 2-2).

Table 2-2. Capital formation as percent of gross national product; typical annual rate in 1970s.

Western Countries	%	Eastern Countries	%
United States	17	U.S.S.R.	18
West Germany	24	East Germany	19
United Kingdom	19	Poland	27
France	24	Czechoslovakia	18
Italy	21	Bulgaria	16
Canada	23	Hungary	21
Japan	33		

Source: Western   Countries—IMF, International Financial Statistics, August, 1978. Eastern Countries—U.N. Yearbook of National Accounts Statistics, 1976.

In talking about profit, a distinction should be made between accounting profit and economic profit. Accountants concern themselves with conventions for reporting the historical economic affairs of the business enterprise. Use of alternative conventions can significantly alter reported profit. Some companies have reported good "profit performance" all the way to bankruptcy. The explanation is not deceit or dishonesty. It is simply that reports of past transactions and present conditions by accounting conventions can be distorted one way or the other by what happens in the future.

Economists, on the other hand, concern themselves with the cost of inputs and the value of outputs in a future-oriented input-output model of the enterprise. If the enterprise is to survive, the value of outputs as measured by receipts from customers past and future must exceed the total cost of inputs past and future. If the input-output model is constructed with all economic costs on the input side, the difference is profit or loss.

Accounting and economics can, of course, be congruent, but often they are not. When they are not, the wise business leader will seek the counsel of the economist rather than that of the accountant if he wants to understand the profit fundamentals of his enterprise. The whole subject of managerial economics is developed in more detail in Chapter 10.

The stereotype "I'm in business to make money" also overlooks the fact that many wealth-creating enterprises simply do not have profit objectives. Examples are hospitals, government technical programs, city public works departments, and the YMCA. Yet such organizations can be highly creative and highly achieving. The stereotype connotes selfishness, manipulation, and individual profiteering related to personal power. Small wonder that it would be distasteful to anyone but the man who uses it in reference to himself. But the successful business enterprise today cannot fit the stereotype. Profit is its fuel but not its destination. It must serve a socially sanctioned purpose to earn the fuel. And that brings us to the conceptual approach: an organized search for the fundamentals, expressed as ideas, on which the success of the enterprise will be built.

Resources Needed
There is no road map for the search, but there are many routes to follow. In recent years the literature on corporate planning has presented a variety of approaches. Most of them tend to be technical, procedural, and data-heavy. A plan becomes a document; documents become bound volumes; and ideas perish in a crush of statistics, reports, and due dates. No motivating concept emerges. So let us begin with what we must bring to our search. Among the needed resources the following four can be listed:

1. A knowledge of managerial economics, national and world macro economics, physical science, engineering, biological science, behavioral science, law and political systems, history, language and culture, philosophy, current events, computer systems, statistics, and futurology.
2. A business audit of the enterprise past and present.
3. An environment or framework for developing conceptual thinking about the enterprise.
4. A knowledge of concept-developing questions.

Just those four. But what a four! The first of them requires people who have studied much, read much, and experienced much. The second can be produced by any competent study team following any of several outlines for such an audit. Alternatively, it can be drawn upon as needed directly from the minds of experienced company people; for we need for our conceptual approach only the fundamentals, not all the precise details. The third requires only the desire to undertake the search. The fourth will be provided by this book—at least, let us hope, to such extent that the reader will be able to carry on with his own concept-developing questions.

One important principle must be apparent from our list of the four needed resources. The conceptual approach will not be created on Olympus and handed down to the multitude. Too diverse an input is needed to be found within the top executive alone. Even more important, there must be broad participation in the process if the concepts are to be accepted and serve as motivations. So there are two good reasons for wide participation in the conceptual process: we will get a better result and we will get a result that can motivate achievement. Precepts from Olympus belong to another age. A little bit of God is in every man and every woman. And therein lies the resource for survival, for growth, and for achievement.

The Search for Fundamentals

What is a workable approach to the organized search for the fundamentals, expressed as ideas, on which the success of the enterprise will be built? The most effective one is to do the problem-solving work in small groups, up to perhaps twelve or fifteen people. Six or eight is an especially good group size, but as few as three or four people can be productive. Such groups can be convened at corporate, divisional, and other organizational levels. Large numbers of company people can be involved in creating a future for their company and for themselves. Collectively they can benefit from the unique skills of individuals.

Initial working meetings of that type have been successful in as short a time as half a day or as long a time as a few weeks. My personal preference based on many experiences is for a concentrated two-day concept-developing session. That can be followed by one-day and half-day meetings over several months with homework between the meetings as needed. In that way a good concept of fundamentals can be developed over three to six months. Broad communication by interface among groups, by large informational meetings, and by letters and publications will be an important part of the effort.

You will need courage to undertake such a program; for, if it is successful, most participants will have changed the way they think about their work and about their company. The organization will be in process of metamorphosis from which it cannot return to the way things are today.

There is a convention that says organization change can be achieved only by changing the top manager, with the new man shaking up the organization and instituting change. The conceptual approach sees that as too simple, often futile, and in defiance of the wisdom of the organization itself. Unless the new man has both a valid conceptual approach and the skill and maturity to develop it in his new organization, the result may very well be change without progress. That result is especially likely because the method of change—appointment of a new manager—suggests a top management unfriendly to conceptual thinking. The executive who makes the change involves neither himself nor his people in the fundamentals of the problem. He merely hands the whole thing over to someone new and probably wishes only a continuation of the present company culture and way of doing things but with better operating results. He is likely to be disappointed.

Another convention says we may need a new man or we may not but we do need outside professional help. A consultant is called in. This convention is wiser in many instances than is the new-man convention. For the consultant convention requires a commitment by top management and a participation of top management in the conduct of the work. If the consultant has been well chosen, he is then in a position to develop and implement the kind of conceptual thinking and program development advocated by this book. But if the consultant "lays it on" instead of "creates it from" the organization itself, management may find itself with a new ship to be manned by an uncommitted crew and an unprepared skipper.

It's no convention, but a wise thought, that you can do the job yourself. The "yourself" has a small "y"—it's not you the manager; it's you the whole organization. It's the president and the whole company, the vice president and his operation, the manager and his department, the supervisor and his group, the professional employee and his function, each employee and his job, and all of those together. Only here, in a collective wisdom, do we have all of the needed resources for our work. So let's begin.

If you are a manager, begin with your department. Your success can then spread from that starting point until it becomes a way for all the company. If you are a professional employee, begin with your function. Your success will spread to others around you because they will necessarily become involved by your way of working. That too can spread throughout the company. If you are a president, start with your corporate management level and extend the work to operations as you develop a way that's good for your business enterprise.

Nothing is more powerful than ideas whose time has come. Such ideas can be mined from the wisdom existing within each organization. They are not even hard to find. It is only necessary to loosen the constraints that prevent their flow. But although they are not hard to find, they are deceptively difficult to recognize. Ideas are both cheap and plentiful. Any good brainstorming session can generate ideas faster than they can be written down, but the few relevant ones among them can remain unrecognized in the crowd. Also, we are searching not only for good ideas but for a good idea system for our enterprise. A good idea is not enough. It must also be relevant to what will become the fundamental idea system for the enterprise. That's what we are looking for—the fundamentals, expressed as ideas, on which the success of the enterprise will be built.

The life of the enterprise depends on relationships. Our fundamental idea system must relate to our present, direct us to our future, serve the changing needs of our customers and our several publics, satisfy the aspirations of employees, contribute to the solution of economic and social issues, and motivate the economic performance that can earn the profit needed to fuel the achievement of our goals.

So, beginning wherever you are in your organization, start to think through the fundamentals of your area of responsibility. To be valid, they will, of course, have to relate to the idea system of the total company. If such an idea system is not in clear focus to you now, don't wait for it. Create one by assumption and then search for your own fundamentals in relation to that assumption. Communicate as widely as you can both your assumptions on the company idea system and the fundamentals as you see them relating your area to the idea system. Your motivation and your increasing level of contribution will add weight to your ideas. If you are shot down, use the experience as inputs to modify your assumptions and your own set of fundamentals and take off again. You will become an agent for change.

If you work at a management level and have others reporting to you, involve them in developing assumptions and in searching out the fundamentals for your area related to those assumptions. Involve the person to whom you report. Change is under way.

A Conceptual Framework

In the remainder of this chapter a conceptual framework for an idea system for a total enterprise is sketched. In the following chapters the framework will be developed in more detail.

Business Definition
First of all we must find an answer to this question: What are we? The question seems so simple that few of us stop to consider that we may not have an answer. Obviously, we know what our business is—we work hard enough at it every day, and we're good at what we do. But, damn it, competition is worse than ever, taxes and regulations are breaking our backs, profit margins are going to hell, business isn't very much fun any more, and where is all that new leisure we keep reading about? Maybe our problems are not our problem. Maybe our problems are telling us that we have not, perceptively enough, found our identity.

We are so busy working, so busy doing our jobs, that we have not conceptualized a fundamental understanding of what we are. And if among the many people who constitute our business enterprise there is no common identity and purpose, we may have more problems than we can find solutions. If we don't know what we are, all ideas are relevant. If we don't know where we're going, any road will take us there. If we have no valid concept of identity, random actions to no end result may consume much of our talent, journeys down dead-end roads may consume much of our time, and solutions to one-at-a-time problems may lead only to an increasing number of such problems. Given a valid concept of identity that is broadly understood and shared throughout the enterprise, individual efforts in meaningful jobs can combine outputs to reach new levels of achievement and success.

Our business identity may be defined either very specifically or quite broadly. There is never a right answer; there are only different answers. Each different answer will produce a different company. What is right or good for a particular business enterprise depends on the internal and external situations. A critical issue is to define our identity at the most meaningful level of generalization. We might, for example, define our business as publishing a daily newspaper in a city or providing communication service for people in a five-county area. A company with the first definition will publish a daily newspaper; one with the second might publish a daily newspaper, operate a radio or TV station, introduce cable TV, or provide home-study courses, a checkless accounting service, a shared-time computer service, at-home shopping service via video and electronic communication, preschool training and education, or automated retrieval and delivery of library information.

Neither definition is adequate as a concept of identity, but the two illustrate the range from the very specific to the very general. Neither is superior as a definition. It all depends. Making a definition too narrow can impose too rigid limits on performance and opportunity; making the definition too broad can result in lack of direction. The history of enterprise abounds with examples of strategic errors in both directions. The railroad industry saw itself too much in terms of railroads and finance and not enough in terms of transportation. The motion picture industry went through years of restructuring and recovery from the challenge of TV, which forced a redefinition of the industry from a product (movies) and distribution (theaters) business to an entertainment business. Had it had a more relevant definition of its business, the industry could have prospered by the advent of TV instead of losing money in its struggle against it.

Both the railroads and the motion picture industry defined their businesses too narrowly. At the other extreme, many contemporary conglomerates defined their businesses so broadly that they could develop no integrating operations concepts. Because they lacked direction, the first unfavorable economic winds drove them onto the reefs of purposelessness. If we are too narrow, we fail for lack of vision; if we are too broad, we fail for lack of purpose. Again, there is no right answer, there are only different answers. Some can lead to failure, others to spectacular success.

Our decision on business definition becomes one of the most fundamental, one of the most important, and one of the most motivating decisions that we can make. Also, it must be not only a decision for the present but even more importantly a decision for the future. All business decisions are future-oriented, and none more so than this one. For our question of identity is not only what we are but also what we shall become. Only when we develop and have a common acceptance within the organization of what we are and what we intend to become can we deal effectively with the strategic issues on which outstanding success can be built.

1. Goods and services to be provided.
2. Markets and client groups to be served.
3. Major areas of opportunity.
4. Resource requirements.
5. Competitive strength.
6. Innovation.
7. Trends in the relevant environment.

Arriving at a business definition is difficult; committing resources to it is challenging. Defining identity requires rigorous thinking, studying, conceptualizing, and testing. First answers must be tentative because the full implications will not be apparent until additional market and competitive data are analyzed and later decisions on goals, strategies, and programs are considered. It is usually necessary to cycle through the whole conceptualizing process several times before decisions are finalized.

Good business definitions are usually expressed in terms of products and services, organizational competences, markets, geography, resources, and relevant environment. The business as defined will be unique as an operating enterprise and related enough in its technology and resource requirements to be effectively planned and operated as a goal-directed, achievement-oriented, profit-and-loss business. A company may define its business in one or many such definitions, depending on the scale and the diversity of its operations. Companies that define their identity narrowly may have volume in the tens of thousands or in the tens or even hundreds of millions of dollars and operate very successfully as one business. A more diversified company may have several separate businesses within it—businesses from thousands or a few millions in size and on up. A delicatessen can operate very successfully as one business, and so can a major coal mining company with sales of more than $100 million. One of our very large and very diversified companies, General Electric Co., on the other hand, operates as some 170 different businesses.

Nothing is more important to the success of the enterprise than the decision on, agreement with, and commitment to the specific definition of business identity. And the decision cannot be avoided or even postponed. If it is not made explicitly, it will develop implicitly. The problem then will be differences in implication. And there we are: damn it, competition is worse than ever, taxes and regulations are breaking our backs, profit margins are going to hell, business isn't much fun any more, and where is all that new leisure we keep reading about?

Business Intelligence
When the business has been defined, we must gain expert knowledge of the business situation. We must understand where we are—ourselves, our competition, our markets, our distribution, our environment—and how we got here. We must understand the significant trends and perceive changes in them as they develop. By understanding the past, knowing the present, and conceptualizing the future, we can identify the opportunities on which we should concentrate our efforts and our resources. Business intelligence helps us select the most promising opportunities for major effort and, at the same time, recognize the obstacles we face so we can be realistic in our determinations and effective in the development of our programs. Through business intelligence we develop the information we need to make final decisions on business definition, goals, strategies, and action plans.

Goals

Once we have a clear concept of our identity and our business intelligence has provided us with necessary understanding, we can determine goals. We usually think of business goals first of all, and often exclusively, in terms of sales volume and profit. Those are important measures of performance, and we should certainly set sales volume and profit goals for future achievement. Our business definition and our business intelligence will enable us to develop those goals. But they are not enough. Performance goals are necessary in all the key performance areas that will determine the future success of the enterprise. Those areas include market standing, profitability, productivity, innovation, physical and financial resources, motivation and organization development, and public and environmental responsibility.

By considering all those key performance areas in the light of our business definition and our business intelligence, we will almost certainly develop very significant goals in addition to sales volume and profit. And those goals will usually be such that all business functions and all company people can participate in a meaningful way in their achievement.

Strategy to Achieve Goals

After goals have been determined, it becomes important to lay out the broad framework for the employment of resources. Usually there are several possible approaches to a major goal. However, in consideration of what we are, our competition, our markets, our distribution, and our environment, there will probably be only a very few approaches that can really be effective for us. Accordingly, it is important to find, articulate, and use them as a framework for all business decisions and action plans. Strategy becomes the operating theme that coordinates many people and many actions in the achievement of goals.

The idea of strategy sounds so simple that we might expect it to be broadly understood and commonly used, but it is not. Most businesses have goals; most businesses have some form of action plans. Few businesses have well thought out, articulated strategies to direct and coordinate all areas of action toward the achievement of goals. Yet every great business success has at its core just such a strategy! Why is so important a fundamental so ignored? There are at least three reasons:

First, although goals are very commonly set, they are often limited to those that can be expressed in financial terms and reported in the company's accounting record. Those goals may be important to the company's operating success, but they are not in a form that is directly actionable by individuals and groups. Although they have meaning for the company—and the top executive—they cannot be related to individual jobs. Therefore, the lack of strategy often begins with a lack of appropriate goals. The solution is to set our goals differently. Summary goals in terms of operating results won't carry us very far. We need a structure of goals that relates to all job functions throughout the enterprise. Given such goals, wise strategy decision can coordinate committed actions to reach exciting achievement.

Second, our Western way of thinking and living is oriented to goals and actions. Our popular how-to-do-it books are mostly recipe books for action programs. They do not teach strategy—a way of thinking, a way of living, a way of working. They teach action programs—step 1, step 2, step 3. In business we often jump directly from goals to action programs with no coordinating framework of strategy to relate the two. Small wonder that so much human effort in our organizations is applied to dead-end, unneeded, nonproductive or even counterproductive work!

Many business planning systems do call for written strategies; for today's planning literature emphasizes strategy as fundamental. But very often what is written is not strategy but a potpourri of goals, business intelligence artifacts, forecasts, and action plans. The blanks in the written business plan have been filled in, but the conceptual thinking has not been done. The integrating concepts of strategy have not been discovered. Perhaps we can borrow from the Eastern way of thinking and living that is oriented to the Way, the Tao. In our business enterprise we need all together—goals and actions coordinated and made attainable through the integrating way of strategy.

Third, there is no impelling operating demand for determining strategy. If we don't have a strategy, no one will really notice. And the effect may not show up for many years. When it does show up, the result most likely will be explained by auditors in quantities and ratios that will comfortably obscure the important point that strategy was missing. The only demand for strategy will come from the discipline we impose on ourselves. The only reason for the discipline will come from a desire for meaningful achievement and exciting business success. Without strategy we will have neither.

Action Plans

Here is the focal point of the whole planning process. Given a common concept of our identity, the knowledge resource of business intelligence, a meaningful structure of goals in the key performance areas, and a unifying concept of strategy, all functions and individuals within the enterprise can formulate supportive plans of actions. In the development of those plans, the specific activities to support the strategy are determined. A plan is a statement of the logical step-by-step flow of actions to be taken expressed in terms of what, by whom, and when.

Action plans must be evaluated as to probability of success in achieving the stated goals and as to practicality—cost in relation to return. The individual responsible for each action plan will continually review and revise his plan so that it is always viable for the period ahead. The period may last days, weeks, months, or years, depending on the nature of what is planned. A sales itinerary may be for days, a production plan for weeks, a cash plan for months, a capital or organizational plan for years.

The individual responsible for the plan must also assure that all those who are involved in implementing the plan adequately participate in plan development. Among that group, communications must be established and maintained to assure a continuing understanding and commitment and a continuing common effort directed by a strategy that will achieve the goals. Note that such work groups derive from the logic of our identity, our goals, and our strategy. They will not be found in the hierarchical charts we customarily draw for our organizations. Such charts may be useful for some aspects of administration, but they are seldom useful for organizing the work to be done.

Motivating Achievement
Our plans will be evaluated by the manner in which they are implemented and by the quality and quantity of the results produced. Success in today's complex, highly competitive, and rapidly changing environment will require the best of the creative skills and energies of everyone in the organization. Those skills and energies can be committed to our goals, strategies, and action plans through a participative management style. Participation throughout the process of determining our identity, establishing our goals, determining strategy, developing action plans, and doing the job leads to commitment and to achievement. The conceptual approach gains commitment through involvement and achievement through common purpose. It is not manipulative by the leadership; it is creative by everyone. Our identity, our goals, our strategy, our action plans, our work becomes all of us together. It becomes a management system of objectives participatively developed and supportively achieved.

With such a structure for achievement we are now also able to give a new kind of future orientation to our action programs. Our identity is future-oriented. It is not only what we are, but what we intend to become. Also future-oriented are our business intelligence, our goals, and our strategies. With that perspective of the future we can examine feedback from our action programs to determine whether we are on the track to the achievement of our goals. That kind of qualitative review will help us make decisions and take action currently that will improve future achievement. That kind of predictive control can be far more effective in optimizing performance than after-the-fact variance analysis and management by exception can be.

The new type of predictive control that is made possible by the conceptual approach is described in Chapter 13. When our action plans are well thought out and specific, our daily, weekly, and monthly results can tell us if we are on the way to achieving our goals. In the whole process nothing is static. The business situation changes and our capabilities change, so we must continually change our action plans, set new or additional goals, and at times change our strategy or even our definition of identity as we move to eliminate weaknesses or maximize newly discovered opportunities.

Customer Sales Planning

The real objective, the real essence, of any business is the creation or the manufacture of customers. Without a client constituency of customers there is no business. Our greatest business asset is our customers; our greatest organization asset is our people. Neither customers nor people appear on the balance sheet that purports to be a statement of our assets. What we are and what we say we are often are quite different things. Our people assets can be developed through a conceptual approach to business planning and business operations. Our customer assets can be developed through customer sales planning. Customer sales planning is a framework for sales operations that applies the conceptual approach at the point of sale. It includes the following steps:

Territory assignment. First of all it must be determined how sales assignments should be established. There are several possibilities:

1. Geographical. The salesman sells all the company products and services in an assigned geographical area.
2. Product or service. The salesman specializes in particular products and services.
3. Markets. The salesman specializes in certain kinds of customers and sells all company products and services to that market.
4. Customers. Selected customers are made the assignment. This approach is very commonly used for very large customers or for national accounts.
5. Development. Developing new customers or customers for new products and services is a specialized kind of selling. A sales assignment may consist entirely of development selling.
6. Maintenance. Maintaining existing business can be assigned as a specialized sales responsibility.
7. Distribution channels. The sales assignment may consist of a particular element in the distribution channel—distributors, agents, retail stores, or a particular kind of retail store.
8. Buying influences. The sales assignment may center on certain professions or key groups that influence the purchase of the company's products or services, such as doctors (for pharmaceuticals), architects (for building products), government agencies (for sales to government contractors), standards authorities (for product specification).
9. Two or more of the preceding possibilities. The sales assignment may have more than one dimension: for example, certain products and services to a particular market. There is seldom one right way to make sales assignments. In a typical business and in a typical sales organization there may be several different kinds of sales assignments. The most productive ap-

proach to sales responsibility assignment will derive from the concept of identity and from the specific goals, strategies, and action plans. Sales responsibility assignment is more than derivatory, however. It is also contributory; for sales is a participant in the whole conceptual process. How sales responsibility is assigned will determine the inputs from sales operations.

Territory examination. Territory examination is a process of assembling all the information about a sales assignment needed to set and achieve sales goals and provide market intelligence feedback to the salesman and others in the organization. It will include brief, summary information on all accounts and prospects; it will include an evaluation of competitive strengths and weaknesses. Although comprehensive, it need not be voluminous—it consists of the information about accounts and prospects and competition most relevant to the selling situation. Primarily, therefore, it represents a task in conceptual thinking. It can be guided by headquarters, but it can be accomplished only through conceptual thinking by the salesman.

Selection of target accounts and prospects. In business operations, concentration is always a key to success. A small percent of the total number will account for a major percent of the total performance. In a sales assignment, performance with a small number of important accounts and prospects will largely determine success in the territory. From territory examination, sales volume goals can be set for all customers and prospects. The most important of them can then be singled out for specialized sales effort. They will not be many. Sales territories may have 50 to 150 or more accounts and prospects, but four or five to eight or ten of them may be the key to territory sales success. For those most important accounts and prospects it is helpful to develop individual sales plans.

Development of target account plans. The plans for achieving sales objectives with selected major accounts and prospects—the target accounts—usually include the following information:

1. Profile. A customer profile comprises the factual data about the customer or prospect that relate to the sales opportunity: company name, address, and phone number; type and size of business; other locations, related businesses; key buying influencers; amount of company products and services used; competition; and history with the account. Other information may be included, depending on what is genuinely important to the marketing and purchasing relationship. Companies that use written sales plans usually develop forms that outline the kind of profile information most important in their kind of business.

2. Goal. A specific sales goal in dollars or units should be set for each target account. By using managerial economics approaches, as described in Chapter 11, income contribution goals can also be established for each target account.

3. Strategy. Sales strategy is the way in which the company plans to commit its resources of time, money, and manpower to achieve the customer sales goal.

Strategy provides overall direction for the specific programs and actions. Effective sales strategies relate the needs and goals of the customer to the benefits that can be provided by the company's products or services. The customer's buying decision then becomes a step toward goals important to him. Sales strategies must, of course, also be consistent with overall business strategies. Congruence is so important that the two sets of strategies are usually determined pretty much together; overall business strategies become those that most effectively relate company competences and resources to the needs of major company markets.

4. Programs and actions. The sales program for a target account consists of a series of actions that will be taken to achieve the sales goal. It includes a statement of what is to be done, who is to do it, where it is to be done, and what is needed to do it. In addition to sales programs for their target accounts, most professional salesmen will also have plans—including profile, goal, strategy, and action plans—for each of their other accounts and prospects. They may be simplified in form, and they are seldom—except for goals—put in writing. Nevertheless, the conceptual thinking that is done provides guidance for action.

5. Evaluation. The territory examination and each customer sales plan is evaluated to assure that it is a reasonable statement of opportunity, that the competitive and customer situation is reliably known, that goals are attainable and yet challenging, and that the selling program is a wise investment of effort and resources with high probability of achieving the sales goals. The evaluation is a continuing process—changes are made in goals, strategies, and programs as they may be appropriate to changed circumstances.

6. Implementation and feedback. Customer sales plans are implemented by sales people, but they are led and supported by first- and second-level sales management. Feedback is provided by personal contact, correspondence, transaction forms (orders, acknowledgments, shipping papers, invoices, and so on), internal reports, and qualitative review of the customer sales plan action programs. By use of that feedback, weaknesses can be corrected and opportunities can be further developed. As is true of the conceptual development of the total business, customer sales planning works best through a participative management style. It provides a management by objectives (MBO) system for field sales operation. It helps all to stand together, move together, and achieve together through meaningful, individual contribution. It assures that the most important business asset—the customers—will be most carefully nurtured.

3

Defining Our Identity— Present and Future

If we have no concept of what we are as a business enterprise, our journey into the future will be haphazard. We will continually take actions, adjust, and react, and with luck perhaps we will continue to survive. If our actions, adjustments, and reactions derive from a philosophy in tune with the world around us, we will find some kind of identity whether consciously articulated or not. But unless that identity *is* consciously articulated and unless it is made central to every action taken everywhere in the organization, we can hardly expect a unity of purpose or a strong thrust for achievement. There will be too many random actions, too many problems, too many roads to travel, too many emergencies, too many projects, too many opportunities. If we have no concept of identity, our problem is not that we become nothing; it is that we become everything. And that's too loose a cloak to clothe an enterprise. The organization will be forever overworked—and forever underachieving.

The Search for Identity

So the enterprise as a whole needs a concept of its identity. To a company president or a chairman the creation of such a concept is probably the first and most important achievement needed if the organization is to be successful. All else becomes possible if there is first created a company identity that is right for both the organization and the world and the times in which it must operate.

Theodore Levitt lists four major functions of management:[1]

1. Choosing a purpose for the organization.
2. Molding the character of the organization.

[1] Lecture at management conference of Hooker Chemical Corporation, May 1967.

3. Determining what needs to be done.
4. Mobilizing resources to accomplish what needs to be done.

Many practical businessmen clearly recognize the fourth function and devote a great deal of their time and effort to it. Some concentrate effort on the third function, too, especially those who support a planning operation. Budgets and five-year plans are typical manifestations of function 3. Functions 2 and 1 often go unrecognized and undischarged. The wisdom of Levitt's counsel is perceived only in part by many businessmen. And because those businessmen are practical, action-oriented, experienced people, they tend to see Levitt's recommended list of management functions from the bottom end and work up. By the time they get halfway up the list, they find things getting sort of theoretical and up in the clouds.

In any case there is much less awareness of Levitt's functions 2 and 1 than of 4 and 3. And the "practical" progression, beginning at 4, soon runs out of capacity for conceptual, fundamental thinking. It's too immersed in day-to-day problems. As Buckminster Fuller has observed, the so-called common-sense approach usually means preoccupation with "minute, superficial irrelevances."[2] Fuller's criticism, if a little too harsh for application to business, can at least remind us that even the most obvious and the most practical should be questioned. And here is an example. When we do start from function 1 and work through to function 4, a very surprising thing happens. Functions 3 and 4 become much simpler. There are fewer problems, and the problems that do arise are more solvable. The practical aspects of operations become much more manageable.

So our first priority should not be our problems; it should be our fundamentals. Only when we start from wisely chosen fundamentals can we expect successful management of our problems and successful development of our opportunities. Without a grasp of fundamentals, every problem is our problem and every opportunity is our opportunity. Almost anything at all can become "what needs to be done," and we very quickly run out of resources. With a grasp of fundamentals, we confront our real problems and select the opportunities that are right for us. "What needs to be done" becomes clearer, and the mobilization of resources to do it becomes a very manageable task. The key to the doing is not priorities or ranking criteria; it is having a clearly established purpose for and character of the enterprise. It's as simple as that and as hard as that. Simple because having a purpose and a character vastly simplifies the programming of resources. Hard because purpose and character do not arise from written words on a sheet of paper. They must be created throughout a working organization of diverse but mutually committed people. And that creation begins with finding our identity.

"What business are we in?" is the question that usually begins a search for

<hr>

[2]"Architecture as Ultra Invisible Reality," in Arthur B. Bronwell (Ed.), *Science and Technology in the World of the Future* (New York: Wiley, 1970), p. 151.

identity. And then the search gets under way with a listing of products and markets and an examination of the transactions between the two. Although that exploration is something that should be undertaken, as a starting point it seems to me too limiting. Times change more rapidly than we do, and our initial search should not be constrained by what we are, what we do, and what we did. It should be as unconstrained as we can make it; its orientation should be to scenarios as well as to records. A good way to begin our search for identity is to pose for ourselves not one question but two:

What are we?

What should we become?

Now the fences are down and we can think broadly. But the guidelines too are gone. We'll have to find new ones for our search.

Conducting the Search

Fortunately, the search need not take us far afield. It can usually be confined to the minds of our people. We need only the knowledge inputs listed in Chapter 2, and we probably have all of them within our organization. We certainly have in people's minds all we need to know about our own company and its past performance. Some of the other knowledge inputs may be missing, especially if our organization is so full of doers that we have not recruited and rewarded those who also think about what they do. If our own people are weak in any of the important knowledge areas, outside people can be brought in to help us with our search. They can be consultants, professors, writers, government officials, editors, educators, clerics, outside businessmen, lawyers, bankers, artists—anyone with knowledge in the areas in which our own knowledge is insufficient. All the following areas of knowledge are relevant to and should be included in the search for our identity: managerial economics, national and world economics, physical science, engineering, biological science, behavioral science, law and political systems, history, language and culture, philosophy, current events, computer systems, statistics, and futurology.

The most productive way to conduct the search is with a small group that meets to consider the two questions:

What are we?

What should we become?

To develop answers to those questions the group is most often drawn from the top management of the firm. It should be small—at least five and probably no more than twelve or fifteen. Even better than one group limited to top management people would be several groups composed of top management people, operations people, and selected others from inside and outside the company. Two days is a good length of time for a first meeting, which should be followed by shorter meetings over several months.

The first meeting can be highly structured with lecture-discussion periods, dialog, and workshop sessions, or it can be unstructured with all dialog and workshop sessions. An experienced meeting leader should be selected for each group if a structured format is to be followed. In most cases he should not be the senior manager in the group. If meetings are unstructured, no leader is needed. In either case, however, a skilled reporter will be needed to summarize the facts and ideas presented and record agreements reached and any work assignments made.

An agenda for a structured session might begin with background information, the conference plan, and a management-style questionnaire, include two full days of work on the two basic questions and related concepts, and end with a half-day wrap-up that includes summaries, questionnaire results, and planning. The work on the basic questions might start with a presentation by a highly qualified outsider before moving into workshops that are later pulled together in reports and critique.

If the meeting is to be unstructured, some open thinking should be encouraged among the meeting participants before they come together for the meeting. A number of books and articles are excellent for the purpose, and one or two of them might be distributed to each participant three or four weeks in advance of the meeting. Some suggested titles are listed at the end of this chapter.

As a specific preparation for an unstructured meeting, one or more participants can be asked to prepare a paper to be presented at the beginning of the meeting. The paper can set forth the individual's views on a specific opportunity or problem area or, more broadly, his proposed answers to the twin questions what we are and what we should become. The paper might also include any supplementary questions that the writer feels must be answered before agreement on the two fundamental questions can be reached.

When the meeting convenes, the first hour or two can be given to a presentation of the papers and a group critique. When the group is dialoging well and has more or less conceptualized the range of subjects with which it will have to deal, a halt in the discussion should be called. At that point, the group is ready to identify the key subject areas over which it must dialog during the session. Those that gain agreement can be listed on an easel pad, and they become the agenda. The agenda must, of course, remain a loose one that is subject to change in the course of the session. By the end of a two-day meeting, all subjects on the agenda should be covered and very important areas of agreement should be reached. Participants can then be given individual work assignments to complete over a one- to three-month period. Completion of the assignments may involve many others in the company. The results will provide the framework for a more decisive follow-up meeting.

Workshop Ground Rules

For workshop sessions, both structured and unstructured, several procedural principles are important:

No one is the boss. Ideas must be considered on their merit, not on their origin. Hierarchical organizational roles should be left outside the door. Around the table we want only knowledge, ideas, and open dialog.

Listening is more than half of communicating. A common situation is for everyone to talk and no one to listen. We sometimes listen only long enough to find an opening in which to insert our own opinion. But if we are to have creative dialog around the workshop table, we must have real listening. That means more than merely hearing what the other person says. It means understanding what he says as he himself understands it. We can neither use nor discard an idea until we know what it is. A few simple rules can help us understand rather than just hear:

- Don't interrupt.
- Ask nonjudgmental, clarifying questions.
- Restate in your own words your understanding of the speaker's idea and ask if your restatement is correct.
- Ask the speaker to restate his idea or to elaborate it further.
- Consciously seek to understand the idea as the speaker understands it.
- Accept the idea as an input to the problem area being discussed.

Focus on problems, ideas, opportunities—never on personalities. So long as the dialog focuses on the subject rather than the participants, exciting progress can be made. Ideas will flow. Observations that would otherwise be smothered by company culture or procedures will open up whole new perspectives. All will contribute. And the end result will usually be an agreement that is neither one person's idea nor a compromise but is instead an integration that belongs to all. The result is better than any one of the participants could achieve alone. It is better conceptually as an idea or agreement and far better organizationally, since all involved in developing it have a common understanding of it, a commitment to it, and a motivation to implement it.

Use a large easel pad to record information, ideas, agreements reached, and individual assignments. Watercolor felt-tip markers are best for writing—they make a strong, solid line and do not soak through the paper to stain the paper or the wall beneath. The easel paper should be large enough for all to read. Use of an easel provides a focal point for dialog and helps to assure mutual understanding. Pages can be posted on the wall with masking tape (to avoid damage to the wall) so that several can be examined and worked on at the same time. Material written on the easel pad will also be useful to the recorder in preparing minutes of the session.

Audit Present Business

One of the important subjects of a first workshop meeting is an audit of the present business—the business we now are. It can be produced entirely from the minds of the participants without advance preparation. Alternatively, a prepared audit can be developed and distributed prior to the meeting. From my own experience, neither approach is superior to the other. We do not need all the nuts and bolts; we need only the fundamentals of the business and what the business does—its major inputs and outputs. Those are uppermost in the minds of company people and need only an appropriate line of questioning to be brought out. The line of questioning might be as follows:

What are our product lines? (List with current volume.)
What are the major markets for each of the lines?
What will be the market growth rate for each line over the next few years?
What is our market position in each line? (By major market countries if the business is international.)
Who are our competitors?
What is our competitive position with respect to our competitors?
Where are our best opportunities over the next few years?
What is our competitive position with respect to our opportunities?
What are our people strengths?
What are our market strengths?
What are our technical strengths?
What are our major problem areas?
What changes or new developments in the following areas may significantly affect our future? Technological, legislative or political, manpower and motivational, economic, markets, environmental.
What are the recent trends and future prospects for sales volume and income?
What are our plant facilities and capacities?
What is our present organization?
What are our financial resources?
What changes or new areas of operations might we consider?
What areas of concentration are most promising for us?

By pursuing such a line of questioning—and not exploring each question to its last detail but identifying only what is most significant—a group of knowledgeable people will develop a good and valid audit of their business in about a half day's time. Much more time could, of course, be used, but it is not necessary. The purpose of the audit is to provide a basis for a dialog that will lead to good answers to the fundamental questions:

What are we?
What should we become?

A half day of concentrated effort should be enough to develop the background and common understanding needed for the dialog. The recorder for the meeting can then summarize the workshop business audit, develop any additional information or data that may be needed, and by the time of the next meeting of the group have an audit of the fundamentals in written form.

Alternatively, an audit can be prepared in advance by using the same line of questioning or an outline such as the following one. This particular outline was used to prepare an audit of a company that, in ten preceding years, had shown a level volume of sales and a slowly declining level of income. The audit was then used in developing a concept of identity and a business plan that, in four years' time, increased volume 80 percent and income 110 percent.

1. Catalog, or product literature, with price list and sales terms.
2. Brief description of each product line or major product.
3. For each product line or major product:
   a. Applications or uses, with percent of total sales for each.
   b. Industries sold with percent of total sales for each.
   c. Distribution method (direct, distributors, agents, and so on—number, concentration, policy).
   d. Sales in past five years and forecast for next five years.
   e. Total industry sales in past five years, forecast for next five years, and company share of market.
   f. Major competitors, with approximate present share of market for each. Rate each + (better), 0 (equal), or − (not as good) on following points: product quality, application technology, customer service, new product development, marketing strategy, proprietary position, raw material position, and manufacturing cost.
4. Total sales, costs, and profitability for past five years and forecast for next five years using marginal costing and income format.
5. Any seasonal nature in sales? If so, what is typical monthly distribution of sales?
6. New products:
   a. New products in past five years, annual sales in past five years, and forecast for next five years.
   b. New products now in development and anticipated future sales.
7. Long-term growth:
   a. Prospects of substitute materials, processes, or products.
   b. Market change.
   c. Environmental change.
8. Changes in industry:
   a. What are major new developments in the industry over past three years? Anticipated in next ten years?
   b. What position will company have in each of above new developments?
9. Company organization.
10. Company facilities.
11. Description of present advertising and sales promotion program, including list of active trademarks and trade names, with products covered.
12. Current budget, long-range plan, and marketing plans.
13. Major problems.
14. Major opportunities.

Applications of Identity

Problem-solving, opportunity-seeking dialog among knowledgeable company people—plus outside people when additional skills are needed—can effectively initiate change and also strengthen the organization to make achievement of the results possible. Nothing is more powerful than an idea, and anything can be achieved by committed people. A dialog approach can develop both ideas and commitment. Let me summarize a few examples.

By using exactly the methods recommended in this book, a small manufacturer of calendered vinyl film confronted its problem: 160 employees, $10 million invested in plant and working capital, a rising rate of sales, and a steady string of monthly operating losses. Over a few months' time a new concept of what the company could be was developed, and over the next few months the concept was implemented throughout operations. The new company—the same company made new by its new concept—(1) changed its product mix, (2) concentrated marketing effort on different markets and selected target accounts, (3) planned products and sales programs to maximize marginal income per hour of calender operation, and (4) improved calender line productivity to increase capacity by approximately 40 percent.

The people were the same, but their company became quite different. And they did it themselves; all of them participated in the dialog and played their roles in their individual jobs to bring to reality the new concept of what they should become. And among the things the company became was profitable. Organization changes were made as the program progressed, but they were understandable and acceptable to all because they fitted the new concept. And as progress and achievement continued, motivation and commitment increased. A come-from-behind victory is the sweetest kind of achievement.

Another company had operated successfully for years on the basis of a tightly held patent position. There was little growth, but there was great security—at least so long as the patents were valid and customers found no alternatives. Management recognized that although that kind of security might be perfect for the present, it was fragile for the future and there must be something better. Dialoging the two fundamental questions, what we are, and what we should become, provided an answer. Management chose to develop a new security based on market position rather than patent position. The present market position was carefully analyzed and a desired new position was conceptualized on the basis of markets, products, and technology. Three new product-market areas were targeted, and technical and commercial programs were initiated to establish them. Starting from a clear recognition of where it was, a new business was created. It was far more secure than the old one, far more profitable, and far more fun to work for.

An overseas company was in the business of building furnaces for industrial customers. In its home country market it was well known and respected as a leader in its industry. A dialog of the two fundamental questions revealed significant variance from the apparent image. Except for a few products and a few markets the company was not in a leadership position. Operationally, it was inefficient. When it was examined by principles of economics, it was even unprofitable, although the income statement managed to show a modest profit. Clearly new concepts of what the company was and what it could become were needed. Dialog sessions and individual homework provided them. The business was no longer one of designing, manufacturing, and selling industrial furnaces. It became one of engineering and marketing heating processes for industry. Certain industries and certain country markets were targeted for major effort. Many old products were discontinued, and marketing effort become more specialized in target market requirements, operations, systems, and needs. Even the company name was changed. The word "furnace" disappeared and in its place appeared the words "process heating." An old and unprofitable product business was becoming a new systems business that sought success through a concept of what it should become. The concept did not make the job easy, but it did make the job possible.

A plastics company, long a leader in its field, faced difficult problems as it approached an important anniversary of its founding. Over several years sales volume had risen slightly when business conditions were good and declined moderately when business conditions were less favorable. Two major attempts at diversification had not yet reached profitable operations and were a significant drain on company resources. With the 1970 business recession, profitability declined sharply.

Management decided to use the dialog approach with the help of two outside consultants who were selected for competence in disciplines important to a consideration of the company's problems and opportunities. One contributed expertise in motivation, job enrichment, and organization development; the other contributed expertise in business planning and economics. Over three months of dialog, with some 70 managers, supervisors, and professional employees involved, concepts of what the company then was and what it should undertake to become were developed.

In implementing the new concept, the company reorganized itself into specialized business areas and concentrated on the specific businesses targeted as opportunities. In a year's time, as dialog continued, new programs that considerably changed the character and the competence of the company were in operation. Adverse trends in sales, income, productivity, innovation, and motivation slowed and then reversed. The company entered its anniversary year on a strong, creative uptrend.

An international company with manufacturing operations in twelve countries, sales subsidiaries in an additional seven countries, and marketing operations throughout the world used the dialog approach to understand its present and conceptualize what is future should become. The dialog process began with a management group drawn from all operations. Over a four-year period there were dialog groups within individual country operations and other groups with all operations represented. Groups were as large as sixty-five and as small as three; sessions were as long as one week and as short as two hours. Many dialog sessions were scheduled as a portion of meetings required for other reasons, such as board and budget review meetings. The result of the dialog was the emergence of new concepts that significantly altered the future of the company. The company changed itself from what were primarily a number of subsidiaries operating in individual national markets to a worldwide marketing company with expertise in both national and international markets both West and East. The stronger emphasis on its marketing skills made possible a multinational growth and diversification of product lines and services.

Such conceptual thinking need not be limited to large company operations. With a history of success and effective ways of doing things and a large investment in the past it is often very difficult for the large organization to loosen up enough to really think conceptually about its future. The smaller, newer operation or the one-man entrepreneur, on the other hand, depends for existence on conceptual thinking. In 1960 Milan Panic was a graduate student in biochemistry at the University of Southern California. Four years earlier he had come to the States from his native Yugoslavia, where he fought as a guerilla during World War II while still in his teens.

As a student, Panic saw an emerging need for radioactive and nucleic acid biochemicals. He began to sell a line of those kinds of chemicals to pharmaceutical companies, built up a financial base, and six years later launched a growth-by-acquisition program to acquire small pharmaceutical companies that could implement his business concept: specialization in nucleic acid biochemistry and biochemical radioactive compounds. In 1961, his first year of business as a selling company, total company sales were $8,000. Ten years later Milan Panic headed ICN Pharmaceuticals, Inc., with a sales volume of more than $160 million and subsidiaries in fifteen countries. All of that was created from a concept that was right for him, right for his company, and right for the world around him. And that conceptual, creative process continues.

Pierre Cardin has long been among the most successful of the Paris couturiers. His enterprise concept well matched his considerable skills in the fashion world. Now that concept has been expanded to embrace new areas. Fashion, after all, is much more than what people wear; it is expressed in everything man creates. "I have found," says M. Cardin, "that it is just as easy to design a table as a dress."[3] And industrial design becomes an area of enterprise.

Over recent years, Cardin has well exemplified creative conceptual thinking as a route to achievement. As the world of *haute couture* became less and less profitable, new opportunities and new ventures were needed. In the early 1960s

[3]*Business Week,* February 5, 1972.

Cardin launched ready-to-wear, a revolutionary idea for the fashion houses of the time but now the major source of income for most of them. In the 1970s, implementing a broader concept of fashion, Cardin moved into the world of industrial and consumer product design, where his talent has been applied to design of baby carriages. Hi-Fi systems, facial tissues, sewing machines, bicycles, perfume, furniture, rugs, wristwatches, chocolates, TV sets, cars, bathrooms, kitchens, and wine. Says Cardin, "There is always something else to design." By the late 1970s the Cardin name and designs were worth at least $250 million annually, with 370 licensees making hundreds of Cardin-designed items sold in 40 countries, including Russia.

The need for conceptual thinking is not limited to business enterprise. All institutions need valid conceptual thinking if they are to have a meaningful, successful future, and dialog is the most productive way to create valid concepts. In 1969 a committee of trustees, faculty, student, and administration representatives of Nasson College, Springvale, Maine, developed a statement of definition, purpose, and objectives for the college. A long-range planning committee drawn from the entire college community annually reviews and updates the statement. By the agreed-upon definition, Nasson is a private, nondenominational liberal arts college that will not attempt to increase in size but will instead concentrate on quality education for students who are capable of "contributing to their education as well as benefiting from it." As the quoted passage implies, emphasis is on the personal approach to education, and so faculty-student interaction is fundamental to the continuing examination of the statement of definition, purpose, and objectives.

Educational innovation will be considered regularly, and the academic program, although the responsibility of the faculty, will be "designed to allow the student the greatest possible freedom in determining his own course of study." The expectation is that Nasson graduates will be "mature, responsible adults" who will have developed "constructive attitudes of self-discipline" and will be self-developing individuals capable of contributing to their own special fields of endeavor as well as to society in general.

Lower-Level Applications

Nasson and the other examples illustrate how an enterprise can find a meaningful identity by drawing on the knowledge and abilities of its people. But what if you are not at such a level in your organization that you can motivate that kind of total organization effort? Is the whole thing then a matter of only academic interest—something "they" should do or do better? Not at all. The same ideas and the same kind of approach can be very useful to you wherever you are in your organization.

Work in organizations does not get done in accordance with the customary hierarchical charts; it gets done by individuals and groups who combine their talents to achieve specific outputs. At any one time a professional, supervisor, manager, or other employee will be working as an individual on some outputs and also as a member of one or more groups of people on other outputs. Such groups typically cannot be identified on the organization chart.

A group need never actually meet to function as a group, although it certainly must communicate. For example, someone in purchasing may procure samples and equipment for someone in engineering to develop a product specified by someone in product planning for a market identified and quantified by people in sales for customers who require specialized delivery service from transportation of the final product manufactured by people in production from raw materials purchased by still others in purchasing and produced by processes determined by someone in process manufacturing. Most outputs require similar collaboration of groups of people. Each individual in his job and each work group can be made effective and productive in proportion to his or its concept of identity. That's where it all starts. Of course, when the company, division, or subsidiary has its identifying concept well thought out, accepted, and in use throughout the organization, all individuals and work groups can see their own identities much more clearly. But even when the company concept is unclear, they can conceptualize identities for themselves. After all, they do know a great deal about their company and its products, services, markets, and way of working.

Beginning with those observable inputs an individual or a work group can conceptualize a summary statement answering the two fundamental questions what we are now and what we should become. Work on the statement can be individual or by a dialog among several people. It can be done for individual jobs, work groups, or organization components. When the concepts are developed, they should be used, along with goals and strategies described in the following chapters, to the extent they can be used within existing organizational constraints. And they should be communicated with next higher levels of management. If disagreement is found, it can be dialoged to find new solutions if necessary. From the whole process can come growth and achievement for the individual, the work group, the unit, and the company. The responsibility is not only "theirs." It belongs to all of us.

Defining the Identity

Whether for a job, a work group, an organization component, or the entire company, dialog on what we are and what we should become can be organized through a consideration of the following enterprise dimensions:

1. Products and services provided—the "outputs."
2. Markets and/or client groups served.
3. People competence: technical, marketing, financial, entrepreneurial.
4. Facilities and capital resources.
5. Geographical scope.
6. Relationship to environmental change.

Defining our identity in those dimensions can be an exciting adventure. For the individual it becomes job enrichment. For the work group and the organization component it begins the journey toward organization development. For the entire company or profit center it becomes the fundamental business definition on which the future can be created. All, of course, are related to one another. And when the work has been done throughout the enterprise (and continues to be done, for it always must be current), we will have a climate for competence and achievement in which we can find our future and achieve it.

The definition we develop will probably not be expressed in all six of the dimensions listed. Although all six should be considered and dialoged, the definition should be expressed in the terms found to be most meaningful. The easiest definitions to arrive at are those expressed in products and services. We seem conditioned to think of our jobs, work groups, and companies in product and production terms. There is nothing wrong with that except that no longer is that kind of a definition enough. We need to add one or more of the other enterprise dimensions, and we need also to add a dimension of time.

So we look at the second dimension: markets and/or client groups served. Usually it is productive to examine them in relation to products and services; for it is in those relations that our definition can become distinctive and meaningful. The relations can be readily developed by matrix analysis:

1. List products and services by appropriate classifications across the top of a piece of paper or on an easel pad if the work is done in a dialog session.

2. List markets and/or client groups served down the left-hand side.

3. Fill in the intersections with appropriate data and information such as, for an enterprise, sales volume, market position, marginal income, market size and growth rate, opportunities, and problems. Figure 3-1 illustrates a format for this matrix analysis.

Totals for the columns are product totals; totals for the rows are market totals. The boxes, or intersections, show significant relations between the two. In using such a matrix we should not look only for snapshot information. We should look for a motion picture—the current information in a time perspective. We need to understand also both past and probable future changes and trends. From that information we can then define our enterprise, both present and future, in product and market terms.

People competence, facilities and capital resources, geographical scope, and environmental relationships need also to be examined—what they are now and what, perhaps, they will or should become. When all six of the enterprise dimensions are examined by a management group, through dialog, surprising things can happen. The enterprise may confirm its past identity, but it is more likely to develop something significantly new. And the new identity can be strong enough and motivating enough to combine talent throughout the enterprise to new heights of achievement. The new identity will be expressed and understood by all, in terms of:

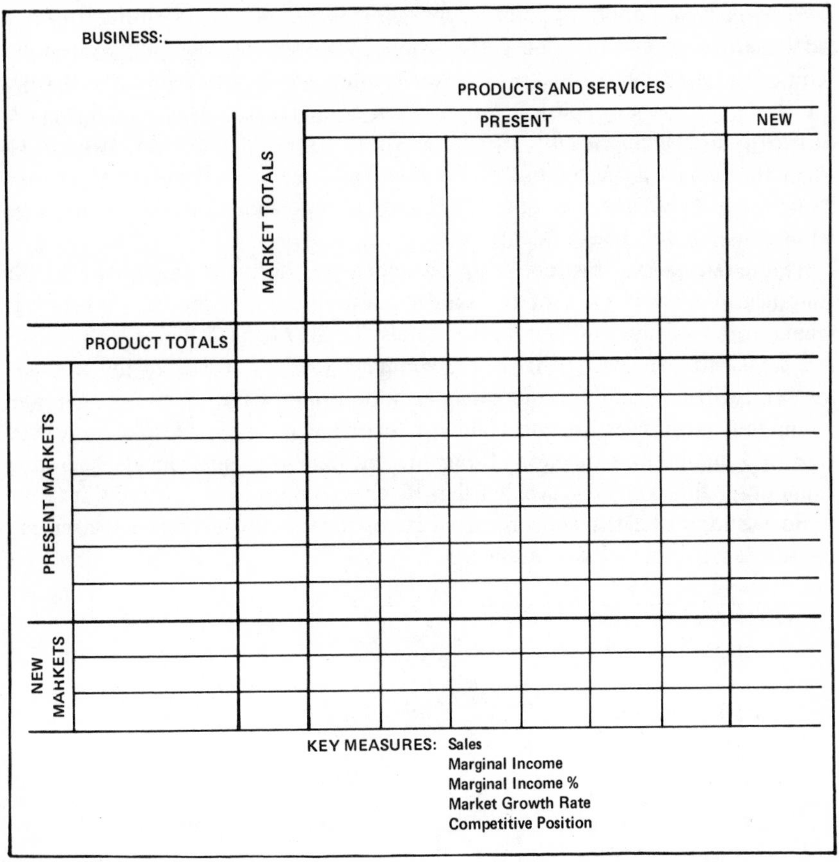

BUSINESS:_____

PRODUCTS AND SERVICES

	MARKET TOTALS	PRESENT					NEW
PRODUCT TOTALS							
PRESENT MARKETS							
NEW MARKETS							

KEY MEASURES: Sales
Marginal Income
Marginal Income %
Market Growth Rate
Competitive Position

Figure 3-1.

1. How we will apply our:
   People skills
   Capital, raw material, and energy resources
   Technology
   Market position
2. To offer superior value to selected markets and target clients
3. Within environmental constraints:
   Political
   Social
   Ecological
   Economic
4. And focusing primarily on areas of change

Growth is an important form of change, and the one on which industry has particularly concentrated for performance improvement. But success can be built also on other forms of change—technological, commercial, economic, social, environmental, political. Success can come from making it *different* (in response to changing needs), as well as from making it *more* (in response to aggregate demand). For the timid, change is frightening. For the satisfied, change is threatening. But for the confident, change is opportunity. Management has to be a profession for the confident.

Figure 3-2 shows this matrix as developed by the management of a South American company. Each of the solid circles represents a product-market segment. Totals of the rows are market totals. Totals of the columns are product line totals. At the lower right are the company totals. For each of the product-market segments, and for the totals as appropriate, basic operating data was assembled: gross sales, marginal income, marginal income rate, market growth rate, and competitive position. From this information and from its operating experience, this company decided that its client values were primarily in terms of marketing strengths and organized its operations by markets served. Each market row became a P & L business.

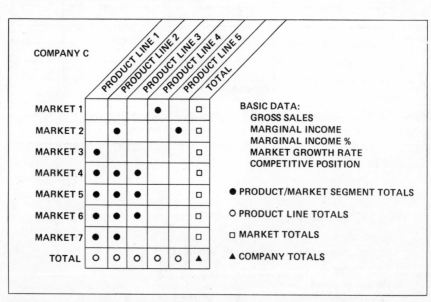

Figure 3-2.

Company D, Figure 3-3, a job-shop manufacturer of components, defined its business into three product groups. There was very little overlap in clients and market segments served. For product groups 1 and 2, superior customer values were defined and each of these was organized as a profit-center business. For product group 3, income performance was poor and no superior customer value was identified on which success could be built. This business was sold.

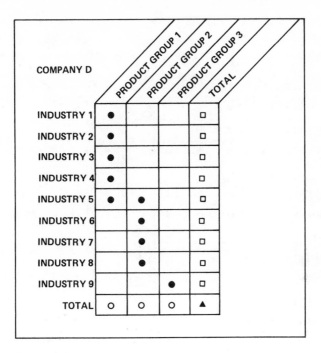

COMPANY D	PRODUCT GROUP 1	PRODUCT GROUP 2	PRODUCT GROUP 3	TOTAL
INDUSTRY 1	●			□
INDUSTRY 2	●			□
INDUSTRY 3	●			□
INDUSTRY 4	●			□
INDUSTRY 5	●	●		□
INDUSTRY 6		●		□
INDUSTRY 7		●		□
INDUSTRY 8		●		□
INDUSTRY 9			●	□
TOTAL	○	○	○	▲

Figure 3-3.

Another company, Company F, defined its very complex customer-product line mix into five strategic businesses partly by product line and partly by market served. These product-market strategic businesses are illustrated in Figure 3-4.

In all three companies, for each of the businesses as defined, the "superior customer value" was identified on which the company could build its business success. And resources were concentrated on those particular businesses and business segments where growth or change was greatest. Use of this matrix in developing strategy is discussed in Chapter 5.

Success, however, can not be only in terms of products, markets, and competition. There also has to be an awareness of and an accommodation with the other environments impacting the business. Survival and future success depend on environmental relationships as importantly as on current profitability. Figure 3-5 shows the diverse environments that comprise today's business environment. There is the company environment operating within the commercial environment of suppliers, clients, and competitors. But our world today is far more than this.

There are also the economic, the technical, the ecological, the social, and the political environments with their regional, national, and international aspects. All of these environments interact with all others to change continually the world of business. In these changes and in these relationships there are opportunities as well as constraints, so we must develop an anticipatory awareness of

47

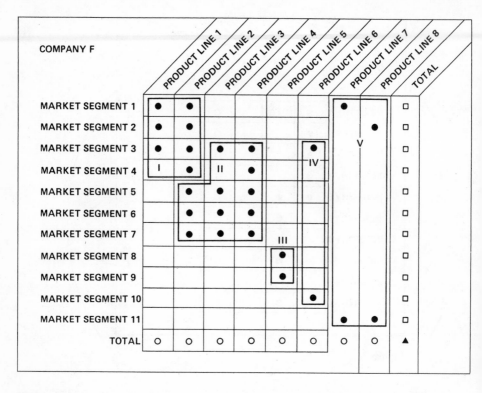

COMPANY F	PRODUCT LINE 1	PRODUCT LINE 2	PRODUCT LINE 3	PRODUCT LINE 4	PRODUCT LINE 5	PRODUCT LINE 6	PRODUCT LINE 7	PRODUCT LINE 8	TOTAL
MARKET SEGMENT 1	●	●				●			□
MARKET SEGMENT 2	●	●					●		□
MARKET SEGMENT 3	●	●	●	●		●			□
MARKET SEGMENT 4	I	●	II	●		IV			□
MARKET SEGMENT 5		●	●	●					□
MARKET SEGMENT 6		●	●	●					□
MARKET SEGMENT 7		●	●	●					□
MARKET SEGMENT 8				● III					□
MARKET SEGMENT 9				●					□
MARKET SEGMENT 10					●				□
MARKET SEGMENT 11							●	●	□
TOTAL	○	○	○	○	○	○	○	○	▲

Figure 3-4.

environmental change and by our actions accommodate the enterprise to this change.

An international company, by using dialog and project assignment among its management group, over a six-month period developed a definition of its identity expressed in terms of people competence and products and services:

IDENTITY

Company AA is a growing, multinational enterprise based on:

1. Technical and commercial expertise in _____ systems.
2. Enterpreneurial skills in business development and diversification.
3. Marketing competence within countries and areas and trading competence between and among countries.
4. Resources in organization talent and its development and motivation.

STATUS

Present Company AA businesses are:

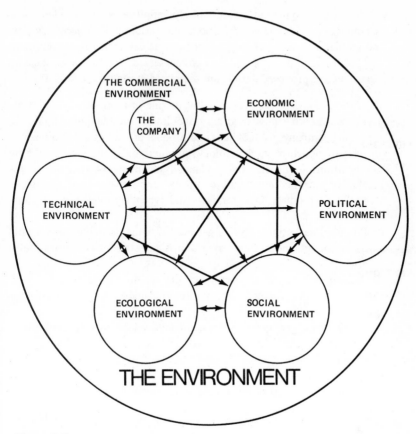

Figure 3-5.

1. Product Group A.
2. Product Group B.
3. Product Group C.
4. Process and product recycle.
5. International trading, contra trade.
6. Diversification enterprises.

The definition describes a company different from the one that prepared it. It includes what the present company is, alters that a bit, and adds some significant new dimensions that specify what the company intends to become. It provides a conceptual launching pad for the articulation of goals, strategies, and action plans. But that will forever be an iterative process. Everything relates to everything else, and as new goals, strategies, and action plans are developed and implemented, feedback will foster changes in what went before. Our normative future can be created, but continuing change will be a part of that creation.

Most companies will define their identities in terms of products as a first step.

Many will stop at that point. But a product-only definition is seldom adequate as a starting point for a success story. Additional dimensions will be necessary if we are to find an identity strong enough to motivate achievement. Most commonly one of the additional dimensions will be markets served. The following checklist is useful in evaluating proposed definitions expressed in products and markets:

1. Does the definition specifically delineate one or more of the following?
   a. Product line business area: a product line or product grouping unique among company product lines and product groupings but as a business related enough in its technology, production facilities, and marketing operations to be effectively planned and managed as one business.
   b. Market area: an important company target market for a range of products, product lines, services, and systems provided by the company.
   c. Product line business area target market: a major market that is within a product line business area and is targeted for concentration of effort.
2. As defined, is the business a significant one for the company?
3. For the business as defined, can the situation analysis worksheet information be obtained?
4. Is there a meaningful rationale for company leadership in this business?
5. Is it appropriate and logical to program research and development for this business?
6. Can productivity objectives be determined for this business?
7. Does a definite group of customers and prospects logically fall into this area?
8. Is it logical to set sales volume, market share, and income goals for this business?
9. Can sales of and income to this business be measured?
10. Can sales and promotion effort be specialized to the market served?
11. Are environmental relationships favorable to the company?

At this point we have developed, by business definition, a concept of our present and future identity, but we have not yet completed our work. The concept may not be the one best for us. To find whether it is, we have some concept testing to do. We can do it by asking ourselves some questions about the business as we have defined it. All the questions will test our concept of our identity in relation to markets, competitors, and conditions and change in the world around us. In our questioning we will remove ourselves from our company or organization and look at our concept of our identity from the viewpoint of related areas in the environment around us. That is hard to do, but it is very interesting and at times even inspiring. In the process of concept testing I have seen exciting changes in concepts of identity emerge.

Again, the concept testing should not be by management decision, it should be by exploration by a number of competent people. Rating scales, checklists, and questionnaries are sometimes used for the purpose, but I find them usually too mechanical and too related to the organizational constraints that we should be testing. One approach that I have found useful is a listing in matrix form of environmental considerations and the business as defined in such terms as business areas, product lines, and markets and market segments. Modifications of that matrix have been specially prepared for developing business intelligence evaluations of different kinds of businesses. Figures 3-6 to 3-8 illustrate the matrix formats.

For each business and market area and target market we must become expert in our knowledge of the business situation. That we can do with situation analysis, which is an organized method of collecting pertinent data, developing the data, and then determining or anticipating their effect upon the business environment. The situation analysis worksheets in Figures 3-6 to 3-8 provide a guide for such studies. Information filled into them constitutes an analysis of where we are (our company, environment, competition, markets, and distribution) and how we got there. It also constitutes an analysis of significant trends and a projected outlook on future condition. The analysis will identify the areas that offer the greatest opportunities. From the opportunities that are available we can select the most promising ones for major effort. At the same time we will recognize the obstacles faced, so that a realistic evaluation of opportunity will result. The situation analysis and evaluation provide us the information we need to make final decisions on business definitions, goals, strategies, and action plans.

Suggested Readings

Ansoff, H. Igor, Roger P. Declerck, and Robert L. Hayes, *From Strategic Planning to Strategic Management.* New York: John Wiley & Sons, 1976.

Drucker, Peter F., *Management Tasks, Responsibilities, Practices.* New York: Harper & Row, 1974.

Gellerman, Saul W., *Management by Motivation.* New York: Amacom, 1968.

Harman, Willis W., *An Incomplete Guide to the Future.* San Francisco: San Francisco Book Company, Inc., 1976.

Herzberg, Frederick, *Work and the Nature of Man.* New York: World Publishing, 1966.

Levitt, Theodore, *The Marketing Mode.* New York: McGraw-Hill, 1969.

Likert, Rensis, *The Human Organization: Its Management and Value.* New York: McGraw-Hill, 1967.

Lippitt, Gordon L., *Organization Renewal.* New York: Appleton-Century-Crofts, 1969.

McHale, John, *The Ecological Context.* New York: Braziller, 1970.

Schon, Donald A., *Beyond the Stable State.* New York: W. W. Norton & Co., 1973.

Steiner, George A. and John B. Miner, *Management Policy and Strategy.* New York: Macmillan Publishing Co., Inc., 1977.

SITUATION ANALYSIS WORK SHEET
COMPETITIVE FACTORS

LRP Business Area _____
Prepared By _____ Date _____

Competing Companies				
Share of Market				
Trend of Market Share				
Reason for Change				
Cost Position				
Number of Salesmen				
How is Sales Dept. Organized?				
Pricing Policy				
Quality of Technical Service				
Product Quality				
Research Department				
Important Recent Innovations				
Major Strengths				
Major Weaknesses				
Strategy Used				

Figure 3-6.

SITUATION ANALYSIS WORK SHEET
MARKET FACTORS

LRP Business Area_____ Date_____
Prepared By_____

Major Market Sectors				
Market Size & Growth Trend				
Seasonal Sales Pattern				
Sensitivity to Business Cycle (Ups & Downs in General Business Conditions)				
Type & Size of Customers				
Degree of Concentration by Size				
Geographical Concentration (Within USA)				
Are There Important Foreign Markets?				
Price Trends				
Profit Opportunity				
Key Buying Influences (Who must we sell or influence to get the business? List in order of importance.)				

Figure 3-7.

53

SITUATION ANALYSIS WORK SHEET
MARKET FACTORS (Continued)

Innovation: a) Significant new products & processes commercialized in last 3 years			
b) Approximate life cycle for new product			
Integration Trends — How do they affect our business?			
Technological Changes — How do they affect our business?			
What alternative products or processes are now or potentially able to serve this market?			
What are the major needs and problems of this industry?			
What are our customers' major markets?			
Is knowledge of these markets important to Hooker? Where answer is "yes," fill out Situation Analysis Work Sheet for the customers' market.			

54

Figure 3-7 (continued)

Relation to other Hooker
or Oxy businesses

Trade regulation or judgment, order or
decree limitations

Health and safety
considerations

Pollution control requirements

Possible harmful consequences
of use and ultimate disposal
of product

Transport, handling,
and storage hazards and
regulatory requirements

Product pre-approvals
required

Figure 3-8.

55

4

The Stimulation of Goals

In defining our identity we conceptualize a purpose. When we find answers to our two fundamental questions, we find a value system and a direction that can stimulate great achievement. In answering the question of what we are, we understand our history, our competences, and our current situation and performance. In answering the question of what we will become, we use the wisdom of our present and awareness of the world around us to determine the purpose for our future. That purpose can then be made specific and highly motivating through the development of organizational goals.

Goals and Value Systems

In all areas of human affairs we see great motivational drive for the achievement of goals when those goals clearly represent value systems people believe in. That kind of motivation, that kind of stimulation can be drawn on by the business enterprise—or any other kind of organization—once it has defined its identity and that identity has been accepted as valid by its members.

As we saw in Chapter 3, validity is not the product of individual brilliance or the province of management. It can only be the product of mutuality and the province of all the people who comprise the enterprise. Communication, involvement, dialog—all those make possible the achievement of a valid identity. And those same processes must be used to develop from the identity the goals that, in their achievement, will confirm the identity.

One business developed a concept of its identity as being a leader in certain segments of its industry but having a need to diversify into at least one major new area in which it could develop a leadership position that would provide future growth. To achieve greater productivity in existing operations that would be required by intensifying competition and to establish an innovative climate that could make possible successful diversification, the organization would have to function more openly and more participatively than it had in the past. Some sixty managers and professional people participated in a dialog to bring into clear focus specific goals most important to the enterprise if it was to achieve that new identity. A limited number of goals were sought, but the goals were significant enough that all areas of company operations could relate to them. In that way, efforts throughout the company could be mutually supportive and the work of each person and unit could contribute effectively to company achievement. Seven such broad goals were developed and agreed on:

1. Maintain or achieve a leading market share in the specific business areas targeted for concentration of efforts and resources. (These were separately identified.)
2. By 19– double operating income with programs then in place and successfully functioning to insure continuing growth in profitability of 10% per year or more.
3. By internal development or by acquisition commercialize two or more new ventures prior to 19– that will: (a) enhance earnings in an existing business area or (b) enable the Company to achieve a leading position in a new growth segment of the plastics industry. By the end of 19– commercialize one of those ventures and have programs for at least one more prepared.
4. Target and achieve experience curve productivity improvements and thereby achieve favorably competitive costs in targeted business area segments.
5. Relate experience curve economics to pricing and develop appropriate pricing strategies.
6. Conduct operations to meet the Company's responsibilities to its employees, the general public, and the communities in which it operates and the requirements of applicable law.
7. Create a participative management environment within the Company that can develop the talent, the will, and the group effectiveness to accomplish Company goals.

We cannot look at a listing of goals such as those and evaluate how good the goals are. How good they are will depend on such considerations as the following:

1. How well accepted are they throughout the organization?
2. How directly can the goals be related to the work of individuals, work groups, and departments?
3. To what extent do the goals recognize the present situation in the enterprise—the concept of what we are?
4. To what extent do the goals fit the environment and the opportunities?
5. Are the goals actionable?

6. Are the goals mutually consistent? Are they consistent with the concept of identity—what we intend to become?
7. Are the goals achievable?
8. Can progress toward the achievement of the goals be measured and reported promptly as an aid to goal achievement?
9. To what extent can all individual operating actions be directly related to and guided by one or more of the goals?

Answers to such questions cannot be known from looking at the goals alone. We must also know the organization. An examination of the seven goals listed earlier, together with knowledge of the organization that developed them, reveals a quite significant reorientation of the company's way of doing business. And the goals were the result of inputs from many people, although that effort did not completely change a long history of rather authoritative management. Nevertheless, a start had been made, and in this particular company further dialog resulted in some new and changed goals within two years. The organization had changed and grown—in competence rather than in number of people. The environmental situation was changing. And the organization was able to rethink its goals to improve their validity and motivational impact.

Once the company has conceptualized its identity and developed appropriate goals, it becomes possible for components of the company to develop goals of their own that, when achieved, will move the company toward the achievement of its overall goals. The management and professional people of a major product group business within the company just described critiqued their business situation and their company's objectives. Over a period of two months they evolved several goals most important for their product group business at that time. The goals were those that could be achieved over periods of from a few months to a year or more. New goals would be established from time to time as the first goals were achieved or as new major problems or opportunities developed. The following were the goals developed by this product group business:

MARKET STANDING

1. To achieve 25% or 11,000,000 pounds of the _____ market for product line _____ by the end of this year. That would be followed by achieving 37% or 20,000,000 pounds of the market by the end of next year.
2. Maintain 60% of the market for product _____.
3. Increase our U.S. market share by 1½ percentage points.

INNOVATION

4. Develop and commercialize new applications for _____ materials by

the end of this year with a potential volume of 15,000,000 pounds per year and sales this year of 1,500,000 pounds.

5. Develop and commercialize a significant new product line by December 31.

PRODUCTIVITY

6. Establish production schedules and manage inventories to provide two-day service on 95% of the orders for materials of the stock and customer stock classifications.

7. Incorporate a target account system in field sales operations with specific sales volume objectives and a monthly report of achievement.

PROFITABILITY

8. Improve product _____ so that the marginal contribution is 50% or better.

9. Achieve an operating income of $_____ this year.

All the preceding specific operating goals for a product group business related to the overall goals of the company. They became, in effect, a budget plan for the product group business. And in carrying out their programs to achieve those goals the product group operating people were contributing to the total achievement sought by the company. All three market-standing goals related to company goal 1 on market share. The first innovation goal also related to company goal 1 on market share; the second related to company goal 3 on diversification. The first productivity goal related to company goal 4; the second related to company goal 1. The two profitability goals related to company goal 2. The dialog method of defining identity and determining goals not only arrived at good decisions but also assured that those decisions throughout the company were related and supportive.

In the preceding example the product group business objectives in turn became the starting points for objectives for subgroups, work groups, and individuals. For objective 1 under market standing, for example, a task force was organized to achieve the agreed-upon objective. Task force members remained in their regular jobs, but they contributed to the task force their individual expertise and their operating capabilities to achieve the objective. An action plan with specific objectives for each member was developed. There were four longer-range objectives to be accomplished over a three-year period:

1. Develop practical molding techniques for high-viscosity materials.
2. Develop electrical materials having specified premium properties.
3. Develop a new generation of general-purpose materials.

4. Develop and improve fabricating methods to more closely approximate current practice for the large-volume materials with which the new product line would compete. (Materials and desired fabrication characteristics were specified.)

The longer-range objectives were chosen as the present actions most important for the longer-range success of the new product line.

To achieve the immediate goal, short-range objectives were established for each task force member. In the first plan developed there were six objectives for product development, seven for sales engineering, three for production, and four for marketing. They would be accomplished in periods of from one month to nine months, and they were very specific to individuals and work groups. For example, the four marketing objectives in the first plan were:

1. Establish new product numbering system by _____ .
2. Develop pricing policy for new line and, with approval, announce and establish the introductory prices when sales program is launched.
3. Prepare advertising and sales promotion plan by _____ .
4. Plan introductory sales program and be prepared to implement program on _____ .

An individual was given the responsibility for accomplishing each of the objectives. As the plan progressed, as objectives were achieved, as the situation changed, and as new problems and opportunities were confronted, objectives too were changed. Throughout the program each task force member had current objectives coordinated with those of others to achieve the overall objective of the task force. And the overall objective was not only achieved but exceeded. In that related, mutually supportive way—from company, to product line business, to work groups, to individuals—a system of objectives can be developed and maintained always current to achieve, in total, the overall mission of the enterprise.

Fundamental Goals

It is always possible to develop a short list of the goals that are most fundamental to any enterprise or group within it at a particular time. It is necessary only to have as a starting point some valid concept of identity as discussed in Chapter 3. From that starting point it is possible to develop the key or fundamental goals that then become the control panel for guiding the enterprise or group. That approach to goal definition and goal achievement, when it is companywide, becomes in effect a budgetary control system in terms of work and achievement. It is a far more effective kind of budgetary system than one expressed in financial terms. It is also far simpler. It avoids any annual ordeal of budget construction, because a work and achievement budget is evergreen. What we most want' in a financial budget—income, expenses, and profit—can be drawn from it any time such data may be wanted.

But to establish a system of goals that can provide us those kinds of benefits, some procedural guidance is needed. We can't just ask ourselves what is most important. We might very well overlook critical areas of performance on which our future success depends. So we should, first of all, ask ourselves what areas of performance we must consider in thinking about specific goals. The first performance areas that we are likely to include on such a list are easy to identify. Our long experience with financial measurement and control will suggest profitability, sales volume, and costs. From there on the going is slower. We know that people are of great importance to the success of the enterprise, but how are company goals related to people? Employees don't appear on the balance sheet or the income statement, and we the people are certainly less measurable than the other inputs to and outputs from our business.

Change and responsiveness to change around us are important too. Our business enterprise exists and functions within a natural, social, economic, and political environment, and so environment considerations may be critically important in the formulation of goals. As we begin to think of all the many areas that may be important to the future of the enterprise, we might easily be overwhelmed by complexity. Instead of a few goals that are fundamental, we may begin to see a great many goals that are important or at least interesting.

Key Performance Areas

A mechanism for thinking through the complexities to the fundamentals was provided for us many years ago by Peter F. Drucker.[1] He identified eight key performance areas on which the success of the enterprise depends. These I have slightly modified in my work to the following listing of seven fundamental Key Performance Areas:

1. Market standing.
2. Innovation.
3. Productivity.
4. Physical and financial resources.
5. Profitability.
6. Motivation and organization development.
7. Public and environmental responsibility.

In developing goals with personnel of various companies, divisions, and units of divisions, I have found that we were consistently concerned with one or another of Drucker's key performance areas. So in more recent years I have

[1]*The Practice of Management* (New York Harper & Row, 1954), p. 63.

begun the investigation with the above listing as a helpful way to get the thinking of the people participating in our dialog productively concentrated on the fundamentals. Dialog, in my experience, is the most effective way to find the specific, most fundamental objectives. Taking in turn each of the key performance areas, we ask: "In consideration of our concept of our identity—what we are and what we wish to become—and guided by our business intelligence, what are the most important objectives for us, at this time, in the key performance area of _____?" A dialog beginning with that question will produce many possible objectives. But among those many there will be a small number that, if they were to be achieved, would clearly be most significant to the company. Usually for a company or for a unit within it the total number of major goals agreed on will be in the range of six to twelve.

Before dialoging each key performance area to arrive at goals, a short time might be devoted to a discussion of the key performance area idea and a brief summary and discussion of each of the key performance areas. The following outline can be used for that purpose.

The Need for Objectives

For every business, objectives are needed in every area in which performance and results vitally affect the success of the business. Objectives in terms of profit and sales volume are not enough. Only by setting objectives in all of the key performance areas that significantly affect business performance can we achieve long-range success. Peter F. Drucker has defined key areas important to all businesses, whatever the economic conditions, whatever the type of business, and whatever the business size or stage of growth. He has pointed out that wisely selected objectives in the key performance areas are the instrument panel necessary to pilot the business enterprise. They become fundamentals that determine the success of the enterprise.

Establishing Good Objectives

In developing specific objectives in the key performance areas, best results can be obtained if:

1. Objectives are arrived at through participation by all those directly involved in achieving the objectives.

2. Objectives are few in number rather than many. For an individual business there will probably not be specific objectives in all of the key performance areas, and the total of all specific objectives will probably be in the range of 6 to 12.

3. Objectives are changed as conditions change. While the key performance areas will remain the same, the specific objectives will change.

4. Objectives are written specifically. They should include quantities when possible, have target dates for competition, and be stated in end-result terms. That makes possible feedback on progress toward achievement of objectives.

The Seven Key Performance Areas

1. *Market standing.* Most businesses should have at least one objective in the general key performance area of market standing. It might be the maintenance or achievement of a target percent of market in a major country or countries. In considering goals for market standing it is very helpful to review the resource strategy matrix. A summary of the resource strategy concept and how it can be used is given in Chapter 12. Listing businesses in the cells of the matrix will provide guidance in setting market-standing objectives. For businesses listed in cell A, objectives for increasing market share are essential; the alternative would be to go out of the business. For businesses in cells B and C, objectives might be to maintain market share. For businesses in cell D, the objectives are generally to optimize or to discontinue.

In addition to market share objectives, specific objectives for sales volume can also be established. The following are examples of objectives in the market-standing key performance area.

Achieve the leading market position in _____ materials by fourth quarter 19–. (Objective for a business in resource strategy cell A.)
Maintain 34% market share in product line _____. (Objective for a major business in cell C.)
Introduce _____ and achieve leading market position by the end of 19–.
Achieve sales volume of _____ in 19–.

2. *Innovation.* We most commonly think of innovation as it applies to new products, but innovation may also be important in services offered and in various functional areas of our business operations. Because change is occurring so rapidly today, innovation must be an important key performance area. Successful products and methods from the past can very quickly become inadequate. The following are examples of key performance area goals for innovation.

Develop and commercialize product _____ by third quarter of 19–.
Shift distribution from agents to company representatives in _____.
Install new process for production of _____ by September 1.
Initiate an achievement-reporting system to replace present operating reports by January 1.

3. *Productivity.* Many firms establish specific objectives for production volume, and for the costs of the required raw materials, energy, and labor. Measures and reports monitor performance against these standards. But while many firms measure production in this kind of way, few firms measure productivity in any kind of way. Productivity is the measure of production in relation to the inputs required to produce it. Productivity requires us to look at all the inputs,

not man-hours alone. We must look at raw materials, energy, capital consumption, and man-hours and understand our productivity performance and trends for each of these input factors, and for total factor productivity. On these measures the successful enterprise will achieve productivity improvement superior to its competitors. This superiority requires awareness, measurement, and a continuing action program. Also useful can be methods for measuring, monitoring, and improving "economic productivity" which can be defined as the costs of all inputs in relation to the economic value of all outputs created. This measure provides a holistic economic summary of total operations that reflects both productivity achievement and product and product line development. Value-added is the key output measure in monitoring economic productivity. Trends in productivity measurements will indicate good performance and areas in which change is needed. The following are examples of goals in the key performance area of productivity.

In 19— increase sales volume per employee from _____ to _____.
This year achieve ratio of value added to employee compensation of 3 to 1.
By September 1 establish experience curve cost reduction goals for three-quarters (by dollar volume) of product production.

4. *Physical and financial resources.* The importance of specific goals for physical and financial resources will depend on the current situation in each company. The following are examples of such goals.

Reduce working capital 18% by September 1.
Meet targeted costs on new plant facility and have it on stream by July 15, 19—.

5. *Profitability.* Most businesses will have one or more specific objectives in the area of profitability. Here are some examples of such goals:

Reverse downturn in profitability by the end of the second quarter.
Increase marginal income rate from 42.1% to 44.0% by December 31.
Achieve operating income of _____ this year.

6. *Motivation and organization development.* One of the greatest opportunities for business organizations today lies within the organizations themselves. Underdevelopment of talent and underutilization of people are common, even prevalent. Improvement in both morale and the use of our human resources can often be achieved by such methods as increased participation, job enrichment, delegation, and stretching—giving people just a little more responsibility than they can comfortably handle. In most organizations there is great unused potential that can be recovered by improved communications, greater participation,

and improved structuring of the work to be done. The following are examples of goals in this key performance area.

Have a participative management by objectives (PMBO) program operating through three levels of management by September 1.

Make available to all management and professional employees at least one educational program this year.

Apply job enrichment approaches to the structuring of work in _____ department.

Increase use of the task force approach to problem solution. Keep a record for each task force of task force membership, purpose, program, and results.

Increase management-labor communication by personal contact (walking tours) and by informational meetings as they are found to be appropriate.

7. *Public and environmental responsibility.* Peter Drucker, in commenting on goals in the area of public and environmental responsibility, says that

objectives in this area, while extremely tangible, have to be set according to the social and political conditions which affect each individual enterprise and are affected by it, and on the basis of the beliefs of each management. It is this that makes the area so important; for in it managers go beyond the confines of their own little world and participate responsibly in society. But the overriding goal is common for every business: to strive to make whatever is productive for our society, whatever strengthens it and advances its prosperity, a source of strength, prosperity and profit for the enterprise.[2]

Specific goals in the area of public and environmental responsibility may relate to pollution control, employment practices, support of community programs, and participation in government affairs.

Application

By dialoging the key performance areas in consideration of the company's business definition, a management group can develop the objectives most important to the success of the enterprise. Those objectives become the starting point for an MBO way of working throughout the company. They also amount to a budget plan in action-oriented operating terms. For example, the management group of a European company whose previous good earnings performance had declined to about a breakeven level decided to use the methods advocated in this book. By a clearer statement of its business definition, the following objectives were developed to deal with major problem and opportunity areas. The objectives and the action programs implemented to achieve them led to substantial improvement in operating results.

1. Maintain number 1 market position in area 1; increase market position from number 3 to number 2 in area 2.

[2]Drucker, *The Practice of Management,* p. 82.

2. Complete audit of product lines and:
   a. Simplify by dropping unprofitable and unpromising lines and products.
   b. Concentrate efforts on: (1) Major lines E, U, and S with high market share to earn current profit. Strategy—optimization. (2) New lines P and F with growth opportunity. Strategy—increase market share.
3. Expand volume of subcontracted production and reduce direct materials and subcontract costs by 5%.
4. Increase prime margin from 32.7% to 35% by November 30.
5. Increase sales volume from 210 last year to 255 this year.
6. Control fixed expenses to no more than 60 this year.
7. Develop and implement a management education and development program by September 1.

The management group of a South American company had a successful record of improving sales and income, but the trends had plateaued and were beginning to decline. By thinking through a viable business definition more clearly and by dialoging the key performance areas in relation to that definition, the management group developed the following specific objectives to get their business back on the track of improved operations:

1. Achieve scheduled production of product A by March.
2. Obtain delivery of in-specification product B in contracted quantities by April 1.
3. Obtain distribution rights for product W to industrial customers at prices that will yield 24% marginal income or more.
4. Start up second D reactor by March 15 and pulverizer unit by April 15.
5. Achieve targeted sales volume objectives in business areas D, P, and C.
6. Successfully commercialize product PR by third quarter.
7. Develop plan and program for diversification by July.
8. Minimize profit effect of new labor and tax legislation.

Objectives and Goals
By beginning with overall company goals related to our definition of our identity, we begin a surprisingly motivating experience. The definition of identity has not been postulated; it has been found through the contributions of many individuals. Having been found in that way, it belongs to all. We then give our discovery specific dimension by developing the key performance area objectives most important to the identity we see for our future—what we intend to become. Through dialog, the talent of the organization has found and formed its direction.

The key performance area objectives of the company then become the specific MBO goals for the chief executive, but many individuals will participate in the achievement of most of those objectives. The chief executive then becomes a sort of task force chairman who helps, coordinates, and supports the achievement of the objectives. For some objectives, an executive reporting to the chief executive assumes responsibility for the achievement of an entire objective. The chief executive's role then becomes primarily supportive. For some other objectives, such as diversification by acquisition, the development of a participative management style, and investor relations, the chief executive himself may have the major role in goal achievement.

Once company goals are established, the next step is to develop objectives in divisions, subsidiaries, departments, business areas, and other components and work groups. Since company definition and goals have been participatively developed through dialog, a broad leadership group now shares a common concept of what we are, where we're going, and the major objectives for achievement on the road ahead. With that perspective, related and supportive objectives can be developed throughout the company. In each division, subsidiary, department, business area, component, and work group the objectives most important for achievement will also be found through dialog. The seven key performance areas and the company objectives in those areas provide a framework for that dialog. In that way objectives can be developed for all company units and work groups to the point of individual jobs.

Each employee and each company unit has then developed the performance objectives that in their collective achievement will accomplish company goals and effectuate the company's definition of its future. Objectives throughout the company are interrelated, mutually supportive, and highly motivational. We have implemented a participative MBO way of working together that makes jobs more interesting and meaningful and much more productive. We have found a way of structuring work different from the more conventional hierarchical organization charting with functional job descriptions and responsibility assignments. Concepts for and experience with this new approach to structuring work are described in more detail in Chapter 8.

Many organizations prefer to make a distinction between goal and objective. It may be made on the basis of organization level or by some measure of significance. I prefer, however, to use the two terms interchangeably. A goal is an objective; an objective is a goal; each is both. The two are the same thing—the targeted end result of achievement. But terminology is as we define it, so each organization may choose and define the terminology with which it prefers to work.

Through the process of establishing an identity and developing objectives throughout the company we have made another discovery. We have found a budget system superior to the conventional financial budget with financial operating reports and variance analysis; for our business definition and goals become both a long-range plan and a short-range operating plan. What is critical in the financial budget appears in our system of objectives also. But we now have a budget plan that is expressed in actionable terms and includes opportunity for feedback that will help in achieving the objectives. We have a budget of the enterprise, by the enterprise, and for the enterprise, its people, and its future. That concept, which I prefer to call achievement reporting rather than budgetary control, is described in Chapter 13.

From identity come objectives. From participation and through dialog come related, supportive objectives throughout the enterprise. In that network of goals everything is related to everything else and everything is related to our business definition, our concept of identity. The stimulation of goals becomes the starting point for organizational achievement.

5

The Strategy Compass

Strategy wins wars, wives, elections, business success, and ball games. It determines how the game will be played or the campaign fought. It's intellectual and empirical, theoretical and practical. It motivates commitment and common action. But for many of us, strategy is misunderstood and misused or perhaps even ignored. We might use the word but tack it onto other notions and thereby lose a powerful motive force for achievement.

We think so much of what we do and we concentrate so much on tangible goals and actions that we are likely to think of strategy as someting that we do or something that we aim for. In many business plans, I have seen carefully stated "strategies" where no strategies were stated at all. What was stated was objectives (to increase participation at this account, to reduce scrap 10 percent, to improve materials handling) or elements of action plans (to conduct operator training programs, to install a second production unit, to hire three more salesmen). Strategy is not a what, where, who, or when. Strategy is a how.

When we define our identity, we answer the two basic questions: what we are and what we intend to become. When we determine goals, we set benchmarks along our roadway to the future. Now, in establishing our strategy, we answer a final question: how we are going to get there. The how question will be answered at all levels for all objectives throughout the enterprise, but it is important first of all to formulate strategy at the top corporate level for the achievement of the major corporate goals. Just as identity and goals at the corporate level provide guidance for the formulation of supportive definitions and goals throughout the company, so the overall corporate strategies provide similar guidance for the strategies that will be formulated and used for goal achievement throughout the organization. Everything relates to everything else. And the more we can relate to well thought out fundamentals the greater the achievement of the enterprise can be. For a business enterprise the fundamentals begin with the thought out, thought through, commonly accepted concepts of identity (what we are and what we intend to become), goals (where we are going), and strategy (how we intend to get there).

By one definition, strategy is the art of using available resources to achieve predetermined objectives. It is the broad framework that provides direction and approaches for the deployment of our resources in the best way to achieve our goals. The resources we have to work with are people, time, plant, equipment, materials, energy, working capital, and information. Resources are all the inputs to our business—all we have and all we can develop, acquire, or create. Strategy is how we use them.

Good strategies are not a one-time thing. They should be changed in relation to opportunity and changes in environment and competition. Some strategy directions can be very sticky and hard to change; some can be flexible and relatively easy to change. A strategy of decentralization of operations to several profit centers commits a big investment in people and facilities and is not easily changed. A strategy commitment to television advertising is much more flexible.

Although flexibility and options for change are important considerations in strategy development, we should seek strategies that can work successfully for us over long periods of time. Good strategies need a life commensurate with definition of identity and goals. Those too can change. But if they change very often or very significantly, we don't in fact have an identity and we don't really have goals. And if our strategies change very often, we don't have strategies. We have confusion.

Successful strategies will usually operate over long periods of time, but the specific actions they guide can change frequently. Several action plans can be in operation in support of one strategy to achieve one goal. There can be and will be flux and change and redirection of action plans, but the plans remain in tune with the strategy and in pursuit of the goal. Among major, top corporate level strategies can be listed those discussed in the following sections.

Resource Strategy

Since strategy pilots our resources toward our goals, useful dialog searching for fundamental strategy decisions should begin with the options for deployment of resources. These will be the probing questions:

1. Which of our products, product lines, businesses, and markets are most important to our operations today?
2. Which have opportunity for growth and for income tomorrow?
3. What that we are doing now has little or no future opportunity?
4. How well does our present mix of businesses match our concept of identity and statement of goals?
5. If there are gaps, how can they be filled? By changing our business mix? To what? By changing our concept of identity and statement of goals? To what?

By searching those questions, the basic resource strategy—how resources will be developed and deployed to achieve company identity and goals—can be formulated. Deployment of resources is the first and most fundamental strategic commitment. It is fundamental because, once committed, resources cannot easily be redeployed. The strategic commitment is long-term; it must be supported by perceptive analysis of the relevant environment. We need to test it against alternative scenarios and identify possible options for maneuverability. But we must make the decision about resource deployment; for if we don't make it intentionally and at the level of company strategy, we will make it piece by piece at the level of capital budgeting. Instead of a resource strategy we will have a mishmash created by accident rather than intent. The concept of resource strategy and how it can be developed for a business enterprise is described in Chapter 12.

Penetration Versus Diversification

A business can grow by doing what it is already doing but doing more of it or doing it better or by diversifying into new markets, new products, or completely new areas. Those strategy options have been well described by H. Igor Ansoff, who diagrams the options in matrix form.[1] Growth can be planned according to the penetration and diversification strategy matrix shown in Figure 5-1. The four "cells"—A, B, C, and D—are segments of the matrix that represent these options:

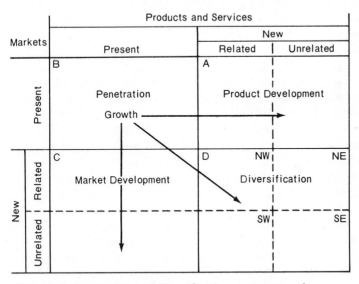

Figure 5-1. Penetration and diversification strategy matrix.

Source: H. Igor Ansoff, *Corporate Strategy* (New York: McGraw-Hill, 1965). Used with the permission of McGraw-Hill Book Company.

[1] *Corporate Strategy* (New York: McGraw-Hill, 1965).

A. We can develop new products to broaden our product lines to present markets—a product development strategy.

B. We can market more of our present products and services to present markets by greater penetration based on customer sales planning principles.

C. We can develop additional markets for present products and services—a market development strategy.

D. We can sell new products and services to new markets. This diversification approach can be implemented by acquisition or by growth from within. If growth is from within, there will normally be some relation between the diversification and present business. That is illustrated by the northwest, southwest, and northeast squares of the diversification cell in Figure 5-1. Related diversification may be different but related products sold to different but related markets (NW); different but related products sold to unrelated markets (SW); or unrelated products sold to different but related markets (NE). Diversification that has some relation to the present business, called concentric diversification, can be accomplished by internal growth or acquisition. Conglomerate diversification—in which unrelated products are sold to unrelated markets (the southeast square)—can usually be best accomplished by acquisition.

There can be a relationship between the penetration and diversification strategy matrix illustrated in Figure 5-1 and the resource strategy matrix described in Chapter 12. Resource commitment must be the first and most fundamental of the strategy decisions. When the resource strategy matrix is used as an aid to reaching that decision, the result is an important conceptual base for the profitable application of the penetration and diversification strategy. The procedure is as follows:

1. For each business as defined and plotted on the resource strategy matrix (Figure 12-2) list in cell B of the penetration and diversification strategy matrix (Figure 5-1) product groups and major products by appropriate groupings and markets and market segments also by their appropriate groupings. Indicate the products sold to each market, as shown in Figure 5-2.

2. Separately summarize sales, marginal income, and market growth rate for each product group and product and for each market and market segment listed, as shown in Table 5-1.

3. Dialog penetration opportunities and identify them in cell B, Figure 5-2.

4. Dialog product development opportunities and list them in cell A. Separetely list probable attainable sales volume and marginal income for each.

5. Dialog market development opportunities and list them in cell C. Separately list probable attainable sales volume and marginal income for each.

6. Dialog related diversification opportunities and list them in the appropriate NE, NW, and SW segments of cell D. Separately list probable attainable sales volume and marginal income for each.

| Markets | | Products and Services | | | | | | | | | |
| | | Present | | | | | | | New | |
		Product Line A	Product Line B	Product Line C	Product Line D	Product Line E	Product Line F	Product Line G	Related	Unrelated
Totals	42.1	11.7	8.1	5.7	4.0	2.9	8.0	1.7		
Automotive	8.8	3.0	2.1	1.6	1.7	0.4				
Bus	2.3	1.6	0.5			0.2				
Furniture	6.5	3.2	2.8			0.5				
Decorative	2.1		2.1							
Construction	4.6				2.3		0.6	1.7		
Converters	4.3	2.1	0.6	1.6						
Footwear	0.2	0.2								
Consumer	12.6	1.5		1.9		1.8	7.4			
Packaging	0.4			0.4						
Luggage	0.3	0.1		0.2						
New Related									NW	NE
New Unrelated									SW	SE

Figure 5-2. Penetration and diversification strategy worksheet.

7. In consideration of the situation and the opportunities identified by both the resource strategy analysis and the penetration and diversification strategy analysis develop strategy decisions for the business as now defined.

73

Table 5-1. Penetration and diversification strategy data ($ millions).

Product Line	Sales Volume	Market Growth Rate	Marginal Income	
			$	%
A	$11.7	6%	$5.0	42.7%
B	8.1	4	2.5	31.0
C	5.7	5	1.5	26.2
D	4.0	6	2.2	55.4
E	2.9	5	0.7	23.1
F	8.0	9	3.1	38.6
G	1.7	5	0.7	40.3
Total	$42.1		$15.7	37.3
Market Areas				
Automotive	$8.8	8	3.0	34.1
Bus	2.3	2	0.8	34.8
Furniture	6.5	5	2.1	32.3
Construction	4.6	9	1.9	41.3
Decorative	2.1	7	0.7	33.3
Converters	4.3	5	1.1	25.6
Footwear	0.2	9	0.1	46.8
Consumer	12.6	5	5.8	46.0
Packaging	0.4	15	0.1	22.1
Luggage	0.3	5	0.1	30.7
Total	$42.1		$15.7	37.3

Product Offer Versus Marketing Offer

The primary aim of any business enterprise is to create customers; without customers there is no business. What the enterprise sells to its customers can vary immensely and so becomes a major strategy determination. The options are given in the following list. If the enterprise offers a service, substitute "service" for "product."

1. Product only.
2. Product plus product guarantee.
3. Product plus specific product benefits to meet customer need.
4. Product, product benefits, and assistance in product use to solve customer problem.
5. Product, product benefits, assistance, and related additional services to solve comprehensive customer problem when the product is one element of the solution.
6. A relationship such that option 5 is continuously available to the customer.

In recent years successful business enterprises have tended to find some of their most successful strategies more toward 6 than 1. Theodore Levitt describes option 6 as the "augmented product"[2]; in Hooker Chemical we call it the marketing offer. Whatever it may be called, it represents considerable competitive strength. Sel-Rex Corp., for example, became the leader in the sale of precious-metal-plating chemicals by formulating and providing a marketing offer uniquely responsive to the problems of its customers in the electronics and decorative industries. What the company produced and sold according to the accounting record was precious-metal-plating chemicals and plating equipment. But what Sel-Rex really sold was a marketing offer that included:

1. Determination of the plating process that best met the customer's specifications.
2. Engineering of equipment to meet the selected process requirements.
3. Production and installation of the equipment.
4. Plating chemicals.
5. Start-up of the equipment.
6. Training of customer personnel.
7. Monitoring of process operation.
8. Technical assistance in solving any problems as they develop.
9. Process optimization.
10. Recovery of precious metals from customer's scrap.
11. Process improvement and new process development to provide still better solutions of customer problems.
12. Design of and contracting for effluent control systems.

All or particular elements of the Sel-Rex marketing offer could be used to solve a particular customer's problem and to establish the kind of relationship listed earlier as strategy option 6.

Option 6, however, is not always superior to option 1. It all depends. What it depends on is the market situation and the business economics, both for us and for the customer. As products and businesses move along the product growth curve, the appropriate strategy option tends to move from 1 toward 6 and then back toward 1. Everything is relationships. But time alters relationships.

Good strategy decisions in the area of product and marketing offer depend on the unique-difference principle. In our strategy dialog we look for opportunity to base our strategy approach on characteristics and capabilities that distinguish our company and its marketing offer in ways that provide unique values to the customers we will serve. The unique characteristics that are dynamic in the opportunity area are the differences that the good strategy will emphasize.

---

[2] *The Marketing Mode* (New York: McGraw-Hill, 1969), chap. 1.

Centralization Versus Decentralization

What is to be centralized and what decentralized and to what extent are important strategy questions. For reasons of the way people work most effectively, a decentralization strategy is a necessity for the effective functioning of the large enterprise. People work and achieve on an individual and work group level, and the strongest motivational climate relates to how work can be structured in a responsible way at those levels. And that requires decentralization.

On the other hand, some functions can be performed for the company as a whole by relatively small work groups, and those groups might be centralized. Examples include finance, research, and consulting service. However, centralized functions will be fewer and fewer as we think less in terms of pyramidal, line structures for our organizations and more in terms of rather tentative structures better suited to the work to be done. Thinking of work groups as they actually function is different from classifying organization groups as we customarily show them on charts. A small group may comprise members working in an inter-related way with members of other groups to achieve particular objectives.

The centralization-decentralization strategy is concerned with the structural location of work groups. Limitations on decentralization are communication, coordination, and organizational entropy. At least that is a commonly held view. But when we stop to think about it, most of us would probably see the same limitations on centralization. The problems of communication and coordination can be resolved through the dialog process of defining identity, determining goals, and developing strategy. That is what keeps the decentralized organization functioning in common purpose to achieve its goals. It can also prevent the occurrence of immense bloopers, a problem considered by some to be a special weakness of decentralization. But we seldom gain security and freedom from errors by more strongly centralizing authority; usually we only limit achievement. Motivation and organization development can prevent organizational entropy, as described in Chapters 8 and 9; they move us in the direction of decentralization.

Whether we centralize or decentralize, everything remains related to everything else. And when we have developed our identity, our goals, and our strategies through dialog, we can arrange those relationships in ways most effective for our enterprise.

Authoritative Versus Participative Management

The matter of management style is related to but different from that of centralization versus decentralization. Centralization is not necessarily authoritative; decentralization is not necessarily participative. But authority requires hierarchy, and participation requires work groups small enough that individuals can relate one to another, so management style will influence organizational forms. By choice, most managements and most organizations prefer a participative style. By actions, the real situation often leans more toward the authoritative. That being so, much more than a strategy choice is involved here. If the choice is for a participative management style, a learning process and a significant change in the way work is done will probably be required.

Regional or National Versus International

The geographic area in which the enterprise will concentrate its efforts is an important strategy decision. It should be thought through, dialoged, and specifically stated as a strategy. As with all strategy decisions, there is no right answer, there are just different answers. And it will be our wise choice from among those different answers that will determine our future success. If we make our strategy choice of geographical area too narrow, we will miss opportunity or lose out to unidentified competition. If we make our choice too wide, we will dissipate our resources and underachieve.

Innovate Versus Follow

Whether we will innovate or follow is not the same question as whether we will change or not change. It is the question how we will seek change. Whether the change is in product, process, product and service systems offered to customers, or functional systems by which organizational work is done, there are two basic strategy choices. We can invent and develop the change ourselves, or we can use and apply change that is invented and developed by others. Of course, our choice need not be all one or all the other, so the strategy decision really involves the kind of innovation, if any, we wish to create. And that strategy question will immediately relate to our first strategy decision on deployment of resources. In the areas in which we choose to concentrate our resources will lie the prospects and the opportunities for innovation that we undertake to create.

For example, if we commit resources to a major growth opportunity, the opportunity may require us to innovate if we are to achieve our goals. IBM committed resources to a growth opportunity in problem solving and innovated in computers and computer systems and ways of making them practical and applicable to solving problems for individual customers. The innovation was both technical and marketing. In the late 1970s, AT&T broadened its corporate commitment to include all forms of communications systems, with specialization by market served. It would continue its historic customer-service productivity-improvement strategy in the regulated telephone utility industry. In addition it would become a competitive, market-oriented supplier of communications systems for the information needs of each of its targeted market sectors. This major new commitment was described by AT&T's chairman as the biggest change in the company's history. It would require innovation in products, in systems, and in the structure and operations of the company. But innovation strategy does not apply only at such lofty levels as computers and information systems. The proprietor of a small diner at an ordinary road intersection invented his own chili-dogs and chili-burgers, served them with a country-kitchen informality and friendliness, and great numbers of people went out of their way to stop at Al's Dog House.

But it is not necessary always to be the creator of the innovation. The important thing is to make use of an idea or invention that is right for us whatever its origin may be—"not invented here" should impose no constraint on "what is used here." Of course, our major areas of business will probably require some kind of effort toward technical and functional innovation. It could be a major research effort to invent, or it could include special assignments, task forces, or consultant assistance for finding innovative ways to improve our goal achievement competence. Innovation of our own will probably be in areas of opportunity in which we have made a significant commitment of resources. Major opportunities will require major innovations. And some of those innovations will be ours if the opportunity itself is going to be ours. It would be hard to follow someone else to the front of the line.

At the same time, we will want to make good use of innovation that's right for us, whatever its source. So an important strategy consideration will be to find innovation and put it to use. We will need both a climate to encourage invention and new ideas and an open attitude that will permit acceptance and use of innovation from all sources. Then instead of thinking of this strategy decision as innovate *or* follow, we might think of it more productively as innovate *and* follow—how much of each?

Specialization Versus Generalization

The question of specialization versus generalization is related to the basic strategy of resource deployment, but it gets more specific. Here we confront the important strategic question of how specialized and how generalized we should be with respect to products and product lines, services and systems, markets served, and geographic area.

With respect to products and product lines we might specialize our resources in selected segments or generalize over a large product category. A successful retail hardware store will generalize over a broad product range to meet many and diverse needs of consumers for the tools, supplies, hard goods, and parts required for household operation and maintenance. A department store may generalize over a broad range of goods and services (R. H. Macy & Co.) or specialize to serve the fashion needs of a market segment or life style (Lord & Taylor). General Electric's plastics division specializes in high-performance materials for engineering applications. The specialization versus generalization strategy decision is not of itself the decision that leads to success. The basic question is why we generalize or why we specialize, and then how we do it.

McDonald's Corp. grew from $54 million in sales in 1961 to $3,738 million in 1977, when it had 4,700 retail outlets. The company specializes in a limited menu of low-priced, quick-service foods that are tasty, reliable in quality, and served in a clean and friendly atmosphere. The limited menu, featuring the staple hamburger in several varieties, is selected to appeal to the taste, convenience, and pocketbook of large numbers of eating-out Americans. But it is more than the specialization that has made McDonald's spectacularly successful. It is how the specialization has been carried out. Every detail of procurement, processing, food preparation, and service has been planned to assure satisfaction to the customer.

The whole McDonald's system, and the retail outlet in particular, is an engineered, personalized process for delivering good food and beverages to its customers. With the quality assured by the procurement and processing system, and the repetitive, tedious elements of the work largely automated, employees can concentrate primarily on the more human aspects of service to customers. In 1977 McDonald's crews handled over two billion transactions. The company's selection, training, and development programs assure that each transaction is carried out with professionalism and friendliness. Crews work as teams, with each member trained and experienced in several jobs and with great stress on both individual and team goals and achievement. The McDonald's system does the work, the employees operate the system, and the McDonald's customers get the kind of food and food service they like. The McDonald's strategy of specialization is supported and made effective by a strategy of engineered and personalized marketing.[3]

With respect to markets served there are many specialization or generalization options. Most business enterprises should formulate a strategy with respect to markets and customers. If the decision is not made, strategy will develop from day-to-day operations and will almost surely be one of generalization to the point of dissipation of resources.

Markets can first be looked at as consumer, industrial, and government, and the first decision will be the desired mix. Next we can become more specific about which geographic areas are best for our commitment of effort and resources. A productive strategy will direct the company's products or services to markets and segments of markets that represent the best opportunity for what the company has to offer as that offer is perceived by customers. That is the positioning strategy described in works on marketing and promotion planning. The following is a seven-step approach to developing specialization strategy.

1. Audit company products and services and those of competitors in relation to market position, need satisfaction, and customer attitudes in each market and market segment.
2. Relate the factors of step 1 to change and developing trends in the markets and segments.
3. Identify opportunities in which market or market segment needs are not or will not be adequately served by competitors and in which the company has a competence advantage to meet the need.

[3]Ibid., pp. 71-78.

4. Develop an augmented product or marketing offer in terms most responsive to the perceived opportunity.
5. Identify communications methods most effective for reaching the customers for the offer.
6. Determine appropriate production, logistic, and distribution support.
7. Concentrate on situations in which change is occurring, or will occur, and in which the company has a competence uniquely responsive to customer needs.

Of those steps, the seventh is one in which great opportunity can be found and costly errors can easily be made. In it are combined competitive comparisons, market awareness and needs, and a milieu of change. Real opportunity can come only from a market situation in which there is change. Major change offers major opportunity for gain and also for loss. The opportunity will come from a unique competence of ours to serve a new or changed need as the market sees the need and our competence. RCA Corporation could not go head-to-head with IBM in computers, but Control Data Corp., by taking a segment approach based on special competence, could be very successful against IBM and all others. Western Union could begin with its competence in and wide recognition for message transmission and establish a major new business in the burgeoning communications industry segment of electronic data transmission. With limited resources concentrated on local market needs and wants, Southwest Airlines could successfully challenge international carrier Braniff in the intrastate Texas transportation market.

The strategy options of specialization or generalization will usually lead to decisions on areas of specialization by products and services offered, by markets and market segments, and by geographical area. Within the target area of specialization there will be generalization of product line appropriate to optimizing sales and income. The broad-line retail hardware store, generalized as it is in products, specializes to a certain kind of consumer need. As in the case of the hardware store, one or another of the three areas of specialization will usually provide the controlling strategy to which the other will relate. And all three, in total, will relate to business economics as discussed in Chapters 10 and 11.

Job Simplification Versus Job Enrichment

People create the outputs of an enterprise by applying their talent and effort to it. That is called work. And work is organized into jobs. But how the work is organized into jobs is a strategy decision that is seldom confronted. Instead, the organization of work into jobs is usually the unexamined and unquestioned result of existing machines and processes, customary ways of doing things, manning tables, union contracts, and historically held assumptions. We build into our organizations a random structure of work without ever considering that there might be strategic alternatives.

What is usually built into the work we do is the result of several decades of evolution of scientific management—the simplification of work to discrete elements and the specialization of those elements into individual jobs. So far as the material and mechanical inputs to our business enterprise are concerned, that has created remarkable achievement. As for the people inputs, it has transformed craft skills that could provide wealth for an aristocracy to mass-production achievement that could provide wealth for the multitudes. But, more and more, it has also provided dissatisfaction in the job.

We are now finding that much of what is simplified and specialized either can be automated or will be accommodated to by schizoid conduct: apathy and anonymity on the job and participation and identity off the job in other activities. We are also finding that the structure of work can be altered to provide participation and identity on the job and, through that, greater outputs for the enterprise. Today an immense opportunity for improvement in company performance lies in providing strategic direction to the organization and structure of work. That important strategy alternative is discussed in Chapter 8.

Short-Term Profit Versus Long-Term Growth

The short-term-profit and long-term-growth dichotomy is often presented as one of the major strategy trade-offs that must be confronted by an enterprise. Fiction. It is not a strategy trade-off; it is an invention of accounting. The invention is useful for managers who want to collect bonus payments determined by numbers in the annual income statement. But the invention only confuses strategic planning. For what we are really saying is that we can do or not do certain things and thereby show a higher profit this year in our income statement. Unfortunately, if we do or don't do those things, we find out later on that we have to pay for it. We are not increasing short-term profit. We are only increasing short-term cash availability by neglecting to recognize certain economic costs and then calling those unpaid costs profit.

Instead of debating a short- and long-term strategy trade-off, we should be looking at the business economics of the enterprise as recommended in Chapters 10 and 11. First of all, we must understand what our real, economic costs are. Then, if we wish to postpone or re-time certain of those costs in the interest of cash budgeting and in this way alter our business plan, we may do so. What appears to be a short- and long-term strategy dilemma is not one. It is only a viewing with myopic vision that can be corrected by the optometry of business economics.

The major strategies for the enterprise will be appropriate to the enterprise's business definition (present and future) and goals. For each major goal a strategy will be articulated. Within a key performance area one strategy may direct the achievement of more than one goal, but there will always be a strategy for the achievement of a goal. And as goals related to and supporting the overall company goals are established throughout the enterprise, so also will the subgoals be directed by appropriate strategies that relate to and support the overall company strategies. The network of goals throughout the enterprise will be matched and coordinated by the network of strategies that directs the programming of their achievement. In that way there will be subgoals and substrategies in such areas as marketing, advertising and sales promotion, product development, market development, sales, pricing, distribution, labor relations, personnel and organization development, production, research, innovation, finance, and public responsibility.

As strategies come into focus and are tentatively agreed to, it is appropriate to examine each one for its relevance to the situation, its appropriateness to the company, its uniqueness in respect to competition, and the operating results probable from its implementation. There can be no absolute measure on those points, but there can be enough understanding to confirm validity. Dialog becomes the best method for reaching that understanding. The following checklist can be useful in evaluating the strategy through dialog:

1. Is the strategy internally consistent?
2. Is it consistent with the environment?
3. Is it appropriate for the available resources?
4. Does it involve a reasonable, or satisfactory, degree of risk?
5. Does it have an appropriate time horizon?
6. Does it work?[4]

Frank F. Gilmore recommends a practical procedure for strategy formulation in smaller companies:

1. Record current strategy.
2. Identify problems.
3. Discover the core elements.
4. Formulate alternatives.
5. Evaluate alternatives.
6. Choose the new strategy.[5]

The overall company strategy must first be developed, articulated, and agreed to. It provides the basic direction for resource commitment; it is the compass directing all company effort. The strategies within components and functions of the company will relate to and support the overall company strategy. Among the most important of the supporting strategies will be marketing, or functional, strategies supporting the marketing plan. For evaluating those marketing strategies through dialog the following checklist is helpful:

[4]S. Tilles, "Evaluating Your Corporate Strategy," Harvard Business School Note, 1962.
[5]"Formulating Strategy in Smaller Companies," *Harvard Business Review*, May-June 1971, p. 61.

1. Does the strategy commit manpower and resources?
2. Is the manpower and resource commitment intended to operate long-range?
3. Does the strategy fit the needs of the customer? Today? Long-range?
4. Does the strategy capitalize on company strengths and competitor weaknesses, that is, the unique-difference principle?
5. When it is successful, can the strategy be readily copied by competitors?
6. What are the directions of possible maneuverability for the company?
7. What alternative strategies could be selected?

For each alternative strategy, answer the preceding questions plus the following three, which compare the alternative strategy with the chosen strategy:

1. What would be the relative cost?
2. What would be the probable five-year sales volume projection under each strategy?
3. What would be the relative marginal income or operating income?

The importance and the value of plotting our business course by the direction of a strategy compass is illustrated in the following quotation:

> With these goals established for our overall operations, we have developed strategy approaches to achieve them. This work is extended throughout our chemicals and plastics divisions and companies so that we have specified goals, strategies and action plans for all of our business areas . . . all of these consistent with and supporting the achievement of these overall company goals, all linked together through strategy. There is much in this approach that is not conventional. But then, we do not intend to be a conventional chemical company. There is nothing in our approach, on the other hand, that has not been empirically demonstrated. It is just that we choose our way from the contemporary and the future-oriented rather than from the old school of past success. In this way we can operate creatively, responsibly, and profitably today. And we can aspire to become the guest of tomorrow's opportunities; not the prisoner of yesterday's successes.[6]

---

[6]William D. Morrison, president, Hooker Chemicals and Plastics Group, remarks at company management meeting, February 1972.

6

Mission—
An Iterative Process

Everything in life is relationships. Everything in life is objectives. Here we have two great ideas that can be greater still in combination. The first is a core idea of Eastern philosophy; the second of Western philosophy. A growing Western interest in the wisdom of the East is a popular recognition of the value of the Way, or the Tao, as well as (or, for many, instead of) the value of achievement. In our business enterprises we certainly have been highly oriented toward the philosophy of objectives. And the great achievements of our enterprise system show dramatically the validity of such a philosophy.

But the dimension of relationships now appears as equally important, equally valid. The first fundamental for business enterprise is a concept of identity—what we are and what we wish to become. A good identity comes not from one mind, but from many. It comes from a relationship of minds. And when it is developed, the concept of identity is not an end result. It is a starting point for the determination of key performance area objectives that relate to the conceptualized identity. The identity relates the objectives so that all the many diverse actions throughout the enterprise will collectively result in them. That is possible because the formulation of objectives has been supported by strategy determination; the basic approach to be followed in organizing and carrying out the work has been established in advance.

Everything is relationships. The identity is related to the company's present situation and to the complex and changing environment in which the company functions. The identity is in turn related to the key objectives, and they to the strategies. Everything is related to everything else. Everything influences and changes everything else: identity, objectives, strategy. As we work through the thinking, dialoging process by stages—first identity, then objectives, then strategy—we find that each new effort influences and changes what went before.

The Nature of Mission

When we define our identity, we develop business intelligence on all important aspects of that identity. And as we study the proposed identity in the improved perspective of greater knowledge, we make changes that make sense to us for our enterprise in the environment that we see developing. Business intelligence also helps us find our key objectives and our strategies. But in the process we will often go back and change something that we have done before. Everything is relationships at the same time that everything is objectives. And when we learn how to learn about relationships, we will have found our Way, our Tao. And we will have found a route to greater achievement.

Three fundamentals—identity, key objectives, and strategy—relate to one another. When they are developed within an organization, when they are articulated, understood, and accepted, they become the strong, integrating, motivating force for the enterprise. They, together, become a mission for the enterprise. If they are developed by the work and inputs of many people in the organization, they will be realistic and at the same time imaginative, fundamental and at the same time actionable, motivating to the organization and at the same time relevant to the total environment, interesting and challenging to individuals and at the same time productive of economic success for the enterprise. A mission that we are all a part of is a great experience as well as a Way to great achievement. It is relationships. It is objectives. It is a value system with goals. Or we can give it some other name more meaningful to us. The name should connote a bringing ɔgether, a motivation, a bond or tie among people, a way of working together, and a concept of present and future identity. Other names have indeed been used:

Business charter has been in use as a term for more than two decades. Often it has been used to define boundary lines between divisions or operations within a company rather than to motivate achievement. It is more administrative than creative in connotation, more historical than future-oriented, more descriptive than motivational.

Strategy statement is a good term that can connote the three basics—what we are, what we intend to become, and how we intend to get there—but sometimes it does not. Often it is invented by the leader without a contribution of the wisdom of the many and therefore lacks the great strength of common purpose.

Corporate policy is often stated at the front of a very fat policy manual. Usually it attracts poor readership, less understanding, and no motivation; it is an advanced product of specialized bureaucracy. When we must have procedures, let's have them. But let's automate them more and talk about them less. When we must have performance, let's be more flexible and more personal.

Company philosophy may be a highbrow term, but it is a good term connoting the right idea. It all depends. The same comments apply to it as were made for the term "strategy statement."

Any other name can be given to the total of the three business fundamentals: definition, goals, strategy. Or, of course, you may wish not to give a name to the summary statement of the present, the future, and the Way of the enterprise but instead simply label it for what it is:

(Company name)
What we are
What we intend to become
How we intend to get there
or
(Company name)
Business definition, goals, strategy

By whatever name it may be called, a simply written statement of that kind can be a big step toward great organizational achievement, provided the very simple statement is developed from the total talents of the organization as described in the three preceding chapters. And it should be written on paper, not cast in bronze. For the same process that created it will cause it to change as knowledge increases, achievement increases, and environment changes. An iterative process developed the statement as new understanding altered the old. The same iterative process will have to continue so that we are always in tune with ourselves, our opportunities, our problems, and our total environment. An action-oriented businessman may see it as time-wasting and inefficient. But if he develops the skills to use it, he will find that it takes less time than whatever else he may be doing now, if "time" is from now to achievement rather than from now to some kind of action.

Application of Mission
Through mission, we will just be using our brains more before we use our pencils or our brawn. And we—all of us, the total organization—will be far more productive and far more achieving. But those are just words, and they may or may not sound good to you depending on the perspectives you bring from your own experiences to the reading of this book. Let me give you some examples.

A plastics company developed a mission through broad dialog among its management and professional people. It defined its business in terms of product groups and markets served but added a new dimension of diversification. It then identified seven major goals most important to that identity. Those goals are listed in Chapter 4, along with a description of how they were supported by related subgoals throughout the company. Twelve major strategies were developed to coordinate direction in achieving the goals.

1. Company D shall concentrate its efforts in business areas and segments of promising growth and in which the Company can achieve leadership

positions. In such targeted areas and segments, the Company shall seek to use particularly bold and imaginative strategies.

2. In business areas whose growth prospects are limited (less than 5% per year), and where the Company has a leading market position, its strategy will be to do that which is necessary to maintain market share. Special attention will be given to extension of activities into related areas where special advantage can be taken of its expertise in the established market. Also, special effort will be directed toward the definition of protectable market segments where the Company can reasonably expect to achieve leadership positions.

3. In business areas whose growth prospects are limited (less than 5% per year), and where the Company's position is minor, its strategy will be to (a) search for protectable market segments in which it can achieve leadership, (b) maximize short-term earnings and cash flow, and (c) if earnings prospects are unsatisfactory, disengage from the business and redeploy resources in business areas promising more rapid growth.

4. By concentration on growth opportunities as stated in the above three strategies, change the overall business mix to make possible the achivement of Company goals.

5. In targeted business areas and segments, the Company will develop positions of technical leadership through research and development programs oriented to Company goals.

6. In targeted business areas and segments, develop systems marketing concepts where such an approach can provide a route to the unique satisfaction of customer needs, increasing value added, and protecting market position.

7. Where there are significant markets targeted by more than one business area, special marketing groups may be established to handle the marketing of all Company products to those markets.

8. Develop and implement the facilities program needed to achieve Company goals.

9. The Company will operate in the United States and Canada but will view each business and segment from an international perspective. In the development and prosecution of international opportunities, the Company will work through and assist the International Group in the establishment and realization of goals.

10. The management team will consist of a highly motivated staff that will provide prompt and firm decision making and effective implementing programs through a participative management style.

11. The Company will recruit and develop personnel who will manage the Company's affairs with vigor, imagination, and independence of thought.

12. Our personnel will be encouraged and deployed to make their full contributions to achieving Company goals, with responsibility and authority

delegated broadly throughout the organization. Personnel will be provided the opportunity for rapid development through varied job assignments, increasing responsibilities, educational programs, and other means, with continuing consideration for advancement on the basis of ability.

The strategies first of all articulate company decisions on resource strategy and then highlight marketing offer, management style, innovation, and specialization as major strategies. The mission statement was developed at a time of problems. After several years of exceptional success, operating results had begun to deteriorate. With the 1970-1971 recession, sales volume declined. Profits fell more than 50 percent. Cost reduction programs were instituted, and several organizational changes were made. Then a new chief executive began to look for strength more within his own organization. He cultivated it with communication, study and educational sessions, and a conscious effort to develop a more participative management style. The development of a mission statement was a first part of his program.

Not all problems were immediately resolved with the finding of mission. A present business situation is the result of several years of history, and change can never be easy. Time will be an important ingredient of even the best of solutions. For the plastics company the beginnings of improvement could be seen within six months. A year and a half later the company was improving rapidly: the organization was much more competent and motivated and the customers were much better served. Business recovery from the recession had improved the external environment and provided new opportunity. But the changes made in the internal environment provided the real growth and expansion of success.

Figure 6-1 shows the steps taken in the planning process by The Coca-Cola Company. The statement of purpose and objectives corresponds to mission. Included in the statement are the general strategies for the achievement of the objectives. Vitally important is the way in which the various steps are carried out to arrive at the statement of purpose and objectives. It is not enough that they are carried out by experts so the final product is technically valid. There must be participation by all the organization so the final product is organizationally valid as well.

The Mission Statement

A mission statement need not be long in words; it need only be sound in concept. The briefer the better. An excellent mission statement can be reduced to one or two pages of writing, provided the thinking has been reduced to fundamentals. Usually, the better the thinking the shorter the document. And the shorter the document the more communicable, actionable, and motivational it can be throughout the organization. Here is the very shortest mission statement of definition and goals I have seen. It was developed by the management

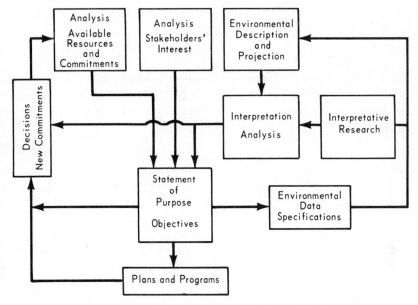

Figure 6-1. Relationships of planning steps, The Coca-Cola Company.

group of a company in Brazil that manufactures and markets plating equipment, chemicals, supplies, and processes.

DEFINITION

Marketing, servicing, and production in Brazil of surface treatment systems for industry.

GOALS

1. To develop an integrated surface treatment business and to be the leader in Brazil in this business, with sales of $_____ million by 19–.
2. To develop people that can achieve goal 1.
3. To become a strong industrial marketing company.

STRATEGIES

The strategies are those of the international group of which this company is a part.

Not only is the statement short; it is highly specific because the opportunity for the business over the next several years is highly specific. That opportunity, very simply, is to concentrate on the present business in the rapidly growing

Brazilian economy. The basic strategy is the resource strategy, described in Chapter 12, by which the company has reached decisions on the allocation of its resources.

That the business definition and goals can be stated very briefly and specifically does not mean the business is simple. It means only that the fundamentals on which success can be built can be simply stated. The management team, guided by its definition and goals, developed for itself 14 key performance area objectives in 6 of the 7 key performance areas:

Area	No. of Objectives
Market standing	5
Profitability	5
Productivity	1
Innovation	1
Motivation and organization development	1
Public responsibility	1

The objectives are, in effect, the company's budget plan, one that is expressed in actionable, operating terms rather than financial terms. But the needed financial data are there, too. They flow from the organization performance described by the key performance area objectives. When they are derived in that way, the financial budget data are not just forecast. They are the result of specific achievement programmed throughout the company to reach agreed-upon goals. All this amounts to a conceptually different way to create a budgetary control system. The "next generation" budget system will even need a different name. It could be called a motivation and achievement system. It can do for us what we have always wanted budgetary control systems to do and have never quite understood why they didn't.

Here is an example of business definition and goals for a company in the same kind of business as the Brazilian one. It also is in Latin America. The two businesses have the same products, services, and kinds of customers. But the way in which the company management groups define their businesses is different, and the major goals are different.

DEFINITION

1. Company P is an organization for marketing, production, and development of systems for metallic and nonmetallic surface treatment in industrial production.
2. Areas of operation will be Countries A, B, C, and D.

1. Maintain market position in Country A and achieve sales volume of $_____ by 19–.
2. Develop markets in Countries B, C, and D and achieve sales volume of $_____ by 19–.
3. Raise the technical level of our industry in all four country markets.
4. Diversify into new opportunities depending for success more on people competence and know-how than on capital resources.
5. Develop the organization competence and individual skills to accomplish these goals.

The Brazilian company has one major area of opportunity; concentrating on its present business in the expanding economy of Brazil. The second company, on the other hand, has three opportunity areas: (1) maintain position in its present business in Country A, (2) diversify in Country A, and (3) develop its present business in Countries B, C, and D. Those important conclusions were reached by the company's management group by following the procedures described in Chapters 3 to 5. On the basis of those conclusions, they have laid out a course for the future development of their business. By continuing to use the same dialog procedures, they can modify and improve their concepts of definition and goals with experience, achievement, and environmental change so that at all times they will have an integrating concept of what their business is and what they intend it to become. In effect, they will continually have—rather than by annual revision—an actionable, achievable long-range plan. And, like the managers of the Brazilian company, they have developed shorter-range key performance area objectives—in effect, a budget plan. Basic strategy is the resource allocation to the three areas of opportunity listed above. Resource strategy decisions were developed by using the approach described in Chapter 12.

As shown by the preceding examples, a mission statement can be very short and quite specific and still be meaningful, actionable, and motivating throughout the enterprise. To develop a short one rather than a long one is harder and usually takes longer. The short one, to be effective, must represent the most fundamental ideas on which the success of the enterprise depends. Even for today's most outstanding companies, each new success must be created. No yesterday assures a tomorrow for business enterprise. What tomorrow will be, what we aim to create, can be determined by the development of a concept of mission—business definition, goals, and strategy—as the basic framework for business operations. Figure 6-2 shows a one-page format that has been used for summarizing a mission statement for divisions and subsidiary companies within a large, decentralized corporation. In that brief format are summarized the definition, goals, and strategy for each business developed as described in Chapters 3 to 5.

1a.	Div. or Co.			1b. Business			
	Prepared by						
	Date						

2. Definition of the business:

3. Objectives:

Volume and income	19__	19__	19__	19__	19__ B	19__ Goal
Sales volume: $—add 000						
Index—1974 = 100						
Market share:						
Income:						

Other Objectives:

4. Strategy:

Figure 6-2. Business plan summary.

Function of the Mission

The point of a mission is, of course, not to find it or write it down. The point is to have it so it can relate the actions of the people throughout the enterprise. It becomes the background of understanding for everything the company does. Whenever a decision is made, it is on the table as a fundamental input. It guides every action. It separates the important from the merely urgent. It provides a framework for transactions throughout the company so they will support a common strategy and achieve the common objectives. It must constantly be communicated and reinforced by everything that everybody does everywhere in the organization. Every problem, opportunity, and action must first of all be related to it. Then it can become the superego of the enterprise, our community conscience that backdrops all we do.

But it need never become limiting. It can always be creative and motivational because we invented it by an iterative dialog among ourselves. And we can keep it newly invented, always us, and always current by the same dialog process. In that way the organization superego will not develop to constrain us. It will continually develop to create us.

The Mission in Action

Over a four-year period in which an international company was developing and applying the concepts described in this book, the idea of mission proved to be very useful. It helped develop an identity and motivate achievement among operations in 15 countries. One of the first steps was the development of what was called a strategy statement. It was the product of lecture-discussion sessions and discussions, workshops, and dialog among management and professional employees from all operations over a period of several months. A year later came a revised strategy statement, and within two years a third statement, called a mission, was developed. Each statement was a change from the preceding one and was arrived at by dialog and in consideration of past achievement, new knowledge, company and environmental changes, and identified opportunity.

Mission is an iterative process. New experience and new knowledge alter our view of the future from an earlier perspective. For the company under discussion the second statement was very similar to the first; it showed only evolutionary change. The third statement, which was developed through a dialog over six months, shows both evolutionary change and restructuring. After a definition of identity in terms of people talent and product areas, the statement goes on to articulate goals and operating principles or strategies that would substantially alter the company. And through the process that developed the mission, the company has not only conceptualized a new future for itself; it was on its way toward getting there. Because the iterative process of mission continues as new change develops, journey and destiny can remain in harmony. The company's mission statement seems to me a very remarkable document:

DEFINITION

Company R is a growing, multinational enterprise based on:
1. Technical and commercial expertise in surface finishing systems.
2. Entrepreneurial skills in business development and diversification.
3. Marketing competence within countries and areas and trading competence between and among countries.
4. Multinational financial acumen.
5. Resources in organization talent and its development and motivation.

PRESENT COMPANY BUSINESS

1. Product Group A.
2. Product Group B.
3. Product Group C.
4. Process and product recycle.
5. International trading, contra trade.
6. Diversification enterprises.

OBJECTIVES

1. To become a strong international marketing company with capability in

all chosen markets and with expertise in transactions between and among countries.

2. To develop and optimize present businesses, including:
   a. Achievement of operating objectives in each operating unit.
   b. Expansion into developing country markets.
   c. Increasing value added by vertical integration.
3. To diversify into significant new business opportunities depending for success more on mental than capital resources.
4. From all operations to grow in sales volume at more than double the GNP growth rates of the countries in which we operate.
5. To achieve annual growth in net income of 15% per year.
6. By 19– to achieve return investment of 20%, with investment defined by the Company method.
7. To maintain and increase communications and technical and marketing cooperation among all related companies.
8. To provide for all Company personnel opportunity for individual achievement and recognition in a framework that will develop the organizational competence to accomplish the Company mission.

OPERATING PRINCIPLES

1. Company R will conduct itself as a multinational organization that respects the national interests and characteristics of its operating units.
2. Operations will be directed according to agreed-upon achievement objectives:
   a. Each operating unit will make regular reports of achievement of agreed-upon unit operating objectives.
   b. Financial statements will be prepared to report group operating results.
3. Operations will be decentralized to the smallest viable units, each with:
   a. Good leadership.
   b. Periodically determined performance objectives.
   c. Operating guidelines.
   d. Feedback for measuring, reporting, and controlling performance toward achieving objectives.
   e. Programs for training and development of people.
4. For Company, manufacturing, marketing, R&D, administration, and other units as may be established:
   a. Performance objectives will be set in relation to the key performance areas of prime margin profitability accounts, people competence and motivation, market standing, innovation, productivity, physical and financial resources, and public responsibility.
   b. Achievement of objectives will be measured and reported on a trend basis.

   c. New methods, change, and simplification will be sought (1) to increase value-added from available resources and (2) to achieve objectives at lower costs.

5. Product Group 3 business will be operated by:

   a. Establishing one development and design center to develop products meeting design requirements for all markets.

   b. Rationalization of production.

   c. International marketing programs.

6. Sourcing will be planned to make maximum contribution of Group resources.

7. The Company's overall distribution strategy shall be the direct marketing of its products with the aim of achieving and maintaining market leadership. Where they are appropriate, the Company will establish major distribution outlets controlled through ownership. A direct presence is desirable in countries in which ownership of a distribution outlet is not practicable. Management shall set standards of performance for all distributors and shall assist and monitor their marketing efforts.

8. Company business will be expanded in developing country and regional markets by individual representatives, distribution facilities, service facilities, and new country or regional companies as may be appropriate to achieve operating objectives.

9. For each product group, international marketing plans and a mechanism to deal with any internal conflicts on product or customer responsibility will be developed and managed by the individual having the international product management responsibility.

10. New business opportunities will be sought from all sources—including acquisition, licensing, agency agreements, research, and internal development. Major diversification will be sought by acquisition. Other new business opportunities with major long-range opportunity will be developed internally in venture groups and mini-enterprises separate from operations and free of company "systems" constraints.

   a. Venture groups and mini-enterprises may operate anywhere in the Company.

   b. Project approval is the responsibility of local management.

   c. Information on the existence, objectives, and results of venture enterprises will be communicated throughout the Group.

   d. Decision to expand or drop will be made at the mini-enterprise level on the basis of local success and other intelligence and appraisal. Local management will determine the level at which decision should be made, in consideration of the potential significance of the decision. Expansion of new businesses will be internationalized as appropriate by the individual having the international product management responsibility.

11. The Company will provide a communication and information system

among all member companies in the areas of: (a) research and development, (b) new product commercialization, (c) marketing and promotional cooperation, (d) business management, and (e) innovation in all business functions.

12. A strong corporate image will be established and maintained through the common identity of individual company names and product nomenclature and common and consistent themes and designs in communication and production.

13. The Company considers that its personnel are an important resource. With a first-class team of people, all other resources can be developed or acquired; all goals can be achieved. The major Company strategy is therefore the development of its personnel and organizational competence:

   a. The Company shall provide an environment for individual development that will create the team ability to conduct the group's activities with vigor, imagination, and determination to achieve particular goals through the agreed-upon business strategies.

   b. Management capabilities will be developed by recruiting quality personnel, by providing varied job experience, and by encouraging continuing education and programs for personal development. Authority and responsibility shall be delegated to individuals with management ability without regard to age, sex, religion, or race.

   c. This will entail the coordination of group training and educational facilities and the continuous budgeting for recruitment of young, professionally qualified personnel in various disciplines.

   d. Managers have a responsibility for training and for making time available for it to be carried out.

   e. The principle of management by objectives is accepted throughout the Group, although it must be operated in a deformalized manner with care to avoid bureaucratic procedures that could lead to a stifling of initiative or excessive staffing to insure implementation.

   f. It is the Company's intention to move toward a more participative type of management and to encourage all employees to take part in this concept.

   g. The "professional excellence" concept shall be developed through high standards of performance for each job.

14. Resource strategy guidelines will be used for developing business decisions on resource commitment. Company strategy is to develop and maintain a mix of businesses and markets that can achieve current and long-range growth and income objectives.

Managers from Company R operations participated in the development of the mission. Since it was from and for their companies, its translation to the national interests and characteristics of each operating unit (operating principle 1) provided both guidelines and motivation. One member company conducted a three-day management workshop on the concepts described in this book and their application to the company. With the parent Company R mission as a resource that they had participated in developing, the company managers were able to summarize the mission for their own company very completely on one double-spaced page:

BUSINESS DEFINITION

1. Three-sentence definition within the scope of Company R definition.
2. Statement of the geographical area of operation.

OBJECTIVES

1. The first objective was to implement the parent company mission in the company's area of operation.
2. The second objective was to achieve selected short- and long-range sales volume and income objectives.

That one-page statement, plus the parent company mission statement, became the mission statement for the member company. From there, the management group of the member company went on to consider the key performance areas and develop short-range objectives for their company. The result was the identification of 24 objectives that became the budget plan for their company and carried them toward the overall objectives of their mission. The shorter-range objectives were set in all seven of the key performance areas:

Area	No. of Objectives
Market standing	4
Innovation	5
Productivity	3
Physical and financial resources	4
Profitability	3
Motivation and organization development	4
Public and environmental responsibility	1

Similar work done in other country operations of Company R becomes the operating realization of operating principle 2: "operations will be directed according to agreed-upon achievement objectives." With the Company R mission providing identity, the stimulation of goals, and the strategy compass, each member company is motivated to achievement and the collective efforts of all member companies link together to accomplish the overall goals of the group. Mission, participatively developed, is a highly motivating experience.

In his book *The Social Contract,* Robert Ardrey argues that humans and other higher forms of animal life share three innate needs that must in some way be satisfied.[1] First in importance is identity, the opposite of anonymity. Each person must see his own importance and his own role in relationships that are meaningful to him. Second is a need for stimulation, the opposite of boredom. He must have in his environment something to which he can respond in ways that are satisfying to him. Third is security, the opposite of anxiety. He must have available to him resources and support that can provide continuity into the future. Those three needs can be met in a person's working life by his participation in developing and carrying out a concept of mission for the enterprise. The mission can provide identity; it can be highly stimulating; and in these uncertain times it can provide the security of membership in an increasingly successful, continuing organization.

[1]New York: Atheneum, 1970.

7

Action Plans That Get Results

The business enterprise is an arena of constant action. Products are manufactured, services provided, products sold, bills paid, shipments made, reports prepared, deliveries received, complaints adjusted, contracts negotiated, advertising prepared, materials processed, wages paid, inventions made, new products introduced, prices changed, purchases contracted, plants built, processes improved, people hired, deliveries invoiced, productivity increased, scrap reprocessed, results analyzed, products tested, production scheduled, promotions launched, and on and on in infinite variety. With everything related to everything else, small wonder there are problems and crises, small, medium, and large. A typical top manager attitude is: "Any damn fool can plan. Give me someone who can solve the problems." And he sees himself as that someone.

The successful businessman is a problem solver. He has an empirical knowledge of each problem area. He knows his organization. He has the authority to act. He is positive and confident in manner. He likes to solve problems. He has solved lots of them. He's good at it. He acts. How well his actions resolve all problems depends on his competence, the management style with which he operates, and his consistency with an overall mission of the enterprise.

Some businessmen operate on the star system. In a brilliant display of positive action they cope with one problem after another, invent creative solutions, launch dramatic programs. But their brilliant display may or may not be related to an integrating concept of mission—what we are, what we intend to be, how we intend to get there.

Others may operate on the bureaucratic system. Every problem that comes up is dealt with by the prescribed procedures. Maybe if it is dealt with long enough, it will go away. Here an integrating concept of mission is almost certainly lacking.

Neither the star nor the bureaucrat will fully develop, much less employ, the

great organizational competence that is potential in any group of people working together toward common goals. But either could greatly improve performance by first of all promoting the creation of a concept of mission. Every action within the enterprise would then relate to the objectives of the total enterprise.

Integrating Disparate Actions

The actions throughout an enterprise are so many and so diverse and involve so many different people that molding them to a common purpose may seem an impossibility. There is in most companies a recognition of both the desirability and the difficulty of doing so. For there are many reminders: resources of one unit unused by another, disparate or conflicting actions by related units, intramural strife on product or investment programs, overlapping and duplication of effort, and what Theodore Levitt calls the problem of the centrifugal enterprise—actions that negate strategy or actions elsewhere and leave employees less productive and customers and other publics less well served.[1] What advertising tells the customer may not be what the customer experiences when he buys the product. What the research department develops may not be what the marketing department can market successfully. What the executive says on the podium may not match the employee's experience on his job. Those disparities are very real and certainly unintentional. The enterprise *will* travel in all directions unless there is an integrating concept strong enough to motivate all actions toward a common purpose. The enterprise will be centrifugal, contradictory, and fumbling unless it is pulled together by an accepted system of values and objectives.

When attention is given to it, the problem of integrating disparate actions is often seen as one of communication. The solution, then, is to improve communication by meetings, company publications, letters from the president, revisions in the policy manual, and perhaps management training programs. But unless an integrating message has been developed, techniques cannot be of much help. Without the message, more communication could make the problem worse.

So first of all we need the message. And the message that has the strength and the authority to motivate and integrate all actions throughout the enterprise to a common purpose is the company statement of mission, the short statement of the fundamentals of:

What we are.
What we intend to become.
How we intend to get there.

When such a statement of mission is developed as recommended in Chapters 3 to 6, it will be understood and accepted because there has been broad participation in its development. It will have the authority of a value system believed in by the organization. It will be simple and fundamental. It will be specific enough that

[1]Theodore Levitt, *Innovation in Marketing* (New York: McGraw-Hill, 1962), chap. 11.

each individual can relate his area of responsibility to the overall company mission.

By beginning with the company mission, each component of the company can for itself conceptualize an identity, goals, and a strategy that relate to and support the overall company mission. That process extended throughout the enterprise will result in a network of unit definitions, goals, and strategies—all relating to and supporting the company mission. For any individual unit the documents need not be highly formalized. The identity will be a short statement or paragraph. The goals will be a listing of a small number of most important objectives. The strategies will probably be the same as those of the company and need not be repeated. One side of one piece of paper will suffice for the writing down, but continuing dialog is needed within each group to arrive at what is written down and keep it always current.

It will not be necessary to assemble such documents from all reaches of the enterprise and evaluate them, edit them, interrelate them, approve them, and authorize them. The documents need be seen and used only within the particular group and shown to and discussed with directly related work groups. They will be developed and used entirely at the operating level. The company statement of mission will provide the overall motivating and integrating authority. Management surveillance of the process is not productive, but management support and participation in the process is essential.

Once the company has developed a mission for the overall enterprise, divisions and subsidiaries can develop missions of their own that are consistent with it. Within divisions and subsidiaries business units can develop their definitions of identity, objectives, and strategy. Each can be very meaningful and also very short. A one-page format is illustrated in Figure 6-2. From such a business plan summary, individuals, with their managers, can develop their performance objectives. At each level the objectives are relatively few: from three or four up to six to nine. They interrelate, and in their achievement they enable the enterprise in total to reach its overall major objectives. All are supportive. The programs and the process of goal achievement becomes a communications system. The problem of communication is resolved by the way the organization works together. Communication is less what we say than it is what we do. It is less technique than climate.

The Figure 6-2 Business Plan Summary is usually derived from a more complete business plan. Figure 7-1 illustrates such a business plan based on the principles described in this book. This format follows the recommended concepts and thinking processes that I have found effective in many businesses. It has helped many business people to think through their business situation and to develop programs that have lead to dramatic successes. Note that it is not a voluminous report—it is the essence of the business plan summarized in three pages.

Each goal throughout the enterprise becomes the starting point for an action program to achieve it, and the Gantt-type format shown in Figure 7-2 is useful

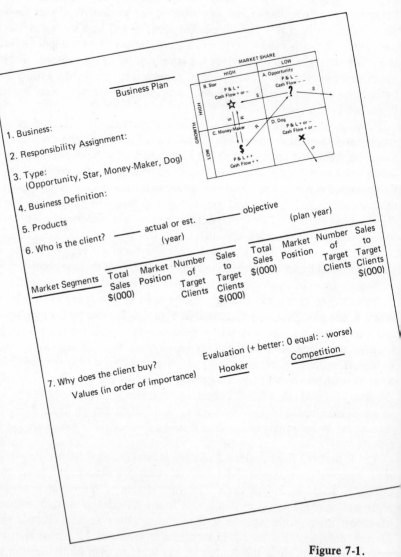

Business Plan

1. Business:

2. Responsibility Assignment:

3. Type:
   (Opportunity, Star, Money-Maker, Dog)

4. Business Definition:

5. Products

6. Who is the client? ————— actual or est. ————— objective

Market Segments	Total Sales $(000)	Market Position	Number of Target Clients	Sales to Target Clients $(000)	Total Sales $(000)	Market Position	Number of Target Clients	Sales to Target Clients $(000)

(year) (plan year)

7. Why does the client buy?

Evaluation (+ better: 0 equal: - worse)

Values (in order of importance)   Hooker   Competition

Figure 7-1.

102

12. Summary of Action Plan:

Programs (Be specific. Show quantities where possible.) | Completion Date | Assigned to

8. Characteristics of the Business: This year   In 5 Years

Market Size

Market Growth Rate

Hooker Sales

Hooker Market Position

Hooker Profitability

9. Major competitors. Estimate Market Position in this business and state the major strength for each competitor listed.

Competitor   Mkt. Position   Major strength

Hooker

10. Fundamentals for Success - What is the "superior customer value" that we can offer?

11. Objectives for _____ (year)

Sales:

Market Position:

Marginal Income:

Other Objectives:

```
Business:

Key Performance Area:

Key Performance Area Objective:



Person having overall responsibility:                    Target completion date:
```

ACTION PLAN

What Is to Be Done	Completion Date	Responsibility Assignment

Figure 7-2. Key performance area objective action plan form.

for developing such an action program. The action programs will be consistent with agreed-upon strategies developed for the statement of mission. Action programs become the responsibility of individuals, task forces, and units. Once an action program is developed, the individuals who undertake specific tasks in it become in effect an informal task force working together to accomplish the objective. One person may work effectively on a number of task forces in discharging his specific job function.

At all levels throughout the enterprise, action programs will be worked out and undertaken to achieve the agreed-upon objectives. The first job of management, at all levels, will then be to assist in goal achievement. That will concentrate management attention on fundamentals, greatly reduce the number of problems and crises, and maximize achievement. Since a network of goals has been developed within the enterprise, there is a corresponding network of action plans for their achievement.

The Performance Budget

The goals and action plans become an actionable budget plan for the enterprise. That kind of budget plan will motivate achievement because each individual has been involved in developing the goals and action plans that relate to his work; each individual has participated in decisions that affect him. But that kind of achievement budget plan is not one that is made up once a year for a fiscal year period. It is made up all the time for many different time spans. It is always being developed, always being carried out, always being changed. It cannot conform to a Procrustean fiscal period because objectives are not achieved by fiscal periods. It only looks as though it can because someone invented financial statements. Financial data can be aggregated to whatever time periods may be desired or required, but achievement must be continuous.

An objective to commercialize a new product may involve many people and groups. The corresponding action plan is likely to be in writing and cover a period of two to several years; it is likely to have much supporting business and technical intelligence and to be continually changed as experience accumulates. In contrast, an objective for production output for the second shift in Department 12 will be very simply stated and the plan for achieving it will be in the minds of the people who do the work. An objective for a sales call and the action plan to achieve it will be entirely in the mind of the salesman.

Depending on the objective, then, the action plan may be for anything from an hour to a year or longer. Important objectives and action plans that involve a number of people may be in writing and be kept up to date as changes are made. Others will be in people's minds and communication will be by words and actions. But all will relate to the integrating concept of mission for the enterprise and to the specific, major objectives developed in support of that mission by each group and by each individual.

That kind of performance budget plan will require a special kind of reporting system that will provide the information feedback needed by each individual and group in carrying out action plans and achieving objectives. The purpose of the reporting system is not to evaluate performance; it is to help people achieve objectives. The new type of performance reporting is described in Chapter 13.

Objectives and the action plans to achieve them will be both written and unwritten. They will be for short time spans and for long time spans. They will continually change. They will be achieved, altered, and abandoned. Action plan achievement, environmental change, and continuing dialog will keep the network of objectives and action plans always current and always consistent with the mission for the enterprise—which itself will change in response to achievement, change, and dialog.

Growth and change are continuing processes. They do not fit the assumption of fiscal year aggregation. So let's deal with them as they are. Let's set objectives continuously. Let's achieve performance continuously. We can then eliminate an annual massive effort to construct a plan for a fiscal year. We can eliminate a periodic massive effort to review and reconstruct a long-range plan. For we will have our plans all the time. From those plans any financial measurements wanted or needed can be summarized for any present or future period very quickly, very easily, and very reliably. Where the objectives and action plans I am describing here are in use, I have seen good financial plans for a fiscal year developed in two hours time. For the future-oriented enterprise, working by mission and for key performance area objectives, the period ahead is always in view.

In all the key performance areas, we understand our present position and how we got where we are. Our objectives describe our short- and long-term destinations. Our action plans lay out the journey. Feedback on achievement keeps us on the right road and gives us an understanding of the trends and changes in trends that are developing in the important measurements in each of the key performance areas. The enterprise becomes a moving picture of all its inter-related variables and how they are synthesizing mission achievement. That is a different picture from what we see when we freeze all the dynamic variables into fiscal period snapshots. Annual snapshots are of little help in managing the affairs of business enterprise. But in the moving picture, every employee can be both a participant and a director.

Effects of Performance Budget

A South American company in an industrial equipment business applied the concepts described in this book to its operations. Major goals were supported by shorter-term goals in each of the key performance areas. Among them were market share objectives in several product lines. A special opportunity was identified in a type of processing equipment, class PG machines. A competitor dominated that market, but new developments from the group's design center in England could provide the company with technical and cost advantages. The management group, in dialoging key performance area objectives, agreed that the company could reasonably aim to achieve the leading position in class PG machines. The product manager would have the overall responsibility. To achieve the objective, the action plan shown in Figure 7-3 was developed by the individuals who would be implementing it. Several observations on that example of action plan are appropriate.

1. Together, the individuals having responsibility for the various actions become an informal task force to achieve the objective.
2. There is no change in individual job assignments; the task force is simply a way of structuring work to be done to achieve an objective.

```
Business: Equipment
Key Performance Area: Market standing
Key Performance Area Objective:
    Achieve No. 1 market position in Class PG machines

Person having overall responsibility:        Target completion date:
    Product Manager                              2 nd Q, 19__
```

ACTION PLAN

WHAT IS TO BE DONE	COMPLETION DATE	RESPONSIBILITY ASSIGNMENT
1. Get specifications from UK design center.	Nov. 1	General manager
2. Analyze specifications and adapt to local market.	Dec. 15	Product engineer
3. Resolve technical problems with UK	Jan. 20	Product engineer
4. Technical visit to UK design center if needed.	Jan. 31	Product engineer or product manager
5. Select machine designs to be offered.	Feb. 15	Product manager
6. Establish prices.	Mar. 10	General manager
7. Economic analysis.	Mar. 31	Controller
8. Business decision to market Class PG machines.	Apr. 3	General manager
9. Manufacture prototype machine.	Apr. 30	Product engineer
10. Prepare sales program.	Apr. 30	Product manager
11. Implement sales program to achieve volume objectives.	May 1 and continuing	Sales manager
12. Coordinate technical and production support for sales program	May 1 and continuing	Product manager

Figure 7-3. Key performance area objective action plan.

3. The task force is made up of individuals from different management levels, including the general manager to whom the product manager reports, a product engineer who reports to the product manager, the sales manager, and the controller, an executive in a different functional area. To achieve the objective, all work for the product manager.
4. The task force functions not by structural authority relationships, but by teamwork relationships:
   a. Mutually accepted and meaningful goals.
   b. Shared decision making.
   c. Mutual confidence and support.
   d. Shared understanding of the situation.
   e. Commitment to a common purpose.
5. In a work group, a manager can work for a subordinate.
6. Performance is more important than prerogatives.

With work structured in that way throughout the company, some surprising things happen. There is greater achievement. There is strong team spirit. There is enterprise and motivation. Problems and crises diminish in number and intensity. We may also notice that we are no longer following some of the management principles that have so long dominated management thinking:

1. We are not working according to a pyramidal organization chart; instead, we have more free form and more temporary work groups.
2. Since one person may be a member or leader of more than one work group, he may very well work for several "bosses" and not just one.
3. With this method of structuring work, "span of control" is not a relevant concept. A manager may lead or participate in ten work groups or one or forty. Competence and the work to be done are what is relevant. Mission and objectives coordinate and relate far more effectively than span of control can.
4. The management job is not so much the management of people as it is the structuring of work to motivate performance.

A plastics materials company had earned the leading market position in one of its major product lines through product innovation and technical and commercial assistance to customers. One of the company's most important objectives was to maintain market share for that product line. As usual, the objective was complicated by the fact that old segments of the market were changing and new segments were developing continuously. To maintain market share would require continuing innovation and wise commitment of resources. Past success could provide resources to work with, but it could not provide all of the direction on resource commitment. Reinforcing the past does not create the future.

But the past does provide experience and know-how as well as resources. New dimensions can be added by business intelligence. Then, by adding the catalyst of innovation, appropriate new objectives can be developed. From business intelligence, the company concluded that new opportunity would come more from the way existing materials were modified, processed, and used than from the invention of entirely new materials.

Increasingly, materials would be modified to achieve desired processing and performance characteristics. They would be filled, composited, alloyed. They would be chemically modified by graft and block polymerizing, engineering of molecular structure, and control of molecular weight and distribution. And with thermoplastics being increasingly cross-linked and thermosets increasingly fabricated by automated methods, the traditional distinction between thermoplastics and thermosets would become less significant.

What would be significant was that plastics are a materials business with, at that time, 39 known chemical families as a basis. Additional new families would be discovered, but the great promise of the plastics materials industry for the years ahead would be in how existing materials would be modified and developed. The world's greatest materials industry, the steel industry, was created from one basic molecule—iron. The plastic materials industry had 39 basic molecules—an ample base for what could become the world's greatest materials industry, one that would surpass steel in volume.

Not only would materials modification be a route to development but new fabricating methods would also be developed to make possible new uses of plastic materials. Fabricating machinery would be automated and linked into complete production systems not only capable of the familiar mass production of identical units but also responsive to the contemporary need for individualization and variety through new techniques for discontinuous automation.

Rapidly accumulating engineering knowledge of the performance characteristics of plastic materials under various conditions and environments would continue to expand the use of plastics in new kinds of applications. That growing knowledge would guide the modification of existing materials to offer great new opportunities for the materials and technology in which the company was strong.

The market share objectives for the company, then, took two directions: (1) a strong development effort to formulate and apply materials to engineering applications in automotive parts and assemblies and (2) new processing techniques and the formulation of materials for those new techniques. For each direction, specific short- and long-term objectives were developed. Task forces were established. Individuals and work groups undertook the accomplishment of actions needed to achieve objectives. Action plans were thought out and dialoged by using the format shown in Figure 7-3. Task force leaders followed progress carefully and made appropriate changes in programs and objectives. But always there was participation by all who were a part of the program. A spirit of enterprise and achievement and a strong team competence developed. The resources from past successes and the skills from past experience were refocused on new opportunities. The company remained the leader because it became a leader in the major, developing new opportunities.

Action Planning of Sales Operations

An area in which many companies emphasize action planning is field sales operations. Through an approach such as the customer sales planning discipline described in Chapter 2, sales volume goals can be developed. The salesman in the professional management of his sales assignment in turn develops the business intelligence about his territory from which he can identify major opportunities. He becomes well informed on all customers and prospects, their requirements and problems, key people, company history with each customer and prospect, and competition. From that information he can determine the next major target account opportunities.

In my company sales is an important profession. The salesman is well trained technically and commercially, and he has broad experience in the market he serves. His sales assignment, depending on the business and our strategy approach to it, may be defined by geography, products or product lines, a market or industry, specific assigned accounts, channel of distribution, maintenance selling, development selling, or some combination. In his assignment he is likely to have from 25 to 50 accounts and prospects, on the low side, to 150 or more. But typically, among all those accounts and prospects from three to ten will emerge as target opportunities. Those targets, determined from the business intelligence he develops on his territory, then become the major focus of his achievement objectives. He will have sales volume objectives for all accounts and prospects, but he will concentrate on the objectives for his target accounts. He will have action plans (in his head) for all accounts and prospects. But he will think out more completely, and perhaps put in writing, his action plans for his target accounts. Three considerations influence putting such plans in writing:

1. The goal and the action plan are important to the man and to the company. Writing them out helps to think them out.
2. A written plan provides a basis for dialog between man and manager to arrive at the best possible plan.
3. Others will be involved. The written plan improves coordination.

Figure 7-4 shows one format for a written target account customer sales plan. It summarizes the important situation information about the account and states the sales goal and the strategy. The strategy will be consistent with company strategy and will be chosen as the one that best relates the needs of the customer to the competence of the company so that in the achievement of the sales goal both the customer's company and our company will benefit. The actions to be taken to implement the strategy and achieve the goal are then thought out and listed. Again the Gantt type of action planning is used as a simple way to plan what must be done and coordinate the work of those involved.

With that kind of action planning, the salesman becomes a professional manager of his part of the company—his territory. He is programming his available inputs, (1) his time, effort, and professional competence, (2) company support, and (3) costs, to achieve targeted outputs:

1. Target account objectives.
2. Other sales volume objectives.
3. Income contribution objectives.
4. Other sales program objectives.

The achievement of those objectives in turn establishes his and our company's number one objective—the creation and maintenance of satisfied customers. For without a client constituency of customers there is no business. Through customer sales planning, our business can be created day by day, account by account.

_____   _____
　　　　　　Customer　　　　　　　　　　　　Salesman

Profile Information

Address and phone number:
Other company addresses:

Type of business:

Any related businesses (parent company, subsidiaries):

Key contacts and titles, stating for each his role in buying decision:

Competition at this account, share of business, strength, weakness:

Sales history with this account:

Year	Dollar Sales	Comments
19 —		
19 —		
19 —		
19 —		

Sales goal:
Sales strategy:

Sales program:

Action	Completion Date	Assigned to

Figure 7-4. Target account customer sales plan.

111

By having a company mission to relate to, each unit of the company can define its own identity and think through its own key performance area objectives. From that the subgroups of the units can do the same thing, and so through the organization until all individuals and work groups have objectives most important for them and are following action plans to achieve those objectives. Collectively, those objectives make possible the achievement of the overall goals of the enterprise. At all times a great interrelated network of action plans is moving the enterprise toward its goals. At all times a closed-loop feedback is used as the basis for altering plans and objectives in ways most appropriate to the mission and most responsive to the environment. Everyone participates. Everyone achieves. Goals and action plans rooted in mission provide a framework for leadership to new heights of achievement for the business enterprise. For that becomes not the way we *plan* our business; it becomes the way we *run* our business. We do not first plan and then act; we plan and act at the same time and continually. Everyone plans. Everyone acts. We are always doing, but we are also always thinking about what we are doing to relate all our actions to the normative future we have found and articulated in our mission.

8

Motivation

The chairman's letter in the annual report often describes people as prime among the firm's resources. It thanks them publicly and credits them as the wellspring from which corporate achievement flows. Get inside the organization and you are apt to find a rather apathetic response to those noble words; for they don't always match employee experiences.

The Importance of Perspective

The employee likes his company and the people he works with. He knows the company is interested in the output of his job. But he's not so sure the company is interested in him. And that the company might welcome initiative on his part to determine what the output of his job should be would probably not even occur to him. He has a good job. He does a fair day's work for a fair day's pay. The terms of the job contract are met; one day follows another; and once a year he reads the chairman's letter.

At high levels of the organization the job contract may look very different. There may be found strong personal commitment and a genuine feeling that job output is very much the individual's concern. What happens in the organization may well be determined by small numbers of people in the more senior professional and management positions. In the middle areas of organization there may be a range of feelings and involvement from the highly motivated to the disinterested. Altogether, a mixed bag—with the achievement of the many flowing largely from the commitment of the few. The proportions of the few and of the many will differ widely from one organization to another. But quite commonly, some pattern of this general type will be found: The many will be somewhat bored until they leave their jobs at the end of the day. The few never leave their jobs, and they would like to get home for dinner more often.

That pattern of job content, job commitment, and motivation is a very natural evolutionary product of our industrial history. But it need not be as it is. We can purposively alter the product of our industrial history to make work more meaningful to more people and more productive for our business enterprises. All that is required is a change in perspective. We must become more creative in reinventing the future for our business enterprise and for each unit and subunit to the level of individual jobs. And only our human resources—the many, rather than the few—can make that continuing process of reinvention possible.

Abraham Maslow's pioneering work helps us understand the pattern of human motivation, the historical perspective, and the very considerable resources that we have among us today.[1] Motivation is not administered externally; it is the result of needs within us that cause us to act as we do. Because people have different needs at different times they will respond differently to the same conditions. Maslow generalized their needs in his now-familiar hierarchy:

Level 5	Need for self-actualization.
Level 4	Need for self-esteem, status, ego satisfaction.
Level 3	Need for belonging, social role, friendship.
Level 2	Need for safety, security.
Level 1	Physiological needs, survival.

According to Maslow, we are first motivated by our physiological needs—food, shelter, and survival. Once those needs are satisfied, safety and security become the major motivators, then participation and role in social groups and society, then status and ego satisfaction, and finally self-actualization.

At the time of the industrial revolution and the development of industry and industrial organizations, the first level of needs was generally prevailing. As our economy developed, the physiological needs were more broadly satisfied, and safety and security became the more prevalent needs until these needs too were satisfied for most people. Today in the developed countries large numbers of people are motivated by needs at levels 4 and 5, but the pattern is uneven. There will be people at all five levels, and despite a developed economy large groups can remain at levels 1 and 2. On the other hand, the intelligent and well-educated people who are motivated at higher levels represent a great new opportunity for improving the functioning and achievement of our business enterprises.

Historically, enterprise regarded human motivation needs as more on levels 1 and 2 and perhaps 3. Only a very small proportion of employees had creative, thinking kinds of jobs. Management had the responsibility to plan, implement, measure, and control, and others had only to do the jobs laid out for them. Until perhaps 1920, that kind of approach was a reasonable match to the needs of employees. But today we live in a different world. The old need patterns have changed and creative, thinking work can be done by many, many more people.

[1]*Motivation and Personality* (New York: Harper & Row, 1954).

In fact, it is being done. The only question is whether it will be done within and for the benefit of the enterprise or elsewhere and for other purposes.

Patterns of operation change slowly. A pattern that has brought success will be continued until its only output can be failure. The pattern is as good as it ever was—probably even better because it has been steadily "improved." But the environment has changed, and the old success pattern no longer fits. Evolution is a process of specialization—to extinction. The motivational pattern of 1920 or 1935 is not the motivational pattern of today.

The bankruptcy of the historical assumptions about people on which much management practice was based was first articulated by Douglas McGregor, a pioneer in behavioral science. McGregor recognized that management, if it was to be a true profession, would have to make use of the accumulating knowledge of behavioral science. Yet he saw very little awareness of the research findings and expertise of his profession among businessmen. He also saw very little interest in business among behavioral scientists. McGregor brought the two together. His book *The Human Side of Enterprise* has probably been read by more businessmen, and has had greater influence on them, than any other book in the field.[2] In it he described the assumptions about people on which conventional management methods were apparently based:

1. People dislike work and will avoid it if they can.
2. People avoid challenge and responsibility.
3. Most of all, people look for security in their jobs.
4. Because people dislike work and won't accept responsibility, they must be directed, controlled, coerced, or threatened to get them to do what they should do.

This set of assumptions, McGregor contended, seemed to underlie much management practice. From these assumptions could come different management positions or types, from hard or strong on the one extreme, to soft or permissive on the other. Hard management is characterized by tight controls, close supervision, and use of coercion and threat of punishment to get the performance it wants. Soft management tries to satisfy people's demands to keep harmony in the organization. Hard management is authoritarian and results in restricted output, antagonism, militancy, and undermining of company objectives. Soft managment in its concern for personal relations produces harmony but ineffectiveness, and a lazy workforce that continually produces less but expects more. McGregor describes both hard and soft management no so much as being wrong but as being irrelevant. Both ignore the findings of behavioral research. McGregor gave the name of *Theory X* to the traditional assumptions about people reflected in both hard and soft management positions. From the

[2]New York: McGraw-Hill, 1960.

work of behavioral science he described another set of assumptions, which he called *Theory Y*. Theory Y assumptions include:

1. Work is as natural for people as play or rest. Depending upon what it is, work can be satisfying or frustrating, and it will accordingly be done willingly or unwillingly.
2. People will work toward objectives to which they are committed.
3. Commitments to objectives relates to need satisfaction.
4. Under appropriate conditions, people not only accept responsibility but seek it.
5. Typically, people have more ability than they utilize in the job.

McGregor pointed out that theories X and Y are assumptions about the nature of man. Neither provides a cookbook recipe on how to manage. Management should seek to understand the reality with which they are dealing and then formulate assumptions consistent with that reality. From those assumptions appropriate strategies can be developed. McGregor felt that Theory X assumptions had become unrealistic for business enterprise. They were self-fulfilling in that, when management acted on the basis of them, people behaved according to them. And those traditional assumptions were very limiting; they permitted businessmen to conceive of certain possible ways of organizing and directing human effort, *but not others*. On the other hand, Theory Y assumptions opened up a broad new range of possibilities. "If, however, we accept assumptions like those of Theory Y, we will be challenged to innovate, to discover new ways of organizing and directing human effort."[3]

Underuse of Talent

Today, when many people are motivated by the needs for ego satisfaction and self-actualization and those needs are not commonly satisfied in many business organizations, underutilization of talent is common. It is, in fact, probably the biggest problem in business organizations today. Or, to take the positive view, it probably offers the biggest opportunity for improving output and achieving higher levels of performance. Frederick Herzberg contends that the organization has three choices with respect to the underutilized employee: (1) it can use him, (2) it can fire him, or (3) it can have a morale problem.[4] The underutilized employee has four choices: (1) he can quit and seek a more satisfying, motivational employment elsewhere, (2) he can conform to the organization's work structure and look for self-actualization away from the job, (3) he can deteriorate—for talent unused will deteriorate, or (4) he can work to change the system. All

[3]Ibid.

[4]"Motivation Through Job Enrichment," film produced by BNA Films, Rockville, Md.

those responses are in fact common. The extent to which they are found in an organization is a measure of the problem of underutilization.

The managers of most organizations feel they have a shortage of people and talent at the very time when much talent within the organization is unused. Instead of adding more people, efforts to make better use of existing people would be a highly productive strategy. There are four excellent approaches to the prevention or elimination of underutilization:

1. *Stretching.* Structuring work to give the person more challenge than he can easily handle is called stretching. Management typically underestimates the abilities of people and does just the opposite of stretching; it reduces the work content of the job to a common level of mediocrity. But in doing and achieving, people grow. The self-actualizing employee wants more challenge. Stretching is not speed-up; it is a means of helping the employee to get away from what is to him an unmotivating way of working. Stretching works. And it is not a one-time thing. It works again and again. It is good for the individual and good for the enterprise.

2. *Participation.* Participation is more than communication; it is more than consultation; it is involvement in a responsible, influencing way. As recommended in the earlier chapters of this book, it is a way of using all of the talents of the enterprise. Participation is not an easy approach for a traditional management to use; for it requires a willingness to be influenced by subordinates. It can best be accomplished through a loose organization structure and continuing dialog.

3. *Delegation.* Passing responsibility and authority through the organization as far as it will go can meet the ego-satisfying and self-actualization needs of individuals and result in much greater achievement for the enterprise. The statement of mission developed and implemented as recommended in Chapters 3 to 6 can provide the integrating force needed to make such broad delegation effective.

4. *Job enrichment.* In job enrichment we begin with the do-it kind of jobs in the enterprise and see if broadening the responsibility by restructuring the work will result in more satisfying, more productive jobs. Few companies can apply job enrichment on a do-it-yourself basis; most companies require some outside professional help. Top management must also be involved; for the end result will be more than making changes in jobs. It will be restructuring the way in which work is done.

Cost Versus Value-adding Behavior

All managements are necessarily very interested in cost control and cost reduction programs. Better utilization of talent can make a great contribution to the objectives of cost reduction programs, but in a unique way. We can think of all behavior and all activities of the enterprise as being either (1) cost behavior—that which incurs costs—or (2) value-adding behavior—that which adds value as measured by income paid to us by our customers. Buying raw materials is cost behavior, and buying raw materials at lower prices is a cost reduction opportunity. Using raw materials is value-adding behavior, and getting more production or higher-value products from a unit of raw materials is a value-adding opportunity.

The need to control cost behavior is obvious, and cost-incurring behavior is usually the concern of cost reduction programs. But success is often limited. A concentration on reducing cost behavior is likely to have little favorable effect on profitability.[5] Value-adding behavior is often overlooked among the cost reduction objectives of management programs, yet there is far greater potential for achievement and for profit improvement in increasing value-adding behavior than there can possibly be in reducing cost behavior. More can be created than can be saved out of what we are already doing. Both ends are served when we successfully put to work the excess ability now underutilized in our business organizations. As that talent is increasingly utilized, it will reduce cost behavior, and it can very significantly increase value-added behavior. Certainly, as we put to work the unused talent among us we are improving the motivational climate. But we are not doing it by motivating people. We are doing it by changing the way we do our work.

Job Motivators

A common and erroneous idea is that if we could only motivate our people better, they would do better work. We would leave the work the same but somehow change the people so they would do it better. If we think that way, we are starting from the wrong end of the problem. People are pretty much what they are, and an objective of bringing about much change is unlikely of achievement. So the question becomes more that of the extent to which the work can be structured in people terms.

Frederick Herzberg conducted an extensive research on job motivators. He and his associates interviewed people in many different kinds of work. The interviewer would ask the respondent to think of a time when he felt exceptionally good or bad about his job, and he would then probe to find out what there was about the job that made it exceptionally good or bad at that time. From analyzing the responses Herzberg found that five factors were the most important determiners of job satisfaction: achievement, recognition, the work itself, responsibility, and advancement. The major dissatisfiers were found to be company policy and administration, supervision, interpersonal relations, and working conditions. From his work, Herzberg developed his "motivator-hygiene theory," which states that the motivators are inherent in the job and in what the person does in his job. The other considerations, the dissatisfiers, all have to do with the environment in which the work is done.[6]

[5] Rensis Likert, *The Human Organization* (New York: McGraw-Hill, 1967), pp. 84-91.

[6] *Work and the Nature of Man* (Cleveland, Ohio: World Publishing, 1966).

Herzberg called the environmental factors—company policy and administration, supervision, salary, interpersonal relations, and working conditions—hygiene factors, and he suggested that hygiene factors led to dissatisfaction because of a need to avoid unpleasantness. When the hygiene factors are good, they lead not to motivation but only to an absence of dissatisfaction. The motivating factors, on the other hand—achievement, recognition, the work itself, responsibility, and advancement—result in motivation and job satisfaction because they meet the need for growth and self-actualization. Work, then, if it is structured according to the motivator-hygiene theory matches the needs of the mentally healthy individual. If the motivators are present in the work itself, the individual will experience successes and over time will achieve personal growth. If the hygiene is good, he will avoid discomforts.

From the work of Herzberg and others, it seems clear that if we undertake to "motivate" people so that the work will then be done better, we are on the wrong track. What is needed is a structuring of the work in such a way that the work will have the motivators in it. The work itself, then, will motivate people and the enterprise will have expanded its capability of achieving its objectives. That is the productive answer to the problem of the underutilization of talent.

Yet in many business enterprises today we continue to structure work in worn-out ways. We simplify tasks to the least common denominator to make them productive. And the long years from the employment interview to the retirement party become long years of wasted and deteriorating talent. Through all that time good professional talent in the industrial relations department is concentrating on the job hygiene factors. Little attention is given to the motivators. That situation is general in business and other human enterprises today. It is not that what we are doing is bad. It is just that what we are doing is not adequate for today. The problems we now confront are vast and complex. They cannot be met by anything less than the full commitment of all the talent we have or can develop—not just management's talent, but everyone's talent. We can no longer afford the systems from our past that waste talent and allow it to deteriorate.

The motivators—achievement, recognition, the work itself, responsibility, advancement—are responsive not only to human needs but also to the needs of the enterprise. The congruence of needs can benefit both the employee and the enterprise. If we recognize that great potential strength in our organizations, we will orient our thinking to human and organizational productiveness rather than to mechanical efficiency. We will invent new management principles to replace those that we have learned from the past and that no longer fit today's needs. We will more successfully use and develop our talent rather than continue to waste that most precious asset.

Achievement is one of the important motivators. But only a small percentage of people have a "natural" motivation for achievement. Natural achievers have been found to have two characteristics in common. The characteristics do not relate to intelligence, education, family background, wealth, or professional experience. They do relate to experience in achieving, beginning with the early years: (1) Natural achievers acted independently early in life. They were not done for; they did things for themselves. (2) They began achieving on a small scale while small in size.

David McClelland has studied the achievement motive in many cultures, at all ages over past history, and among many kinds of people. He has traced the rise and fall of cultures as related to the rise and fall of the prevalence of the achievement motive.[7] He has found that self-motivated achievers have three common characteristics in the way they work:

1. They set their own goals.
2. Their goals are within their achievement ability; that is, they represent some kind of optimum risk as being both achievable and challenging.
3. They get specific feedback on how they are doing in the achievement of their goals.

McClelland also discovered that training and development and experience can raise the achievement motivation of people. Specifically, that can be done by:

1. Adding acceptable risk to the job to provide a challenge for the achievement of attainable but meaningful goals.
2. Providing prompt and reliable feedback on progress toward the goal achievement.
3. Giving recognition for achievement.
4. Having the achievement mean something significant as seen by the individual.
5. Relating the goal achievement to the achievement of group goals to reinforce individual satisfactions with an esprit de corps.

Organizational Climate

All the achievement-learning principles are a part of the concept of business operations recommended by this book. The company, in conceptualizing its mission and developing goals and strategies throughout the enterprise, develops the motivational environment identified by such pioneers as David McClelland, Frederick Herzberg, Douglas McGregor, and Abraham Maslow. It develops a way of creating a congruence between the motivational needs of people and the needs of the enterprise to create stronger people and a more achieving enterprise.

By operating that way, management creates a climate within the enterprise that will not be the authoritative, highly directive kind that limits and constrains

[7]*The Achieving Society* (Princeton, N.J.: Van Nostrand, 1961).

talent. It will be open, participative, and supportive. Rensis Likert, after a study of many companies, has classified management style as follows:[8]

System 1	Exploitive authoritative
System 2	Benevolent authoritative
System 3	Consultative
System 4	Participative group

Likert has found that, as companies move more toward the system 4 style of management, achievement and profitability increase. System 4 managment is built on three basic concepts:

1. Supportive relationships throughout the organization.
2. The use of group decision making and group methods of supervision.
3. High-performance goals for the organization.

By supportive relationships Likert means:

The leadership and other processes of the organization must be such as to ensure a maximum probability that in all interactions and in all relationships within the organization, each member, in the light of his background, values, desires, and expectations, will view the experience as supportive and one which builds and maintains his sense of personal worth and importance.[9]

The contrast between the authoritative systems 1 and 2 and the participative system 4 can be illustrated by the measuring and reporting methods used. In the authoritative system employees are not trusted; they are told what to do and trained to do it properly. Appropriate measurements are made to assure that they have done it right. The implicit distrust quite understandably creates resentment, disinterest in the work, and waste of talent. In the participative system the primary purpose of measurement is to provide managers and other employees with information they need on their progress toward the achievement of their objectives as a guide to decisions and action.

Likert identifies four conditions required of an organization if it is to coordinate the work of various people and components effectively and achieve objectives:

1. It must provide high levels of cooperative behavior between superiors and subordinates and especially among peers. Favorable attitudes and confidence and trust are needed among its members.
2. It must have the organizational structure and the interaction skills required to resolve differences and conflicts and to attain creative solutions.

[8]Ibid.
[9]Ibid., p. 47.

3. It must possess the capacity to exert influence and to create motivation and coordination without traditional forms of line authority.
4. Its decision-making processes and superior-subordinate relationships must be such as to enable a person to perform his job well and without hazard when he has two or more superiors.[10]

Those conditions cannot be met by the authoritative style of management. They can be met only by the system 4 participative style of management that therefore can and does, according to Likert's findings, produce higher levels of organizational achievement.

Changes in Organizational Climate

A century ago, when large industrial organizations were developing, the pyramidal, authoritative organization structure developed as an effective way to get the work done. It met the generally prevailing motivation level of workers by providing for physiological needs and also, more than before, for safety and security needs. Within the hierarchy, bureaucratic procedures were followed to get work done and assure order, consistency, and equal treatment of workers. The pyramidal, bureaucratic organization was well suited to the environment and values of its era and represented an advance over the cruel early years of the industrial revolution. As years passed, it has continued to evolve in response to a changing world. It has grown less authoritative. It has accommodated large numbers of professional employees, whose work has been organized to meet higher levels of human needs. Its procedures have, to some extent, become less bureaucratic. Although it still cherishes its pyramidal organization charts, it does more and more of its work interfunctionally with groups of people not directly linked by the chain of command.

But the evolutionary change has not been enough to keep the pyramid contemporary. Its problems have accumulated faster than its competence to resolve them. Those problems result from major new forces in the environment:

1. Rapid change in all areas of human affairs, often so sudden as to be discontinuous from past experience.
2. Sophistication of modern technology.
3. Vast increase in size, diversity, and geographical scope of business organizations.
4. Increasing numbers of well-educated people working at higher levels of psychological need.
5. Interdependence among business organizations, government, other institutions, and the physical environment.
6. Complexity of problems and opportunities confronted.

[10]Ibid., p. 158.

In response to those forces the authoritative pyramid structure will continue to change; it will increasingly be replaced by contemporary structures consistent with Likert's participative management. But whether by change of the old or creation of the new, successful business organizations will more and more be characterized by

1. Integration by common purpose more than by executive authority.
2. Temporary work groups to achieve specific objectives.
3. Recognition of competence more than of rank.
4. Participation in making decisions and programming action.
5. Supportive relationships, mutual confidence, and openness.
6. High performance standards.
7. Effective team-building relationships.
8. Structuring of jobs in human terms.

Many will dismiss such new ideas as impractical, but it is easy to get hung up on what is practical and what is not. For most of us, what is practical is what we know and are comfortable with. In the real world what is practical is what fits the situation. And the situation that exists may be much different from our view of it. In invoking the real world to support an historic position, we can be invoking a fiction. About the pyramidal, chain-of-command, authoritative, bureaucratic organization, for example, we "know":

1. There is a maximum span of control for one manager.
2. No employee should have more than one boss.
3. Management's job is to organize, direct, control, and reward or punish.
4. Performance appraisal is important.
5. The income statement measures performance.

In short, we "know" many principles that fit the traditional bureaucratic pyramid but do not fit the new organizational ways of working. Such principles seem practical because they are so much a part of our heritage. Now we must open our minds to new ways; for these are times that call for innovation. The innovations of the past that now seem so practical must merge with contemporary innovation to develop new forms and new ways that are practical today.

The traditional approach to organization study is to begin with functions to be performed; the contemporary approach is to begin with objectives to be achieved. The traditional approach is to structure functions in an organization chart; the contemporary is to structure work to be done. The traditional approach is concerned with responsibility and authority; the contemporary with competence. We can contrast the two approaches as follows:

Traditional	Contemporary
1. Inventory and analyze functions.	1. Determine mission and objectives.
2. Develop organization structure.	2. Analyze existing organization.
3. Assign functions to components.	3. Formulate long-range target.
4. Prepare management position guides.	4. Organize meaningful jobs related to mission.
5. Outline man specifications.	5. Determine method of change.
6. Staff the organization	6. Develop phase plans.
	7. Implement.

In the traditional approach to organization the work to be done is analyzed and then arranged in simplified elements that can be professionally managed within a pyramidal organization structure to aggregate to the achievement of a desired output. That approach is the synthesis of scientific management at the macro level of organization. It is so obviously right that it is quite difficult to see that it is, really, entirely wrong.

It is only *after* jobs are classified, ranked, and staffed, and after results fall short of expectations, that we turn our thoughts to the motivation of the humans who operate the organization machine.[11]

Jobs have been made more efficient—and less human. A job that is specialized and simplified may no longer be significant enough to the job holder to motivate his achievement and his identification with organization objectives.

Participative Management by Objectives

In the new, contemporary approach to organization, functions are not structured as simplified elements of a highly engineered industrial machine. For when they are and we add people, the machine just doesn't work the way it should. Work has been organized for our material resources. It should have been organized for our human resources!

In an enterprise, organization that is determined by structuring the work to be done will flow from a concept of mission—what the enterprise is and what it intends to become. Organization of a unit within the enterprise then flows from the unit objectives, which are supportive of the overall mission of the enterprise. When we have the objectives, we can program the work necessary to achieve them by writing action plans. The work will then be structured; it will be done by individuals who have the competence to do it and work together to achieve the objectives. Work groups will form and change as objectives change. We will

[11]Douglas S. Sherwin, "Strategy for Winning Employee Commitment," *Harvard Business Review*, May-June 1972, p. 42.

have less of the pyramid and more of the free-form, temporary work group kind of organization. Individuals are likely to be members of more than one such group at the same time. Our organizations can become far more productive as we concentrate on structuring the work and less on structuring the people. Structuring the work through a participative management style will help us develop new ideas about what is practical. We may not need organization charts at all. And we may find identity and achievement principles much more helpful than management principles.

When the enterprise, each unit of the enterprise, and all work groups and individuals have a sense of identity and a commitment to objectives, the climate throughout the enterprise can be highly motivating. The development of identity and objectives is described in earlier chapters. At the level of the individual, that kind of management approach is management by objectives. But there are many MBO styles: some are directive, some participative; some are highly proceduralized, some informal; some are used to evaluate performance, some to get work done. The kind of MBO that I find works best is participative, informal, and used by the man and his manager and his work group associates to get work done. I call it participative management by objectives.

Participative management by objectives (PMBO) is a way of working with people. It is not something to do in addition to managing; it is a way of managing. So we should not think of it as a company program with forms to fill out and procedures to follow. Instead, we should think of it as a way of getting the job done. Managers who have successfully used PMBO have found it effective in increasing output, improving the achievement of goals, and furthering morale and job satisfaction. There are five key elements in an effective PMBO program:

Trusting climate. A PMBO program requires a climate of mutual trust between manager and subordinate. Such a climate of trust develops when there is respect for the other person's judgment. That develops from experience and is encouraged by continuing use of PMBO programs. Also, it is important that both manager and subordinate know not only what is done but the reasons or motives behind doing it. Understanding of those motives can come only through open discussion and leveling between manager and subordinate. Integrity too is essential. There must be no discrepancy between what is said and what is done. Consistent performance and behavior are important to establishing an atmosphere of trust.

Job understanding. Written job descriptions are really not adequate guides to performance. In a successful PMBO program the individual's job is described as to areas of responsibility. But in addition to that, and far more importantly, specific major objectives are developed. The job description and the objectives then comprise the overall job understanding.

Job descriptions may be either written or oral, but it is usually desirable to have brief written descriptions that include the name of the positions and the position to which the job reports, a list of responsibilities, and a statement of the specifically established job objectives. The listed objectives will be few in number—probably three to seven. They will change as they are achieved or as conditions change. Objectives for a job should not be determined only for the fiscal year.

Although jobs are most commonly described in terms of responsibilities and functions, a more contemporary and often more useful way is in terms of outputs and client groups. Outputs are what the work done on the job should produce. Client groups are those who receive the outputs from the job. That method of describing jobs is the starting point for job enrichment. It is also helpful, in describing management and professional jobs, as a starting point for the determination of specific objectives.

If you are preparing objectives for yourself, a good way to start is to write out a description of your position as you see it before you think through specific objectives. Use either of the two methods described above. Also, if you are asking your people to prepare objectives, you might ask them as a first step to write descriptions of their jobs. Then in your meeting with each individual you would include a discussion of the description with that of the proposed objectives.

Mutually agreed-upon goals. Objectives seem to work best when they are (a) set by the subordinate, discussed and critiqued with the manager, and approved by the manager; (b) few in number; (c) changed as conditions change; and (d) written specifically. The manager will usually set the stage for the development of objectives through discussion of the company situation, goals, and strategies. Normally the objectives should number from three to seven, and they should be the most important ones for the position in the immediate future. Usually all of them are job objectives, but it may be appropriate to have a personal development or stretch objective—something that is not normally a part of the job—among them. They should include specific quantities when possible, should have target dates for completion, and should be stated in end-result terms. That enables feedback on progress toward their achievement.

Here are two questions to ask yourself about each objective as written: How will I know when it's done? Can a subordinate know performance without his manager having to tell him? In regard to dates, while we normally think of our jobs in relation to the annual budget, most objectives should be for a shorter time period—from one to six months. Few objectives should have a targeted completion date as long as a year. An individual's list of objectives then continually changes as old objectives are completed or changed and new ones are established.

Frequent discussion about progress toward goals. Once objectives are established, the manager and subordinate concentrate on the achievement of the goals. Their conversation and their work together should focus on the situation and the work being done to achieve the objectives. Discussion should be descriptive, not evaluative; it should address the problem, not evaluate the subordinate's performance. Two-way dialog is essential. Feedback on progress should come directly to the subordinate so that both manager and subordinate are aware of progress being made. The feedback must be current and reliable, not weeks or months old.

When progress is reviewed and it is found that the subordinate is not succeeding in the achievement of one of his objectives, the most important rule to remember is, "Don't criticize." The point of PMBO is the achievement of goals, not the evaluation of people. And as long experience with performance appraisal systems has revealed (to those who care to look perceptively), criticism is one of the most negative motivators of achievement ever invented. A progress review should constitute a participation in goal achievement, not be a performance evaluation. With that more positive attitude in mind, four general rules can be helpful in dealing with situations in which the desired objective is not being achieved:

1. Spell out the problem. Describe the problem in objective terms that avoid evaluative good or bad inferences about performance. It is important to deal with the situation, not the person. Spelling out the problem should be a mutual effort so that together the manager and subordinate clarify the problem.
2. Get the subordinate's reaction. If he is defensive, ask for his feelings about what you've just said. Ask other questions to establish open dialog dealing with the situation; be conversational, open, nondirective. Don't attack excuses that are offered. Listen. Accept. Restate. Mutual understanding will emerge.
3. Dialog what to do. Once the problem is clarified, next steps can be worked out.
4. Summarize. To conclude the discussion ask the subordinate to summarize his understanding of the problem and what is now to be done. With understanding, you have arrived at the best solution that can at this time be developed through the competence of both participants. The focus is on the situation. The manager is supportive. Such dialog can be highly motivating of achievement.

Summary-reward discussion. As a part of a PMBO program there should be periodic discussion in which the subordinate summarizes his performance and is told of any salary change. Salary increase should be linked to achievement of goals, but the linking should be qualitative rather than mechanical. It is not a good approach, for example, to say that, since a man achieved 60 percent of his goals, he should get 60 percent of a merit increase. Instead, a qualitative evaluation should be presented in consideration of goal achievement, how goals were achieved, changes in the situation, the man's individual situation and future promise, appropriateness of reward, and the manager's judgment.

The summary-reward discussion should be short. It should include reasons relating to goal achievement and the considerations listed above, but there should be no discussion of performance improvement.

PMBO Application

Participative management by objectives seems simple but is actually very difficult. Only a very mature kind of person can use it effectively, and usually a good organization needs a couple of years to really begin to get benefits from it. A good way to establish a PMBO method of operations is to begin with the top management levels or with a decentralized operation or subsidiary. As experience develops, the method can be extended.

The work my company has done in individual and organization motivation in recent years developed from a marketing need. We were finding too many instances in which goals had been set, programs developed, commitments made, and goals not achieved. There were always reasonable explanations—there were competitive changes, changes in business conditions, technical problems. Sometimes the goals had been "unrealistic." But all things considered, too many times our performance had not been what we had intended.

Our aspirations were not for the average and the ordinary. We aimed for high levels of achievement. But it appeared that we needed more than good objectives and programs. We needed to do something that would improve our individual and organizational competence to achieve our objectives and programs. It seemed that the behavioral sciences might be helpful. To explore that area, we conducted attitude surveys. We organized company conferences and workshops led by consulting professionals. We studied motivation, management by objectives, work structure, manager-subordinate relationships, and career development. From the conferences and workshops, specific areas for further work were defined and specific projects were established.

Today many of our organizations and many of our people have learned new ways to increase our ability to determine and achieve significant goals. Some of our organizations have made very effective use of PMBO methods. We have had excellent results from job enrichment concepts applied in some laboratories and in some production operations. Several of our divisions and subsidiaries have worked hard to develop more participative management styles, and those efforts we believe have contributed significantly to improving levels of performance.

As a company we advocate motivation and organization development methods. In those areas we organize task forces on specific projects and provide and encourage participation in educational programs. From all that our knowledge increases and so does our ability to change the way we work together to make effective use of the accumulating knowledge of human behavior. That I find extremely important to us in increasing our competence to achieve and therefore to define and create an exciting and meaningful future for our enterprise and our people.

But what we have done so far is only a beginning. We have much to do to expand those practices within our company and to acquire new knowledge. None of what we have learned or accomplished to date can be reduced to a simplified technique and broadly applied by executive order. It must be learned, developed, and applied by many people, so there must be many teachers, consultants, and helpers. We use outside professionals, and we have an increasing number of company people who are becoming knowledgeable in those areas and who contribute substantially to our growing competence.

My present conclusion is that motivation and organization development is one of the essential key performance areas determining the success of any enterprise, that much learning and development effort is required and that it takes time, and that for both those reasons all organization components at all times should have at least one specific major objective in this key performance area.

9

How to Handle Change

In America we have very special resources for using change, responding to it, or causing it. We need not be overwhelmed by Alvin Toffler's *Future Shock*[1] or fall victims to the chaos of extrapolated futures of energy crises, lethal pollution, depersonalizing congestion, cataclysmic destruction, or starvation. Toffler very dramatically describes the impact of technical and social change on individuals and cultures that evolve in their responses more slowly than the environment around them. In the early years of this century Henry Adams examined various measurements of change—the rate of scientific discovery, steam power application, coal production, electric power generation. Everything he measured followed the familiar law of squares. Change occurred exponentially. The acceleration of the seventeenth century he found rapid, that of the eighteenth startling, and that of the nineteenth almost unmanageable. The expectations for the twentieth he found almost incomprehensible:

> Yet it is quite sure, according to my score of ratios and curves, that, at the accelerated rate of progression since 1600, it will not need another century or half a century to turn thought upside down. Law, in that case, would disappear . . . and give place to force. Morality would become police. Explosives would reach cosmic violence. Disintegration would overcome integration.[2]

More recent extrapolist futures are similar. By extension, social trends lead to such scenarios as Aldous Huxley's *Brave New World* and *Brave New World Revisited*.[3] With the advent of the computer and its immense capacity for manipulating variables, simple extrapolations have been replaced by models and the

[1] New York: Random House, 1970.
[2] "The Rule of Phase Applied to History," in *The Degradation of the Democratic Dogma* (New York: Macmillan, 1919).
[3] New York: Harper & Row, 1960.

assumption inputs have been combined in various relationships. For example, Prof. Dennis Meadows and his associates at the Massachusetts Institute of Technology developed a computer simulation model of global interactions of population, natural resources, pollution, capital, and food production. In whatever combination the variables were projected there was no escape from catastrophe.[4]

Response to the Challenge

Yet we are not without resources to respond to the increasing challenge of change at the workday level in our business enterprises and in relation to the macro-scale problems of world dynamics. That wise observer of the American scene, Alexis de Tocqueville, observed that special attribute of Americans more than a century ago when he casually asked a sailor why American ships were built to last only a short time.

The sailor answered without hesitation that the art of navigation is making such rapid progress that the finest ship would become obsolete if it lasted beyond a few years. In these words which fell accidentally from an uneducated man, I began to recognize the general and systematic idea upon which your great people direct all their concerns.

The significant point here, and our significant asset, is not the much criticized acceptance of the idea of product obsolescence. It is the willingness and naturalness with which the idea of change is accepted and believed in. Tradition is less honored than change; the old is less respected than the new. A common greeting on seeing a friend or acquaintance is, "What's new?" Perhaps that orientation to the new and to the future stems from our national history. Anyone not satisfied with his lot in his homeland could make a new start in America. Anyone not satisfied with his life in America could make a new start on the frontier. The nation was expanded across a continent by courageous people seeking something new. The new frontiers are today's complex problems, and we have that acceptability of change as a considerable cultural resource for their solution. It is a resource we can use within our business enterprises.

Areas of Opportunity

In the enterprise, three broad areas of change will give us future opportunity of future shock:

Technological change.
Environmental change.
Organizational and people change.

Each can be constructively cultivated or randomly reacted to. Each can provide our growth or cause our destruction. Each is amenable to understanding. We

[4]Donella H. Meadows, Dennis L. Meadows, Jorgen Randers, and William W. Behrens III, *The Limits to Growth* (New York: Universe, 1972).

must actively seek that understanding if we are to cultivate change to provide for our growth. And as we find that understanding in our business enterprises and in our other human institutions, we will escape Aldous Huxley's *Brave New World* for a more fulfilling residence in the noetic humanism envisioned by his brother Julian.

By what methods of perception will we see the dynamic specifics and the developing central tendencies of the three areas of change? How can we learn the understanding that we need?

Observers of the world scene see our world now in a period of restructing and rearrangement. Continuation of present trends extrapolates to catastrophe. But restructure and rearrangement can create a world different from the extrapolated one. Jonas Salk in his wonderful little book, *The Survival of the Wisest*, describes our world today as at the transition area between the A Stage and the B Stage of the sigmoid curve, common in biological growth. In the A Stage, all feedback says "grow, expand, increase". At the transition area, feed-back becomes confused—"grow, don't grow, change". In the B Stage, a transition is completed and stabilization achieved. Applied to man—if we are genetically programmed or intellectually able to respond to this changing feed-back—we will in years hence have made the transition from an A Stage "quantity, to a B Stage "quality of life."[5]

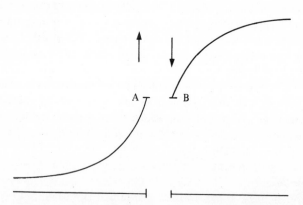

So we now are in a period of change new to us as individuals, and perhaps unique to our history. One of the major positive contributors needed to achieve the change demanded in our time can be the business enterprise. And as it contributes to this change, the enterprise itself will change. There will be change in technology, but different from what we have seen in the past. There will be change in job structure and in the way people work together in groups. And the enterprise will assume a responsibility that is ecological as well as economic.

[5] J. Salk, *The Survival of the Wisest* (New York: Harper and Row, 1973), p. 18.

Technological Change

As for technology, our experience has now developed to the point where we can see technical change ahead more clearly. And we see this change being determined in consideration of its societal and environmental significance, as well as the technical and the economic. Technology today hears not only the A Stage feed-back "quantify" but also the B Stage feed-back "qualify." In our business enterprises we will see technology change predicted, developed, and directed through the use of five important concepts of technological forecasting:[6]

Intuitive forecasting
Trend extrapolation
Normative forecasting
Dynamic modeling
Monitoring

In these concepts there is both the freedom to create, and the discipline of direction. Intuition can be organized into patterns of meaning through Delphi techniques. When we define significant technical attributes, our history has been that we can and usually do achieve performance improvement in these attributes at an exponential rate. Typically, we see change from mechanical to electromechanical, to electronic, to optical with often discontinuity in the rate of change when one new technology impinges on another.

In normative forecasting we see the growing recognition and application of our technological experience which demonstrates that much of the technical change we have seen has developed in response to need. It has been estimated that some 80% of technology has had its origin in perceived need. In the past, that perception has been the A Stage perception of growth and quantity. For the future it will be more the B Stage perception of the husbandry of resources and quality. Indeed, in the demonstrated response of technology to need lies a very considerable hope for the future. New needs, now being perceived will determine its direction.

Dynamic modeling provides methods of "thinking ahead" of the possible and probable relationships in technology change and needs. It applies a systems methodology to technological forecasting. Through monitoring of areas of technology, and monitoring of the social-political-economic-natural environment we see the clues that become the cues that influence the events that form the trends that become our future. In this time of changing modes and conflicting signals, an alert monitoring is essential if the enterprise is to find and develop its future.

---

[6]See James R. Bright, and Milton E. F. Schoeman, *A Guide to Practical Technological Forecasting,* (Englewood Cliffs, N.J.: Prentice-Hall, Inc., 1973), and Joseph P. Martino, *Technological Forecasting for Decision Making,* (New York: American Elsevier Publishing Company, 1972).

So the achieving enterprise must do technological forecasting. It is implicit in every decision involving technology; every response to technological change. We can no longer leave such important matters to implied assumptions. Technological forecasting forces explicit consideration of the technological future by management, by functional departments, and by technical personnel. It is based on methods of reasoning that can be analyzed, tested, challenged, and refined. It leads to a better understanding of the forces that drive or control technology in one's field, and requires consideration of the interactions between technology and societal change. And it demands that forecast participants and users think beyond the immediate problems of today, to the creation of a normative future from today's actions.

As we learn the value of change, "future shock" can become "future transformation" to a world that uses technology to new ends, providing great, new opportunity for the achieving enterprise.

Environmental Change

Often, in our businesses, we think of environment as something "out there" that causes problems for us, often dramatically, and usually unpredictably. Perhaps we could relate better to environmental change if we altered our views of the relationships involved. For, in reality, environment is not something "out there" constraining us. Environment is something we are a part of, and environmental constraints are the interacting relationships that we must manage. I favor not only thinking about environment in this way—I favor putting environment on our organization charts as a part of the structure of business enterprise. Figure 9-1 shows how this can be done for a business unit.[7]

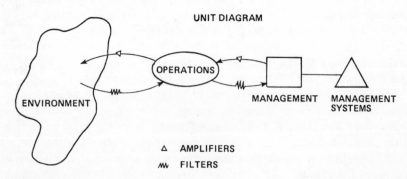

Figure 9-1.

[7]This unit diagram is described further in the final section of Chapter 13, "A Structural Framework for Achievement Reporting." The diagram model was developed by Stafford Beer and is described in his book *The Heart of Enterprise* (New York: John Wiley & Sons, Inc., 1979).

The elements in the unit diagram are operations, management of those operations, management systems which organize information in consideration of mission, and environment which is the world in which the unit functions. Arrows indicate information flow. Sensors at each end of each arrow sense and transduce the data. Filters reduce the variety of the vast amount of data into meaningful information. Operations can't know everything that's out there in the environment, but must know all that matters. Management can't know all the data generated by operations, but must know what matters. Amplification makes possible effective communication of information from management to operations, and from operations to the environment.

An enterprise's operating connectivities with the environment are crucial, and well deserve recognition on the organization chart. And it is not one environment, but several. It is the commercial environment of customers, competitors, vendors, distribution, labor market, resources, and capital markets which we have always recognized. But it is also the economic environment, the technical environment, the political environment, the social environment, and the ecological environment. All of these are the environment of business, and they all interrelate and interact one with another and with business, as shown in Figure 3-5. Our mission provides us a way of managing these important environmental linkages. For our business will clearly be seen as a part of the larger system of these environments, and environmental change will be dealt with in our key performance area objectives, in our strategies, in our action plans, and in our performance measures.

Organization and People Change

We adult human beings can grow as individuals throughout our lives, through accumulated experience, knowledge, and skills—a continuing process of change. This "psychological growth" continues for a lifetime. Similarly, business organizations greatly expand their competence and their achievement through a continuing process of change—and only through a process of change. The stereotype of the rigidly conformist corporation with its "organization men" exaggerates an organizational climate that can, and does, exist. But it is not the business organization that belongs to today, and that will most contribute to building tomorrow. The contemporary corporation is very much an agent of change that contributes to the growth of its people, and of itself. How can the organization bring about this kind of constructive, purposeful change?

First of all, it recognizes the need for change. It recognizes that the enterprise itself through its past efforts and its past achievements has created the three conditions most resistant to the changing of group performance:

Age of the organization (not the age of the people—the age of the organization)

Size
Success

But while the people of our country have learned from the traditions that created the past, they built a new nation by accepting and believing also in the idea of change.

Douglas McGregor altered our views on motivation by revealing that the traditional assumptions about people cause the behavior rather than the other way around. Theory X assumptions become self-fulfilling. They create the environment in which the observed behavior of employees confirms the assumptions. Different assumptions will create a new environment, and behavior also will be different. And so it is in regard to individual and organizational resistance to change. It is commonly known by observation that people and organizations resist change. But perhaps that knowledge and its basic observations result from our assumptions. It may be closer to reality to say that people, in the American tradition, *like* change but *dislike* the methods used by management to put change into effect. What a loss of opportunity! What a misuse of available talent! At a time when we probably have the competence to conceptualize and achieve a normative future for our business enterprise, we tie ourselves too strongly to our past by the ways in which we confront the problem of change.

Why do we continue to impose those constraints on ourselves? Surely it's not for lack of knowledge of them. For many years the data necessary to refute our Theory X type of assumptions about resistance to change have been available. Years ago Alvin Zander identified some of the reasons for resistance to change in organizations:[8]

1. The purpose of the change is not clearly understood.
2. Persons affected by the change are not involved in planning for the change.
3. The change causes anxiety over job security.
4. There is poor communication.
5. Existing work customs and work group relationships are abruptly changed.
6. The appeal to change is based on loyalty rather than on problem solution or goal achievement.
7. There is fear of failure.
8. Work pressure is excessive and the change is seen as intensifying the pressure.
9. The change is seen as requiring too high a personal cost or providing inadequate reward.

[8]"Resistance to Change—Its Analysis and Prevention," *Advanced Management*, January 1950.

10. A vested interest of the individual or his work unit is involved—the we versus they problem.
11. Respect for and confidence in the person or group initiating the change are lacking.
12. There is prevailing satisfaction with the status quo.

If we reflect on those reasons for resistance to change, we can see how they would be created by methods commonly used in our organizations to bring change about. With that understanding, we can then view the reasons for resistance to change in a more positive way. We can see how different methods could enlist those reasons *for* rather than *against* change. Gordon Lippitt has described how resistance to change can be lessened and a climate receptive to change developed:[9]

Involve employees in planning for change. Participation will stimulate ideas from people closest to the problem and most aware of opportunities for and difficulties in making change. It will provide common understanding of the situation, the need for change, and the program of change that is decided on. People understand and believe in what they create, so a program of change developed participatively by those affected by the change becomes more than just a proposal or a plan. It becomes a commitment to cause the change to happen.

Provide accurate and complete information. Rumors fill any vacuum left by absence of information. Withholding information affecting employees leads to mistrust and resistance. Bad as well as good news should be communicated. Both kinds of news are inputs to change. Both kinds help employees to know where they stand.

Give employees a chance to air their objections. Gripe sessions can be helpful just for blowing off steam. They can also provide feedback and involvement in improving and implementing the program of change.

Always take group norms and habits into account. They are not necessarily resistance factors; they also can contribute to the change. Perhaps more compatible work groups can be established. Perhaps value norms will be supportive of the change. Whatever the existing norms and habits, they are important inputs to a program of change.

Make only essential changes. Changes that are trivial, unneeded, or unrelated to the achievement of commonly understood and accepted goals will not be welcomed. Employees who will accept and participate in change for the sake of meaningful achievement may be very resistant to that which they see as change only for the sake of change.

Provide adequate motivation. Change provides opportunity for motivation. The two go together. We won't achieve planned change without motivation, nor will we achieve a motivational climate without planned change. Motivation—in

---

[9]*Organization Renewal* (New York: Meredith, 1969), pp. 149-161.

theory and practice—bears a fundamental relationship to the whole process of change. We may more productively think of change in terms of motivation than in terms of management decision making. For a more complete statement on motivation and its relation to change see Chapter 8.

Let people know the goals of and the reasons for change. People need to know not only what is happening but why it is happening and what goals are being sought. That they should learn as part of the change process from their participation in the process. And if we have developed our concept of mission—identity, goals and strategy—and our key performance area objectives as recommended in this book, the people concerned will also have been informed of and involved in the fundamentals motivating the change. Understanding and support will come more from participation than from telling and selling.

Develop a trusting work climate. Trust comes from openness in communications, a free flow of information, and supportive relationships between superiors and subordinates and among peers. A trusting climate is essential if an MBO approach to achievement is to be used productively.

Learn to use the problem-solving approach. Technical problems can be solved by individuals, but organizational problems can be solved only by the organization. The decision maker may feel he has solved the problem, but the solution will depend on what the organization actually does. Power and achievement are not necessarily the same. President Kennedy is reported to have once listened to a proposal advocated by a visitor, a proposal that he also supported, and remarked, "*You* agree with it, and *I* agree with it, but will the *government* agree with it?" The decision maker always confronts a similar problem: Will the organization agree with it? Using the problem-solving approach within the organization will help assure that the organization *will* agree and *will* perform to achieve the objectives sought by the decision.

Role of Dialog

For an organization, the problem-solving approach applies the scientific method through the group dynamics of dialog, confrontation, search, and coping. Dialog is an open, issue-oriented talking together. For a business the issues may be either problems or opportunities. The focus of dialog is always on the issue, and each participant contributes his knowledge, his ideas, and his suggestions stimulated by the ideas of others.

Dialog is the method; confrontation is the focus. We confront the problem or the opportunity and all aspects of it. Dialog starts the whole process by helping us first of all to identify the problem or the opportunity and to perceive it in a similar way. Dialog continues in our search of all the significant dimensions affecting our response. In the search, participants level with each other; they are respectful of others as individuals.

By confronting the problem and searching its dimensions, we become able to cope with it. Through coping we come to common understanding, arrive at agreement, and effect action. Throughout the process, dialog is the method. Through dialog, confrontation, search, and coping, the organization itself can apply the scientific method to problem solving:

1. Defining the problem.
2. Obtaining and analyzing information.
3. Formulating possible solutions.
4. Testing alternatives.
5. Reaching decision.
6. Developing action plans.
7. Carrying out the program.
8. Obtaining and evaluating feedback on performance.
9. Modifying plans as appropriate.

As a problem-solving approach dialog, confrontation, search, and coping can resolve the common and demotivating experience of the win-lose confrontation. In the problem-solving approach the problem is confronted and resolved by the competence of the group. In the win-lose situation individual positions contend for a victory confirmed by management decision. As institutionalized in traditional management practice, the win-lose confrontation uses too much time, wastes talent, and limits the performance of the organization. Typically, a proposal is developed for presentation to the next higher level of management, where the presentation itself becomes a win-lose situation. The proposal is accepted (win) or rejected (lose). Or it may be accepted after some further work or changes (win, with struggle). It may then go to a higher management level for a repetition of the same kind of win-lose confrontation. A single proposal may run the obstacle course of three, four, or more levels of win-lose confrontation. Small wonder that authoritative hierarchical organization structure can stifle initiative and discourage change.

A more constructive approach is for decisions to be made throughout the organization and to be coordinated and motivated by mission and key performance area objectives. Then win-lose situations can be avoided. Instead of them, the management levels concerned with the problem will develop their solution through dialog, confrontation of the problem (not of individuals), search, and coping. Instead of a hierarchical series of win-lose sessions, there will be one problem-solving session of those who will make and carry out the decision. One or more proposals may be inputs to the dialog process, but the output will be a solution to the problem, not a yes or no on a particular proposal.

The innovative, achieving organization avoids win-lose situations; it focuses the competence of its members on the opportunities and the problems through dialog. In the achieving organization, all members can participate, all members can contribute, and in that way all members can win.

In most organizations change is the product of individual brilliance only when the individual can stimulate the organization itself to change. Perhaps that is one of the reasons why so many long-range plans are so much better on paper than they are in the plant and the market. Through a talent of leadership an individual may initiate change and stimulate the organization to achieve it through the processes previously listed. Or the leader may develop the listed processes to find and develop change through the competence and contribution of the group.

> People just naturally want to improve things. So when one thinks about it, it is strange that "resistance to change" is what is reported by observers of organizational behavior when actually "change" presents the best chance employees have to satisfy their psychological needs! The key to this paradox is that change is great when you are its agent; it is only bad when you are its object.[10]

When we think about change in organizational terms, we are beginning to get close to what change, for our business enterprises, is all about. Too long have we thought of change as the product of executive decision or scientific invention. But change is much more than an idea or an invention. Change is what people do with the one or the other. So it is not so much the decision or the invention or the idea that counts. It is what the organization does that counts. That is why ideas—good ideas—are plentiful but innovation is so scarce. Ideas flow in free supply from many individuals, but only organizations—people in groups—innovate.

Organization Development

The organization is an operating system of people in groups. If that operating system has the characteristic orientation to function, it will have an inertial resistance to change. Decisions, inventions, and ideas will find the soil too barren to sustain them, and innovation will flounder. But if the operating system is oriented to mission—what it is, where it is going, and how it will get there—it will have an entrepreneurial eagerness to change and will welcome and cultivate innovation.

When the manager makes a decision or the scientist makes an invention, he provides an input to the organization. Corporate development, research and development—those too are inputs. Innovation is what the organization does. Managers express an awareness of that reality when they note that, however difficult making the decision is, making the decision a reality is much more difficult still. That reality requires organization change. In recognizing that such change depends on what the organization does, not on what management does, we are not diminishing the management job. We are adding another dimension—organization development.

We need more than an idea input from R&D and from corporate development or a decision input from management. We also need an operative climate

---

[10]Douglas S. Sherwin, "Strategy for Winning Employee Commitment," *Harvard Business Review*, May-June 1972, p. 46.

for change and innovation from organization development, including idea inputs from all. That is, organization development must be cultivated if change and innovation are to be encouraged. Yet organization development is seldom discussed in boardrooms, seldom becomes the concern of management, and, so far as I have seen, is not monitored in periodic operating reports. It is fundamental but forgotten. It is a real need assumed out of existence by a Theory X type assumption that people just naturally resist change.

A good technique in problem solving is to deny assumptions. If we use that technique here, we might hypothesize the reverse of our assumptions on resistance to change and assume that people just naturally like change. Then we might think less of the decision and more of the implementation. We might value less the invention and more the innovation. We might from a different assumption base begin to confront the great opportunities in organization development. Through organization development, people in groups maintain a responsive attitude to the environment around them and develop the individual and group competence to achieve organization objectives and fulfill the mission of the enterprise. Innovation becomes welcome. Change is not only accepted; it is created by the organization. Organization development becomes a continuing renewal of the organization. And it becomes one of the essential concepts for motivating business achievement.

John Gardner, from his experience in developing organization competence, points out that organizations need not stagnate; that they can continuously renew themselves. He describes nine rules for organization renewal:[11]

1. There must be an effective program for the recruitment and development of talent. Well-trained, highly motivated individuals must be continually brought into the organization. And they must not be boxed in or allowed to deteriorate. They must find positive programs for career development so that their talent and motivation continue to grow and benefit both the individual and the organization.

2. There must be a hospitable environment for the individual. Individuality is a value for each person and a resource for the organization. Individuals who feel like cogs in a machine will not be the creators of change.

3. There must be built-in provisions for self-criticism. Gardner states that a basic principle of human organization is that the individuals who hold the reins of power cannot trust themselves to be adequately self-critical. There is an ever-present danger of self-deception, of inability to see problems, even of a refusal to see problems. The best defense against that danger is to create an environment in which each person can speak openly. From its members, through dialog, the organization and its leadership can find reality.

Gardner points out that most ailing organizations have a blindness to their own defects. They suffer not because they can't *solve* their problems, but be-

[11]"How to Prevent Organizational Dry Rot," *Harper's*, October 1965, pp. 21-23.

cause they can't *see* their problems. He proposes four ways to overcome that functional blindness:

a. Bring in an outside consultant.
b. Encourage internal critics.
c. Bring new blood into a few key positions.
d. Rotate personnel between parts of the organization.

4. There must be fluidity of internal structure. Most organizations have a structure that was developed to solve problems that no longer exist. Jurisdictional boundaries and lines of authority tend to become rigid and prevent change and achievement. Although organizations require both structure and specialization, there must always be a fluidity that permits and encourages change and achievement.

5. There must be an adequate system of internal communication. Communication makes possible the combination and recombination of many diverse talents to achieve the objectives sought by the enterprise. Communication does more than provide information; it provides a way of solving problems.

6. There must be means of combating the process by which men become prisoners of their procedures. The procedures persist long after the reasons for them have changed or disappeared. They accumulate to frustrate achievement rather than encourage it. The vital, achieving organization does not allow itself to become encrusted with procedures.

7. There must be means for combating the vested interests that grow up in every human organization. Vested interests exist at every level in an organization—privileges, status, authority, function, working relationships. They exist among work groups, at supervisory levels, among professional employees, and at management levels. The organization capable of renewal must find ways of subordinating those interests to the interests of the enterprise. One way to do that is to find greater interest in the new, in the achievement of mission, than in interest vested from past achievement.

8. The organization capable of continuous renewal is interested in what it is going to become and not in what it has been. An orientation to the future cannot be left to research and development and to individuals and groups concerned with long-range planning. The whole organization must be looking toward the future.

9. An organization runs on motivation, on conviction, or morale. People have to believe in what they do. They have to care.

All nine rules for organization renewal can be applied by using the concepts advocated in Chapters 3 to 9. Organization development through continual renewal is fundamental to achievement. It begins with mission. It finds its way and develops through key performance area objectives, action plans, and motivation. Feedback provides information to modify and renew mission and objectives. Techniques described in the following chapters may be employed. The whole process is iterative and continuing. Organization development becomes mission achievement becomes organization development becomes mission achievement as we find our way to a meaningful future.

An Example of Organization Renewal

Organization renewal concepts are not just ideas; they are used in many organizations. TRW Inc. has several years of experience with organizational development as a route to achievement. The TRW Systems Group has developed a managers' guideline to organization development to help its people develop and strengthen organizational competence. Included as a policy statement in this guideline is the following:

Organization life has many dimensions including economic, marketing, technical, physical, and behavioral—the way people act and relate to each other. All of these dimensions need systematic attention.

In the behavioral area, Systems Group has organization values and objectives which are consistent with and necessary to the Group's established general goal of protecting and expanding our resources, and applying them to the best advantage of TRW Inc., the stockholders, our employees, our customers, the government, and general public, in an appropriately balanced fashion.

These behavioral values and objectives include:

1. Continuous growth in the effectiveness of individuals and organizational teams.
2. Open and direct communication across organizational boundaries, to the end of strengthening mutual support and resolving conflicts constructively.
3. Conscious development and monitoring of the human systems which are an inextricable part of our internal systems and subsystems.
4. Avoidance of depersonalization, loss of personal influence.
5. Encouragement and reinforcement of individual responsibility for action in the interest of the total group.

The behavioral values and objectives listed above are recognized as an integral aspect of achieving TRW Systems Group's general goal. Further, it is believed that the untapped potential in human systems and individuals is very large, and for practical purposes, inexhaustible.

It is therefore the policy of Systems Group to:

give balanced and systematic attention to our behavioral values and objectives,

continue to improve our capability for so doing,

and make general use of this capability.

We have developed methods and skills which are directly helpful and relevant. These are included in the field commonly known as "Organization Development."

Successful implementation of these methods involves a commitment to values which are consistent both with the methods and with the behavioral values and objectives of this Group.

They include:

viewing people as inherently motivated, constructive, responsible, and caring, trusting their ability and motivation to act in the interests of the organization, responding to normal needs for consideration and confirmation,

recognizing and enhancing people's natural potential for continuous change and growth,

valuing and making creative use of individual differences,

viewing people not simply as means of carrying out stated roles but as possessing a wide range of talents and insights for helping the organization and each other,

valuing feelings and their appropriate expression,

choosing direct and open communication over "maskmanship," manipulation, and tactics for out-maneuvering the "opposition,"

directly confronting ineffective performance and behavior rather than sacrificing organization objectives and passively permitting the person concerned to continue living with harmful illusions,

using status to further the effectiveness of the organization rather than as a wall protecting personal power, prestige and isolation,

facilitating the innovative risk taking which is part of organizational and individual adaptability and growth,

giving appropriate values and attention to critiqueing and improving the interpersonal processes by which work gets done, and

placing more emphasis on the personal strength and skill required to achieve collaborative working relationships, as opposed to competitive.

The widespread incorporation of these values requires a long-range continuous effort. A quixotic approach is clearly ineffective. However, the person who acts from such a set of values and premises makes more possible corresponding behavior in others.

The important contribution of organization development, organization renewal, or organization theory—however we may wish to name or define it—is that it is increasingly providing for us knowledge about work in organizations that can be applied to increase our competence to achieve significant objectives. As we learn how to handle change, we will learn how to invent our future and how to make the invented future come true. Achievement of mission becomes, in reality, continuing organization development.

Management in an Environment of Change

Integrating today's rapid change into a process of growth for our people and for our enterprises will require a different kind of management from the traditional management which created our past successes. This new kind of management has been clearly perceived and described by Igor Ansoff. Listed in Table 9-1 are some of the characteristics of this "new" management, in contrast to the traditional, as described by Ansoff.

We are not as yet very much into this future management style. But we are departing significantly from the style of the past. We stand today somewhere beyond a known management style that brought us spectacular achievement through the "A Stage" of our growth. We are now moving tentatively into a new style for the future. My work, in companies throughout the world, has demonstrated that this new style of management today is better for our people, and better for our business enterprises. For today's climate it is pragmatic, not theoretical. It works. It uses the process of change to provide growth for the individual and achievement for the enterprise.

One company, in taking a futures view of its operations, used the occasion of our nation's two hundredth anniversary to review company past performance and to look ahead to changes that could be opportunities, or problems, in the future. From that company's July 4, 1976, report:

Developing now is a renewed nation with the talent, the capital resources, the competitive strength, and the cultural heritage to cope successfully with our problems. But this will mean a process of change. And in this process, and in these changes, can be found new opportunity. At this time it may be rewarding to consider carefully what some of these changes may be, and what they may be as challenges or opportunities for our company. This is not just an academic exercise. If we can perceive significant change before it becomes obvious (either as a problem or as someone else's achievement) we may by actions taken now capitalize on the change to achieve new successes for our company.

Table 9-1. Characteristics of Management.[12]

Past	Future
Values and Attitudes	
Surrogate Owner	Professional
Committed to laissez-faire	Committed to social value of free enterprise
Profit optimizer	Social-value-optimizer
Seeks economic rewards and power	Seeks job satisfaction
Seeks stability	Seeks change
Prefers incremental change	Prefers entrepreneurial change
Basis of Managerial Authority	
Surrogate asset ownership	Knowledge ownership
Power to hire and fire	Expertise
Power to reward and punish	Ability to challenge
	Ability to persuade
Management Decision-Making	
Change absorbing	Change generating
Risk minimizing	Risk propensive
Triggered by problems	Triggered by opportunities
Serial diagnosis	Parallel diagnosis
Convergent	Divergent
Consistent with experience	Novel
Incremental	Global
Sequential attention to goals	Simultaneous attention to goals
Satisfying	Optimizing
Systems	
Financial	Human resource accounting
Capital budgeting	Capability accounting
Expense budgeting	Capability budgeting
Historical control	Action budgeting
Long-range (extrapolative) planning	Strategic entrepreneurial planning
	Forward control

[12]I. H. Ansoff, Management in Transition, in *Challenge to Leadership, Management in a Changing World* (The Free Press, 1973), pp. 40-42.

Changes Now Perceived as Probable	Company Opportunity
1. New technologies revolutionizing old technologies	Applying these to our chemistry and to the needs we serve to minimize energy and materials usage for utility provided
2. Inadequate supplies of crude oil (depletion, growth in demand, political disruption)	Exploration and discovery; alternate energy and feed-stock sources; more productive conversion in the satisfaction of needs
3. Shortages of raw materials, energy, equipment	Sensitivity to supply/demand trends; purchasing arrangements to assure supply; vertical integration; improved productivity; new technology to lessen usage requirements
4. Shortages of food and nutrients	Greater agricultural productivity, new forms of agriculture, new sources for calories and nutrients
5. Talent shortages	Structure of work to attract and motivate high achievers
6. Inflation (deflation?) and shifting exchange rates	Understanding monetary data in "real" terms and using this reality in the decision process to preserve assets and to develop opportunities
7. Recurrent wage-price controls or other forms of incomes policy	Constructive participation with government; increasing value-added in relation to inputs of energy, materials, capital and man-hours
8. Socially and politically imposed responsibility for maintaining the environment	How to make husbandry of the biosphere contributory to company success
9. A shifting from a competitive world of abundance toward a cooperative world of scarcity; a transition from "exploitation and growth" to "conservation and quality of life"	Increasing value-added while decreasing use of materials and energy
10. The "New World Economic Order" developing through the work of IMF, UNCTAD, OECD, GATT, UN, and other international bodies, and by the actions of individual nations and groups of nations	How to contribute to LDC goals in achieving company goals; equitable distribution of created wealth
11. Worker participation in management	Use of talent to enhance achievement of company goals

146

Changes Now Perceived as Probable	Company Opportunity
12. Multinational chartering and regulation of business	New measures of accountability that can contribute to company success
13. Increasing importance of state-managed economies and state-managed enterprises both as suppliers and competitors	Developing modes of trade that can provide acceptable values to all parties
14. Motivation from the work itself	Use of all talent to formulate and achieve business goals
15. Increasing diversity	Ability to deal successfully with ambiguity
16. Decline in effectiveness of hierarchical organization and line-staff relationships	More task-oriented, free-form organization with authority from competence more than from position
17. Deterioration of urban environments and their ensuing reconstruction	Business opportunity in urban renewal; jobs for urban populations
18. Intermediate technology that can make towns and villages viable	Development and production of tools; development and dissemination of know-how
19. Measures other than GNP to measure the achievement of nations	How to contribute in appropriate ways to the new achievement criteria

Understanding change requires for its inputs the knowledge of the philosopher plus specific techniques of the scientific investigator. It requires a focus of knowledge and skills on the fascinating and fundamental reading of the future. Its results will not be predictions; they will be scenarios describing possible or probable futures. Scenarios, once developed, provide a projected path against which actual change and experience can be measured. The measurement then contributes to the continuing recasting of the scenarios; it confirms some futures and revises others.

Here we again see at work one of the fundamentals advocated by this book—what matters is trends and changes in trends, not discrete events and periodic summations. We should watch the future of our business as we watch all other measures of it—as a moving picture of a system rather than as snapshots of events. That concept of forecasting and measuring is essential if we are to manage change. Our business planning should be normative; that is, we should be identifying the future we intend to achieve. For that we need scenarios and measurements to light the way and to illuminate alternative futures and possible detours, changes, or other ways. The study of the future has over recent years become almost a profession itself. Many publications and organizations are now established for professional futurists and others concerned with futures research.

Among the helpful publications are those listed at the end of the chapter. Also listed are a number of interested organizations.

To handle change, our first task is to develop an awareness of the future, construct scenarios, and monitor current change. That is not a task for a professional planner or a subject for a report to management. It is a task for all the organization and a subject to relate continuously to our concept of mission—what we are, what we intend to become, how we intend to get there. We can perform the task by operating through a participative management style and by dialog. In that way, the entire organization can develop an interest in and desire for change.

Planned Versus Unplanned Change

Changes may be unexpected and unplanned, as are fire and flood, loss of a major customer or market, and the sudden appearance of disruptive competitive or government action. Unexpected change requires reaction from the organization. The tradition-oriented organization will seek to adjust and reestablish conditions as they were before the sudden change, to the degree that it can. The change-oriented organization will take a more creative approach. Instead of seeking merely to adjust and reestablish conditions, it will try to compensate and find new achievement that will move it further toward the goals it has already set for its future.

In planning our participation in and response to technological, people, and environmental change we are concerned with the invented future that we have set for ourselves in our concept of mission. Our identity is our normative view of our future. Our goals are our norms. Our strategies are our way. And traveling that way will require a process of change. In business we usually call the map for that road corporate planning. We might greatly accelerate our progress along the road if we called the map organization development, embracing in our structure of work technological change, environmental change, and organization and people change. It's not the planning that makes us go; it's the people. The structure and leadership of work is the task of the new management so that, through change, our people grow and our enterprise achieves.

Of Interest to Futurists

PUBLICATIONS

Appropriate Technology, Intermediate Technology Publications Ltd., 9 King Street, London WC2E 8HN, U.K.

Business Tomorrow, Special Studies Division, World Future Society, 4916 St. Elmo Avenue, Washington, D.C. 20014.

The Center Magazine, bimonthly publication of The Center for the Study of Democratic Institutions, 256 Eucalyptus Hill Road, Santa Barbara, Calif. 93108.

The CoEvolution Quarterly, published by Point, a California nonprofit corporation, Box 428, Sausalito, California 94965.

Future Abstracts, Frost & Sullivan, Inc., 106 Fulton Street, New York, New York 10038.

The Future: A Guide to Information Sources, A Directory of Organizations, Individuals, Books, Education Programs, Films, and Other Resources, World Future Society, 4916 St. Elmo Avenue, Washington, D.C. 20014.

Futures, The Journal of Forecasting and Planning, published quarterly by Iliffe Science and Technology Publications Limited, U.K., in cooperation with The Institute for the Future, U.S.

The Futurist, bimonthly publication of the World Future Society, P.O. Box 30369, Bethesda Branch, Washington, D.C. 20014

Futurscan, Management Data Services, GE-ISBD, 401 North Washington Street, Rockville, Maryland 20850.

Long Range Planning, Journal of the Society for Long Range Planning, London, published by Pergamon Press, Ltd.

Manager, Journal of the European Society of Corporate and Strategic Planning, Via Glason del Majno 20, 20146 Milan, Italy.

Technology Forecasting and Social Change, published quarterly by American Elsevier Publishing Company, Inc., 52 Vanderbilt Ave., New York, N.Y. 10017.

The Teilhard Review, an international journal of integrative studies concerned with the future of man, published by The Teilhard Centre for the Future of Man, 3 Cromwell Place, London, SW 7 2 J E.

ORGANIZATIONS

Cambridge Research Institute, 17 Mount Auburn Street, Cambridge, Mass. 02138.

Center for Futures Research, University of Southern California, University Park, Los Angeles, Calif. 90007.

Center for Integrative Studies, State University of New York, Binghamton, N.Y. 13901.

Center for the Study of Democratic Institutions, Box 4068, Santa Barbara, Calif. 93103.

Committee for Economic Development, 477 Madison Avenue, New York, N.Y. 10022

Congressional Clearing House on the Future, 3692 House Annex #2, Washington, D.C. 20515

Futures Group, 124 Hebron Avenue, Glastonbury, Conn. 06033.

Hudson Institute, Quaker Ridge Road, Croton-on-Hudson, N.Y. 10520.

Industrial Management Center, 1411 West Avenue, Austin, Texas 78701

Institute for the Future, Sand Hill Road, Menlo Park, Calif. 94025.

Irades, Via Paisiello 6, 00198 Rome, Italy.

Mankind 2000, Via Paisiello 6, 00198 Rome, Italy.

National Planning Association, 1606 New Hampshire Avenue, N.W., Washington, D.C. 20009.

Russell Sage Foundation, 230 Park Avenue, New York, N.Y. 10017.

S.E.D.E.I.S. Futuribles France (Société d'Études et de Documentation Economiques, Industrielles et Sociales), 52 Rue des Saints-Peres, Paris 7, France.

SRI International, Business Intelligence Program, 333 Ravenswood Avenue, Menlo Park, California. 94025

World Future Society, P.O. Box 30369, Bethesda Branch, Washington, D.C. 20014.

10

Discovering
Managerial Economics

Managerial economies—the economics of business management—is a discipline different from accounting. All business enterprises use accounting in a professionally competent way. Few employ managerial economics with equal professional competence. Both accounting and managerial economics use much the same internal data base, though economics uses external as well as internal data. Both use what appears to be a similar vocabulary. But the two are conceptually different. And they serve different purposes.

Purposes of Accounting and Economics
Accounting is designed to meet the requirements of cash transactions, government regulations, and tax administration. It also provides a methodology for financial analysis, although much of that kind of analysis can be done in a different way by the methodology of managerial economics. Because of the volume, variety, and importance of cash transactions and regulatory and tax administration requirements, accounting must develop and standardize a system of common practice that will serve all those requirements effectively and as required by daily operations and public policy. The requirements of accounting are historical and so are the measurements. To serve its function, it must codify, measure, and report past transactions of the firm in money terms.

Managerial economics, on the other hand, aims to understand, measure, and report the total functioning of the enterprise in present and future money terms. Whereas accounting is historical, managerial economics is future-oriented. Managerial economics provides an input-output model of the enterprise—value of resources in, value of goods and services out, all in future-oriented terms related to environment and in consideration of relevant constraints. The model comprehends the present and provides an approach to reading the future.

Whereas accounting is needed for the past, managerial economics is needed for the future. Managerial economics provides essential input for decision making and action planning. Accounting can be accomplished within a specialized function and used primarily at the functional and top management levels. Managerial economics should be a part of all positions throughout the company wherever actions are taken or decisions are made.

It is easy to confuse the two very different but apparently similar disciplines. Organizationally, the function for both is often assigned to the same group, which may then be called financial or control to indicate a broader function than accounting alone. Computer services and management information systems may also be assigned to the same function, since it has the greatest use for them. In operation, however, the requirements of the specifically prescribed discipline of accounting are so consuming of time and talent that the discipline of managerial economics may be almost completely overlooked. Worse, it may be proceduralized in an accounting way and practiced throughout the enterprise by rote instead of reason. And, of course, since economics focuses on the future, which cannot be known, it should be a thinking and conceptualizing process rather than a procedure.

A fundamental measure of business success is profitability. But profitability for purposes of tax payment and public regulations and profitability for purposes of decision making and business management are not the same thing. The accountant needs the answers prescribed by authorized procedures; the economist needs the answers that will help the enterprise make wise decisions and take effective actions. Those purposes are not the same, and the measurements needed to serve them are not the same.

Both accounting and economics are very much concerned with profitability. Both have a similar concept of what profit is—profit is what remains after costs are paid. Both are concerned with the same inputs to the enterprise—land and natural resources, capital, human resources, and purchases of goods and services. Both are concerned with the same outputs from the enterprise—goods and services produced as measured by sales to the enterprise's customers. But the measurements will be different and the profit calculations may be quite different. Both are right for the purposes each intends to serve. The requirements of law do not permit the use of economics calculations of profit for tax purposes. But a businessman may, if he wishes, use accounting measures of profitability for business decisions. Many business people do use such measures without recognizing that there is another, better alternative.

In the long run, of course, both economic profit and accounting profit will tend to equal out. But as has been said, in the long run we are dead—except that a corporation, granted its life by legal process, may escape biological fate. A helpful aid to corporate longevity or immortality can be provided by an economics approach to management and operations. Managerial economics will help us see operating results and trends from the perspective of the future. It will identify profit opportunity or profit problems before they show up on an accounting income statement. It can prevent such surprises as an apparently profitable enterprise suddenly finding itself in great financial trouble or a very large "extraordinary charge" appearing in one year to sharply diminish or eliminate that year's reported income.

Accounting makes sudden revaluations that have, in reality, been accumulating over time. Economics makes such revaluations currently. Big-bath accounting does in bunches what economics can do day by day and month by month. Accounting reports according to convention, and it may select the convention for the resulting appearance in the operating report. Economics is more concept than convention. It seeks reality. In short, if we use managerial economics wisely in our present operations, we can assure that in the long run neither economic nor accounting profit will equal out at zero or loss.

Differences Between Accounting and Economics

There are several important areas of difference in the accounting approach and the economics approach.

1. *Concepts of costs are different.* The economist will consider opportunity costs in alternate employment of capital and human talent. The accountant will not. The economist will probably consider interest cost on equity, which the accountant will include as profit. The economist may include salary and income paid to the owner-management or other top management as profit, whereas the accountant will include such payments as a cost. Both the accountant and the economist are right in their treatment of costs. Each is right for the purposes he serves, but the purposes are different.

2. *Treatment of depreciation is different.* The accountant will deal with historical costs of assets and with methods of depreciating those historical costs prescribed by public regulation. The economist, oriented to the future, will think of present and future replacement costs for equivalently productive assets, and his equivalent of the accountant's depreciation will provide for that replacement. In periods of changing price levels great differences between accounting and economic profits will result from the different valuation of assets. Correspondingly, capital gains and losses as reported for accounting purposes and as considered by the economist will be very different.

3. *Different use will be made of current and historical methods of valuing assets.* The accounting record will consist of exact tallies of past transactions. The economist will be thinking of present and future transaction values. During periods of changing price levels, revaluations will show up in the accountant's income statement as assets are turned over. With rising price levels—the history of the past three decades—the accounting method of valuing assets will result in higher reported profits than will the methods of the economist. The accounting method, because it uses actual transaction values, permits exact calculations. The economist conceptualizes those values at current and future purchasing power, an impossible calculation but a quite possible approximation.

The difference in reported profit can be great, as can be seen from the effect on reported profit of two different, accepted accounting practices for valuing inventory—LIFO and FIFO. Both are historical transaction measures and do not meet the requirements of the economist. But they do illustrate the effect of a time perspective. In the LIFO method (last in, first out), the most recent costs go into cost of goods sold; in the FIFO method (first in, first out) earlier costs are used. In periods of rising costs the LIFO method will give a lower reported income, since the costs used will be higher. Both methods are historical, but the LIFO-FIFO differences illustrate the significance of time in the valuation of assets for profit calculation. For the business economist, concerned as he is with the future profitability of the enterprise, inventory valuation will be on the basis of replenishment cost. His value is projective, not historical.

4. *For multinational operations, currency translations will be dealt with differently.* For overseas operations in which business is done in other national currencies, accounting procedure will usually consolidate all operating data in the currency of the headquarters company—for U.S. multinational companies, dollars. Included will be translations of sales volume, costs, depreciation, capital gains and losses, and asset valuation, along with all the local problems listed above, to another currency by an administratively determined exchange rate. Accounting procedures include different conventions for such translations that can result in quite different amounts of profit expressed in the translated currency.[1]

But translation techniques will not have changed economic profitability, whatever that is. The economist might calculate (or estimate) profitability in quite different ways. He is likely to question both the validity and the purpose of consolidating at all and instead think more of profitability within individual countries and resource flows within and among company operations in various countries.

The accounting discipline confronts great difficulties in accounting for multinational operations to fulfill its objectives of public regulation and tax administration. But it does accomplish the task, and it is a participant in the growing public debate on multinational corporation operations, motivations, and constraints. The economics of the multinational enterprise is a new frontier where creative work is still much needed to provide guidance for business decisions and wisdom for public policy decision.

Effects of Inflation
Periods of inflation can result in a dramatically higher statement of income by accounting procedures than the economist would arrive at by using his concepts of costs. The difference results from the historical transaction values contrasted with replacement valuation. This difference can be so great that in a period of inflation a company can be reporting a high and increasing accounting income

---

[1]Donald J. Hayes, "Translating Foreign Currencies," *Harvard Business Review*, January-February 1972.

while its economic income—a measure of its capacity to earn future income—is low, decreasing, and perhaps even negative.

One such period of inflation was the decade of the 1940s. In a study of three large companies, leaders in their industry, reported accounting income and real economic income in the years 1935 to 1947 were compared.[2] In 1947 the total income for the three companies was reported as $90 million (in 1935 dollars), whereas the economic income was calculated to be $120 million *less* than that. In economic terms, the three companies in total were operating at a loss! But reported accounting income was high. The post-World War II years were years of turmoil, but enough economics was known and applied to make changes beyond what would have been suggested by the accounting record alone that most enterprises were able to survive the turmoil. They got a beneficent assist in their efforts by generally favorable business conditions over the postwar adjustment period. Still, that postwar inflation period brought a decline in profitability levels from which industry has never fully recovered.

In the late sixties and seventies we again experienced significant inflation. And again we saw accounting income reported higher than "real" economic income would be calculated. The 1970-1971 recession substantially depressed reported accounting income, but that was only a partial reflection of what was happening to real economic profit. The following period of inflation resulted in another rachet downward in the economic profitability of enterprise. The 1974-75 recession and the following recovery along with high inflation rates again sharply reduced the economic profitability of many enterprises, despite reassuring reports of accounting profit. The disparity was particularly great in capital-intensive businesses. In the years of high inflation in the 1970s the disparity between accounting profit and economic profit become so great that accounting measures of profitability rapidly lost credibility as a valid indication of a firm's profit performance.

Inflation Accounting

A significant step in the direction of economics, inflation accounting, is now being practiced and further developed in several countries outside the United States and increasingly in the United States. A number of European companies regularly calculate the amount of "depreciation deficiency" resulting from inflation. In their published statements they reduce reported income by that amount to arrive at "real" income as distinct from accounting or taxable income. N. V. Philips, the multinational electronics firm headquartered in the Netherlands, for example, has published replacement cost measures for asset valuation and income determination in its annual reports since the 1940s.

Many countries encourage inflation accounting by allowing frequent revaluation of assets and permitting extremely liberal depreciation. Sweden permits

---

[2]Joel Dean, *Managerial Economics* (Englewood Cliffs, N.J.: Prentice-Hall, 1951), p. 25.

generous reserves against obsolescence. Brazil, after several years of substantial inflation, developed inflation accounting to a sophisticated level. Everything is keyed to the minimum wage rate; and as that rate is changed, appropriate adjustments are made in costs and valuation of assets. The Brazilian approach has proved to be quite manageable, and it avoids the distortions that would result from conventional accounting. A company losing money in Brazil could, with ordinary accounting methods, be reporting a profit, but the problem is avoided through price-level adjustments. That approach enables the firm to cope with inflation, but the problem for the economy is to manage affairs so that the feedback mechanisms do not spiral unmanageable inflation.

In England, the Institute of Chartered Accountants has developed a procedure for companies to convert their main assets and costs on their financial statements to current price levels by using the government's consumer price index. Beginning in 1974, companies report income by this new method of inflation accounting, as well as by the conventional accounting procedures still used for tax purposes. The need for more reality in profit accounting is evidenced by a report of Distiller's Co., Ltd. The chairman of Distiller's, Sir Alex McDonald, reported fiscal year real profit as being some 20 percent ($17 million) lower than the profit figure reported by conventional accounting when appropriate adjustments were made for the effects of inflation:

Erosion of the value of our total assets by inflation during the year was £8 million. This is the amount which we would require to appropriate from conventionally computed profits to maintain in terms of today's prices the same volume of physical assets as we had a year ago. The position as we see it is:

	Conventional Results £000	"Real" results £000
Conventional consolidated profit	62,189	62,189
Appropriation required to counter inflation		7,082
"Real" profit		55,107
Taxation	25,020	25,020
	37,169	30,087
Minority shareholders' interest	171	152
	36,998	29,935
Proportion of profit of the United Glass subgroup similarly adjusted	1,323	746
Proportion of profit of Bakelite Xylonite Limited similarly adjusted	199	(22)
Total net profit attributable to the Company	38,520	30,659

I must again draw attention to the charge for Taxation which was not 40% but over 45% of the "real" profit. I welcome the steps taken by the Accounting Standards Steering Committee of the Institute of Chartered Accountants to encourage the development of the techniques involved in inflation accounting.[3]

In late 1973 petroleum prices quadrupled, and over subsequent months this sharp increase in price worked its way through energy and petrochemical costs to impact dramatically industry performance measures expressed in dollars. Figure 10-1 shows the rapid increase in prices for industrial chemicals. At the beginning of 1974 the producer's price index for industrial chemicals was only 6 percent above the 1967 base. By the end of 1974, just twelve months later, the price index stood at 195, up 84 percent in just one year! Dollar sales figures were simply no longer comparable with previous periods, yet such comparisons continued to be made in financial reports. But the greatest discontinuity was in reported profitability. Table 10-1 shows data for 1973 and for eight months of 1974 for one chemical business. Financial statements reported income of $8.8 million for 1973, and $14.6 million for eight months 1974—a dramatic improvement. But adjusting for the effects of inflation showed 1973 income to be considerably overstated and for the eight-month period, 1974, showed income not up, but down, with operations at about breakeven! These adjustments, while lacking the precision of historical accounting methods, are much closer to the real economic situation. The company was using LIFO materials costing so the adjustments for materials costs were moderate—the difference between last in and replenishment costs. The big adjustment was for capital consumption allowances based on the current value of assets employed rather than on their historical cost.

Table 10-1. Inflation adjustment of income statement, capital intensive company, millions of dollars

	1973	8 Months 1974
Reported Income	$8.8	$14.6
Adjustments:		
Capital Consumption Allowances	(5.7)	(13.1)
Materials	(0.24)	(1.71)
Supplies	(0.29)	(0.61)
Manufacturing Labor	(0.07)	(0.07)
Total Adjustments	(6.3)	(15.5)
Economic Income	$2.5	$(0.9)

An industry study of 1976 profit performance found that when 1976 income statements were adjusted to include costs on a replacement cost basis, four tire

[3]"The British Case for 'Inflation Accounting,'" *Business Week*, October 14, 1972.

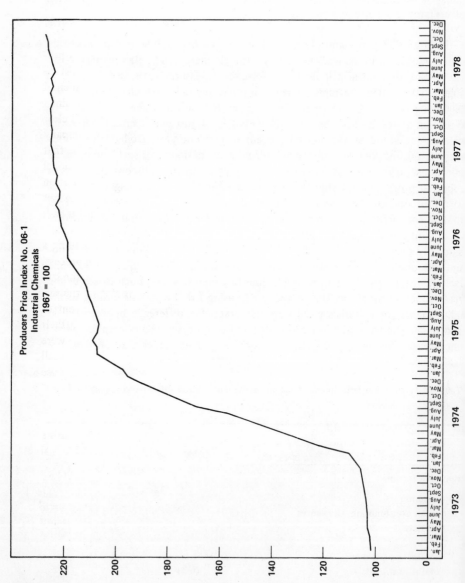

Figure 10-1.

and rubber companies who reported total profits of $161 million actually lost $179 million. Thirteen steel companies who reported total profits of $1,103 million actually had a real loss of $422 million.[4] Especially for capital intensive companies, inflation has a devastating effect that simply is not seen by historical cost accounting.

In early 1979 the Financial Accounting Standards Board announced a proposal to require the nation's largest corporations to account for the effects of inflation on assets and operations and to include this information as supplemental data in annual reports to stockholders. While many technical problems remained to be resolved, there has been a clear trend toward inflation accounting—a clear trend in the direction of managerial economics. If we are to preserve company assets and employ them wisely, we must manage them through the measures that can be provided to us by managerial economics. These must be the informational inputs to our decision making. If we remain unaware of the impact of inflation we will, over time, convert the assets of the company into cash and pay out this cash in taxes, dividends, and expenses not recognizing that what we think is cash available from profits is in large part a liquidation of assets.

For firms which use it, inflation accounting is very effective in building a bridge back to the reality needed for the management decision-making process. The use of inflation accounting for internal company use grew rapidly in the late 1970s, especially among capital-intensive companies most sensitive to the distorting effects of inflation. One survey indicated that about forty percent of such companies were using inflation-adjusted accounting in 1978 in their strategy decision making.[5] I would estimate that a much smaller number were using such information regularly in their day-to-day decision making, at all management levels. And this is what is needed, and can be accomplished by use of managerial economics.

Application of Managerial Economics

Economics measures a moving target. The economist is concerned with future costs. His measurements are speculative. To the economist, past transactional values are irrelevant, except as they can be useful in forecasting future costs.

> Decision-making costs can be found from traditional accounting records only by reclassifications, deletions, additions, recombinations of elements, and repricing of input factors in the process of shaping the cost to fit the concept of cost relevant for the management planning choice. . . . Records of historical outlays . . . need to be drastically reworked for decisions about the future.[6]

Professor Dean, whose book *Managerial Economics* is still a pioneering classic

---

[4]John C. H. Woo and Shirish B. Seth, "The Impact of Replacement Cost Accounting on Financial Performance," *Financial Analysts Journal*, March-April 1978.

[5]William E. Hill & Company, Inc., Management Consultants, New York, N.Y.

[6]Dean, *Managerial Economics*, pp. 250, 251.

and ahead of most practice many years after its publication, points out that there are significant valuation problems as inputs to business decisions and also that the kinds of costs to be considered will vary with the alternative programs considered:

> A single piece of equipment will have different values in terms of its disposal price, replacement cost, value in its present job, and value in alternative jobs. The only values that are irrelevant for all decisions on what to do with a specific asset are its original cost and its book value.[7]

Yet it is those irrelevant values that often dominate in the decision-making process when the objective is a favorable effect on the current income statement (an accounting record) rather than a favorable effect on the economic profitability of the enterprise. The accountant is much concerned with sunk costs; they affect the income statement. To the economist sunk costs are irrelevant; they do not alter the income available from alternative programs. The economist has found that the best way to recover a sunk cost for the accounting record is to ignore it in the management decision. Paradoxically, including the sunk cost in the decision process may so constrain the decision process as to limit or prevent the recovery of the cost.

The difference in approach can be quite readily understood if we take as an example a typical research program. Let's say that $1 million has been spent and certain technology has been developed. The accounting question is, "How can we best recover the $1 million?" The economist's question is, "How can we optimize income to the company from the new technology?" Whether the income opportunity is $0.5 million, zero, or $10 million, the economist's question provides the best answer to the accounting question by ignoring it.

Separation of Accounting and Economics

Because accounting and economics are different disciplines that serve different purposes, we might be wise to separate them functionally in our organization structures. There is a required accounting function. There is a needed financial function. There is a needed data processing and management information service. And there is a very useful managerial economics function. We tend to think of all those things as facets of the same diamond and put them together as one. What if they were separated? As a spur to some creative thinking on the possibilities, what if:

1. Data processing and management information are a part of industrial relations, manufacturing, or marketing (depending on the size and scope of those functions)?
2. Economics is a part of the president's office?
3. Accounting is a part of data processing?

[7]Ibid., p. 251.

4. Accounting is a part of government relations?
5. Accounting is a part of legal?
6. Financial is a top management responsibility without responsibility for data processing, management information, accounting, or economics?
7. Financial and economics together are a top management responsibility?
8. Economics (future-oriented) is a part of marketing (also future-oriented)?
9. Accounting, data processing, management information, and industrial relations are all the responsibility of a top management administrative officer?

The list could go on, but it illustrates the point. We should be thinking differently about accounting, data processing, and economics. They are three important functions, all different, that have become, in many operations, too much oriented to financial and not enough oriented to operations. It's time for us now to employ our talent assets in those areas more productively, beginning with the very much underutilized area of managerial economics.

Since economics is conceptual and future-oriented, it can be very different to different practitioners. In recent years several procedures that could be applications of managerial economics have become quite commonly used.

1. *Return on investment analysis.* This can be historical or future-oriented when it is used for decision making on new investment. Projected future earnings from the new investment can be discounted to a present value by using a management-selected rate of return as an interest cost of capital. In many businesses, return on investment analysis—commonly referred to as ROI—has become highly proceduralized and automated. Although it is valid economically in its future orientation, it nevertheless confronts difficult conceptual problems in regard to historical, present, and future valuation of assets, costs, and income. ROI control has the asset valuation problems dealt with precisely by historical accounting and tentatively by future-oriented economics. To the extent that ROI recognizes the tentativeness of the future measures and appropriately revalues the historical measures, it can provide a useful guide to business action. The limitations of ROI control have been well documented by John Dearden.[8]

2. *Cash flow.* An enterprise must know reasonably well what its future cash requirements will be, and it must plan to have cash available for those needs. Cash flow projection becomes an important part of that planning. It is future-oriented. It can be derived from an input-output model of the enterprise, which is economics. It can be broad—for the entire enterprise—or it can be narrow—for a specific investment. In either case it is a required component of ROI control. But as the limitations of ROI control are more and more recognized, the major value of cash flow analysis will be for purposes of cash budgeting. The economist and the accountant will differ on the cost and income calculations. Both will recognize that taxes will be paid according to the accounting calculations, so it will end up that cash available will be as determined by accounting practices.

[8]"The Case Against ROI Control," *Harvard Business Review*, May-June 1969.

At the same time, it would be wise to look at cash flow from the viewpoint of the economist to see how much of it is real in consideration of the future functioning of the enterprise. Cash available by accounting methods may be in part a liquidation of assets when viewed in economic terms.

3. *Venture analysis.* New products and new ventures are a requirement for success of most business enterprises, and the appraisal of a potential new venture is clearly future-oriented. Here the discipline of managerial economics should apply. And perhaps we do find more economic appraisal here than in other areas of business operations. Many systems and approaches for venture analysis have been published or are now available for a fee. DuPont has made its highly successful venture analysis methods available to others as a handbook.[9] Trade and business publications provide many case history examples. Business consultants can provide technical and business economics assistance to clients on their new venture problems.

Much has been done; much has been learned; much is available; but the user of venture analysis will have to be a sophisticated chooser. For what is available ranges from the economically valid to quantified nonsense, from perceptive identification of opportunity and constraints to ritualized checklists. And there is not only the problem of venture analysis, which is largely economics, but also the problem of venture achievement, which is largely motivation.

Theodore Levitt, a keen observer of venture management, has written extensively on the organizational considerations most productive of new venture success.[10] Venture management is probably the area of business that is today most open to the discipline of managerial economics. But even there, economics is less used than it is required—a fact that may contribute to the poor performance and failure of many new ventures.

There are many areas of business management, operations, and executive decision in which economics can make a valuable contribution. It is only necessary to keep in mind that economics is not accounting. And it is also necessary to develop and apply our managerial economics in a way that makes it readily usable by people throughout the enterprise as they confront such problems as:

Price determination	Inventory management
Plant expansion	Make or buy
New product investment	R&D program expenditure
Product or business area profitability	Off-list price
Manpower addition or reduction	Agent versus direct sales
Changes in sales force	Export versus domestic sales
Investment in new process	Process or plant optimization
Expenditure for promotion program	Sales terms

[9]*DuPont Guide to Venture Analysis* (Wilmington, Del.: E. I. du Pont de Nemours & Company, Inc., Education and Applied Technology Division, 1971).

[10]*The Marketing Mode* (New York: McGraw-Hill, 1969), pp. 129ff.

Product line simplification

Organization change

Cost increases

Transfer pricing

Purchase-resale terms

License proposal

Labor negotiations

Marketing planning

Managerial economics concepts are particularly useful in coping with such problems as those listed above. It provides an integrated system for analyzing and understanding the economics of the enterprise. It makes use of the historical accounting record, but in ways that can provide futurity for business decisions and actions. It also provides a way for simplifying masses of data to fundamentals that are actionable at the top management level and also at all levels throughout the organization where decisions are made and actions are taken. Managerial economics can make available an economics input to the decision process at all levels throughout the enterprise. Chapter 11 describes managerial economics concepts and their application.

11

Applying
Managerial Economics

Managerial economics, because it is conceptual and more approximate than specific, looks like a better subject for the textbooks than for business operations. Unfortunately, it is as poorly treated as it is practiced. Each failing may to some extent explain the other, but the time for correction has come. While the discipline of managerial economics remains inadequately used, we have elaborated systems of financial measurement to almost meaningless profusion. In the wind tunnel of change, our rococo financial measurement systems just don't fly very well. Instead of adding more detail, we need to strip down to the fundamentals of economics.

Basic Principles

In both managerial economics and accounting economics the definition of profit is the same. It is what is left over after all costs are paid. But managerial economics and accounting economics have different perspectives, and the way they identify and define costs is different.

Accounting economics measures past transactions. It is the historical record measured in terms of generally accepted accounting principles. Managerial economics, on the other hand, is looking to the future, since the economics of decision making must deal with what decisions are about, and decisions are about the future. Whether the future is short range—an hour, a day, or a week—or longer range, the economics of decision making deals with the economic consequences of present actions. Managerial economics can help make these consequences favorable and consistent with the company mission. Because accounting economics deals with the recorded data of past transactions, its primary method is analysis. For the future (which is the province of managerial economics), however, we do not yet have performance data. But we do have a great deal of information. How we process this information into decisions requires conceptual thinking more than analysis. Managerial economics provides a framework for this conceptual thinking.

The managerial economics that I recommend to you begins with the recognition of five important principles:

1. Profitability is a function of the total business unit, not of individual products or product groups.
2. Costs are managed according to how they behave:
   a. Variable costs, which are those costs that are incurred because of the transaction and which vary directly with volume (such as raw materials, energy, commissions, freight, royalties) will be assigned to the individual products and transactions that incur them.
   b. Fixed costs, which are all those costs incurred by management decision and which are changed by management decision instead of by changes in transaction volume, will not be allocated to individual products or product groups, but rather will be assigned to the organizational units which incur them.
3. Income is managed according to market demand and competitive opportunity for the products and services provided by the company, for:
   a. Market segments
   b. Individual clients
4. Profitability is managed according to the interacting relationships between internally incurred costs and externally generated income. These relationships can be expressed and measured in an income model that will identify points of action for profit management and for profit improvement. Actions will be in the form of both cost control and output change or increase.
5. Evaluation of what is important will relate to the company's mission—its definition of where and how it will build its success.

In organizing the economics of the enterprise by these principles we are managing costs according to the way in which each cost is incurred (an operations orientation); we are managing income according to how income is generated (a market orientation); and we are managing profitability according to how we influence and control the interrelationships between the two. We can define, measure, and manage these complex interrelationships by using a rather simple income model.

Classify Costs According to How They Are Incurred

The five principles listed above have been known for many years to work successfully in business operations. They provide a systems concept that profit is a function of the total business unit, that there are many interrelationships within the business and between the business and its environment, and it is these inter-relationships and connectivities that must be managed if we are to make a profit. These relationships can be organized for any business unit in a very practical income model. To construct this model we first classify all costs incurred as either variable costs or fixed costs:

VARIABLE COSTS

Definition: Costs that are incurred because of the transaction
Examples: Materials (replenishment cost)
        Energy   *"*
        Direct labor   *"*
        Variable burden
        Royalty
        Packaging
        Freight
        Sales commission
        Duty, and other border crossing costs
        Interest cost on receivables

FIXED COSTS

Definition: Costs that do not change because of the transaction but continue until changed by management decision
  1. Constant Fixed Costs: Time oriented and difficult to change in the short run—the basic organization and facility costs incurred to be in business
Examples: Organization costs:
        Salary expenses
        Headquarters expenses
      Plant and equipment costs:
        Depreciation a. Accounting—based on cost
                         b. Economic—based on current value
        Maintenance
      Social costs:
        Taxes
        Regulatory compliance costs
        Pollution control
  2. Programmed Fixed Costs: Costs incurred by management decision but variable over a shorter time span
Examples: Advertising program
        R & D projects
        Marketing program
        Project activity

Variable costs are those that vary directly with output or activity. In manufacturing, they usually include materials, direct labor, energy, variable elements of manufacturing burden, and royalties paid to outsiders. Maintenance and supervisory costs that vary with output are also classified as variable costs.

The distinction between fixed and variable costs is well understood, so costs can usually be assigned appropriately. However, the important consideration is how costs behave in actuality, and it is often necessary to observe cost behavior before making a classification. That can be done by plotting cost versus activity over a period of time as shown in Figure 11-1. Scatter diagrams of that type will indicate the variability of the cost, and they may also show both a fixed and variable component as in the scatter diagram for maintenance cost. Such data were commonly used in the 1930s and 1940s for flexible budgeting, a concept largely lost in the complexities of the variance analysis of more recent years. Now, however, we can again make very practical use of the distinction in the behavior of costs with output through managerial economics.

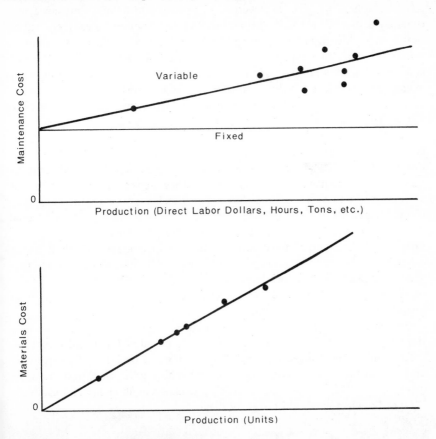

Figure 11-1. Cost versus activity.

One consideration will be the direct labor classification. While we commonly think of manufacturing labor as a variable cost, in many countries—and increasingly in the United States too—it is behaving as a fixed cost. In the world's most competitive economy, Japan, it has traditionally been a fixed cost. Analysis by using the scatter diagram approach will show whether direct production labor is actually controlled as variable, fixed, or largely fixed and partially variable, and the cost can then be included in our marginal income accounts accordingly. Alternatively, practice can be modified to a desired control basis. How costs perform provides us the framework for managing them.

In addition to variable manufacturing costs, all costs in other areas of operation that vary with output will be included. The most common such costs are commissions, freight, and returns and allowances.

Fixed costs are those that accrue with time rather than output and for that reason are often called period costs. Fixed manufacturing costs include depreciation, property taxes, utilities not going into output, manager and supervisory salaries and benefits, plant engineering, all or some portion of maintenance, and other costs that do not vary with output. In other functional areas there will be similar costs. Identifying them as fixed costs does not mean that they cannot be varied; it means only that they are approximately fixed for the budget period and the anticipated range of operations, perhaps ±20%. They can be changed by management decision, and they normally do change if the level of output rises or drops by 20 percent or more. A given level of fixed costs cannot continue to support an expanding level of output without some increases.

In considering fixed costs, it is important to make a distinction between fixed costs that are constant and those that are programmed by management decision. Constant fixed costs include the costs of plant, equipment, offices, and organization—the basic framework of the enterprise. They are the costs that obtain now as a result of past decisions, and they are changeable only with difficulty; they comprise the cost of being in business as we are now operating. For managerial decision making, these costs must be revalued for price changes as described in Chapter 10. Programmed fixed costs, on the other hand, are increments to the constant fixed costs to achieve certain objectives. Examples are a promotion program to increase sales, a research program to develop a new product, an engineering project to improve or expand a manufacturing process, and a computer program to install a new cost system.

Programmed fixed costs can be increased or reduced more easily than constant fixed costs can be. They can also be determined and managed to achieve specific management objectives, including specific and beneficial changes in the income statement. Managerial economics provides a great simplification in the management of the programmed costs by providing a methodology for establishing specific achievement objectives for them.

The Income Model

Having defined and classified costs as variable or fixed according to how they behave, we can now prepare an income statement in marginal income accounts,
using these costs. Here is an income statement for a company with a profit
problem, shown in the conventional format, and then recast into marginal income accounts:

COMPANY P

Conventional Income Statement ($ add 000)			Income Statement by Marginal Income Accounts ($ add 000)		
Sales		$7 745	Sales		$7 745
Customers		7 565	Variable Costs		4 953
Intercompany		180	Marginal Income		2 792
Cost of Goods Sold		7 257	Marginal Income Percent		36.05%
Gross Profit		488	Fixed Costs		3 419
SGA Expenses		1 115	Manufacturing	2 304	
Selling	455		Distribution	350	
Distribution	350		Selling	455	
Development	95		Development	95	
Administration	215		Administration	215	
Operating Income		(627)	Breakeven (Fixed Costs		
Other Income/Expenses		7	divided by MI%)		9 484
Pretax Income		(620)	Sales Above (Below)		
			Breakeven		(1 739)
			Operating Income (Sales		
			Above or Below		
			Breakeven x MI%)		(627)
			Other Income/Expense		7
			Pretax Income		(620)

The key measures and variables in the income statement by marginal income
accounts are:

Sales: gross sales billed
Variable costs: costs varying directly with transactions
Marginal income: sales minus variable costs
Marginal income rate: marginal income divided by sales
Fixed costs: costs that do not vary with transaction volume, but rather have
   been incurred and are varied by management decision

Breakeven: fixed costs divided by marginal income rate
Operating income: sales above (below) breakeven times marginal income rate

We can now prepare an income model:

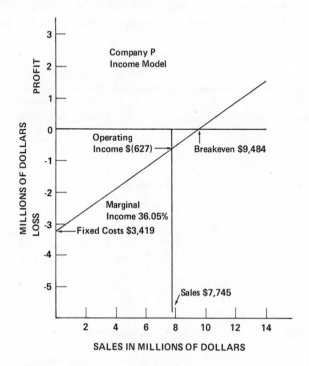

Figure 11-2.

Looking at this model we can dialog its interactions and connectivities to help us determine whether and how improvements can be made. There are three and only three possibilities:

1. Sales can be increased
2. Fixed costs can be reduced
3. Marginal income rate can be increased by:
   a. Reducing variable costs
   b. Increasing prices
   c. Improving mix by shifting toward the more profitable transactions as explained below

If the income of a profit center has declined below satisfactory levels, the explanation for this decline similarly can be determined by looking at recent changes in the model. For the decline will have been caused by some combination of:

1. Sales decrease
2. Fixed cost increase
3. Marginal income rate decrease, caused by:
   a. Increased variable costs
   b. Lower prices
   c. Poorer mix

Dialog of all the income model variables applied to the specific business situation can develop the best approaches for profit improvements. Seldom are the best approaches limited to cost reduction. I have worked with eighteen profit center businesses to develop and implement profit improvement programs. In ten of the eighteen businesses, breakeven or loss situations were changed into profitable operations; in eight, unsatisfactory profit levels were improved. In only two of the eighteen was cost reduction the major part of the profit improvement program. In sixteen of the eighteen the actions taken were more in what we created (output increase or change) rather than in what we eliminated (cost reduction). In all cases, the model was used to help determine the significant leverages on profitability.

Exploring the three variables of the income model will lead to alternative actions each of which can be appraised as to its effect on income directly from the model. In dialoging the alternatives it is necessary to keep in mind that everything is related to everything else and that changes in one area may cause changes in other areas also. Price changes affect both marginal income rate and sales volume. Investment (an increase in fixed cost) may improve marginal income by reducing variable costs and may also support expanded sales. The marginal income accounts and income model provide a methodology for quantifying the system changes and projecting their effect on income. The overall marginal income strategy can be summarized in the simplified income model and statement of principles given in Figure 11-3.

In many profitability problems the transaction mix is an important key to profit improvement. In thinking about mix, we usually think first of all about product mix. And often this is as far as we go. But there are many dimensions to mix:

Product mix
Customer mix
Market segment mix
Geographic mix
Domestic/international mix
Distribution channel mix

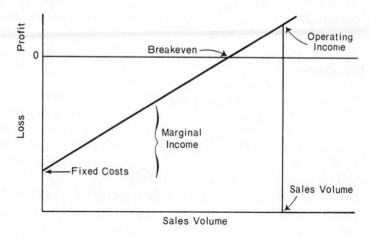

Basic formulas:

1. Sales volume — variable costs = marginal income

2. $\dfrac{\text{Marginal income \$}}{\text{Sales volume \$}}$ = marginal income %

3. Breakeven = $\dfrac{\text{fixed costs}}{\text{marginal income \%}}$

4. Operating income = sales over (under) breakeven x marginal income %

Three ways to improve operating income:

Increase sales volume.

Reduce fixed costs.

Increase marginal income rate by (a) increasing price, (b) reducing variable costs, or (c) improving mix.

Figure 11-3. Income model and strategy summary.

Order size mix

International mix (by country or geographic area, market segment, product, customer, distribution channel, order size)

Other combinations of the above

With managerial economics we can determine the probable effect on profit from any change or combination of changes in these elements of mix simply by "putting the changes on the model" and projecting the probable effect on all of the variables.

For Company P, which had had a consistent record of losses, we explored possibilities in all of the variables in the model to find opportunity for profit improvement. Sales volume increase offered little opportunity since, all else remaining the same, capacity was inadequate to support the sales volume that would be required. Nor was fixed cost reduction the answer. To achieve profitability by fixed cost reduction would require such drastic cuts that there would simply be no adequate plant or organization base remaining. So if the business

172

could be profitable, the leverage would have to come from improving the marginal income rate. We could find little opportunity in variable cost reduction (primarily raw materials), or in the pricing of existing products. This got us to the important question, and opportunity, of mix. And here we found opportunity for success. We could increase marginal income rate by concentrating on a different mix of products to be sold to a different mix of customers. This led to organization and program changes in development, production, and sales, with new objectives for each. Feedback reporting related to these new objectives. Three months later our reporting told us we were "on course" even though the company was still losing money. By a year later this business was profitable, and it has been highly profitable over subsequent years.

The achievement was more than economic; it was also motivational. For it had begun with a concept of mission—what the business was, where it was going, its goals, and its strategy. The mission and its implementing programs had been developed by dialog—and by hard work. There was broad participation throughout. A wide understanding of the problem and of the programs developed for its solution was developed. As work progressed, there was feedback to all on progress made. A faltering but potentially good team grew together, developed, and became a superb team. And the business became profitable. One of the most helpful tools was a change from traditional full costing to marginal income accounts to permit dealing with all inputs and outputs in operational terms.

In looking at product mix it can be very helpful to keep in mind three basic optimizing concepts:

Situation	Optimizing Concept
1. Normal operations	Marginal income rate
2. Limited capacity	Marginal income dollars per hour of the constrained facility (such as MI $/hour of reactor time)
3. Limited raw material	Marginal income dollars per unit of the limited material

These optimizing principles are unknown to many managers who are schooled only in full-cost accounting which does not have, and cannot see, these measures. Yet these measures are extremely useful—I would say even essential—if we are to manage profitability successfully in these times of fast-paced change. One reservation, however. These optimizing principles have to be applied consistently with company mission. Our decisions must be good over the long range; not just for today.

One further, important consideration . . . if we as managers are to understand clearly the profit consequences over time of our present decisions, we must understand the effect of changes in the value of money. We must know what is real, with the effects of inflation (or deflation) removed. Adjusting for these changes, managerial economics may arrive at very different definitions of costs from the accounting definitions we are accustomed to. The effect of inflation on historically reported income statements prepared by generally accepted accounting principles is to considerably *overstate* profits. When inflation rates are as high as six or ten percent, real profit may be only a small fraction of reported profit—or may even be negative—though reported profit looks very good. The long-term consequence of this delusion is the conversion of fixed assets into cash which is used for taxes, dividends, and operating expenses; in effect, a steady liquidation of the business. To correct for the effects of inflation (or deflation) the most important adjustments are:

Depreciation: depreciate the current value of all assets employed rather than the historical cost of assets "still on the books." Most appropriate concept of current value is replacement cost of equivalently productive assets. Use of this concept requires an engineering approach. An alternative is original cost adjusted by the appropriate cost index, less an allowance for productivity improvement. Although depreciation can not be calculated in this way for tax purposes, it becomes essential to look at it this way for decision purposes—if we intend to be successful beyond today by adequately providing for the replenishment of fixed assets.

Raw materials: use replenishment cost rather than historical or "standard." From sales must come adequate cash to replenish raw materials inventory. Second best method is "current cost." Third best is LIFO.

Labor: as for raw materials, use replenishment cost rather than historical or "standard."

The above are the major adjustments. In addition it would be necessary—if we are to do a complete job of adjusting to a managerial economics "real" base—to adjust other variable and fixed costs in similarly appropriate ways.

How to Use the Income Model

Once we know and begin using this income model concept in the business unit, all decisions and all actions can be related to it. We relate each decision to the income model, and determine what the probable effects will be. We look at all of the relationships and connectivities, not just the immediate and obvious ones. Many decisions go wrong not for what was considered, but for what was not considered. Using the model we can test all probable responses against a range of possible actions to find an optimum decision. For each proposed decision we test the effect on the model: What will be the effect on sales volume? What will be the change in fixed costs? What will be the effect on marginal income rate through changes in variable costs, prices, or mix? This kind of a thinking process not only helps us to make the decision, it also helps us to set goals to be achieved as a result of the decision. If we use the income model to help us reach a decision to add additional salespeople, we also arrive at sales objectives to be achieved. If we use the model in quoting a particular job, we also arrive at cost objectives to be achieved in production. If we use the income model in setting a price for a product, we also determine a sales volume to be achieved.

Another important consideration—the income model can be used even when we don't know exactly what the numbers are. We still know what the interactions are and what the connectivities are, and what sort of changes will result from a particular action. We also know generally the kinds of leverage different actions will have. In the case of Company P, the leverage was in improving marginal income rate by changes in mix, and this is frequently a point of leverage for manufacturing businesses with broad product lines, extensive markets, and large numbers of customers. But some businesses are low marginal income businesses. For these, the major leverage for profit improvement is cost reduction; efficiency improvement. Leverage is more in cost control than in volume increase or change. On the other hand, for high marginal income businesses the greater leverage is in increased volume, and additional cost can profitably be incurred to achieve greater sales volume.

I have described profit as what remains after costs are paid; total revenues minus total costs is profit or less. In a typical business enterprise the mix on the revenue side is very complex, the mix on the cost side is very complex, and all interrelate. But starting from where we are, changes in the mix and magnitude of revenue plus or minus changes in the mix and magnitude of costs will yield changes in profit or loss. A way of planning and programming those changes is provided by managerial economics.

A very simple first step in translating a typical accounting income statement into an income statement by marginal income accounts can be taken by dividing the cost-of-sales figure into its fixed and variable components. Because the variable costs of manufacture are prime costs, this first step provides us with an income statement by prime costing accounts that can be used for business decisions and action planning just as marginal income accounts can be used. More useful, however, is to include all variable costs, not just the variable costs in manufacturing, in our calculations, in our income statements, and in our income models. A good general but simple format is the following:

1. Gross sales
2. Variable costs
    Materials
    Direct labor
    Energy
    Royalty paid to outsiders
    Other variable manufacturing costs
    Commissions
    Freight
    Returns and allowances
    Other variable nonmanufacturing costs
3. Marginal income (item 1 minus item 2)
4. Marginal income percent (item 3 divided by item 1)

5. Fixed costs
   Manufacturing
   Marketing
   Distribution
   Research and development
   General and administrative
   Other
6. Breakeven (item 5 divided by item 4)
7. Sales above or below breakeven (item 1 minus item 6)
8. Operating income (item 7 multiplied by item 4)
9. Other income
10. Other expense
11. Net income before taxes

The list of marginal income accounts does more than simply divide a cost-of-sales figure into its variable and fixed portions. It includes among variable costs not just the manufacturing variable costs, or prime costs, but all the costs that vary with volume in whatever functional area they occur.

Application

To use the income model and managerial economics in the decision process I recommend the following steps:

1. Clearly define the business unit profit center to minimize common fixed costs with other profit centers.
2. In the business unit profit center classify costs as variable or fixed, and prepare monthly income statements by marginal income accounts.
3. Monitor variable costs and marginal income:
   a. by transaction
   b. by product
   c. by product line or product group
   d. by client
   e. for total business unit profit center
4. Monitor fixed costs:
   a. by organizational unit
   b. by program
   c. for total business unit profit center
5. Monitor trends for:
   a. sales volume
   b. fixed cost
   c. marginal income rate
   d. breakeven
   e. operating income

6. Prepare an income model of the business unit each month and analyze and dialog this model in consideration of the information provided by the trend monitoring from (5) above. This process will identify any changes needed in: (a) prices, (b) cost reduction, (c) mix, or (d) business programs.
7. Test decisions arrived at on the income model to project probable effect. Use this testing process to set objectives to be achieved by the implementation of the decisions made.
8. Monitor performance against objectives set in (7), making appropriate changes in objectives, and making additional decisions from experience and in consideration of all information listed above.

The steps listed above provide an outline for organizing the transactional data of the business so that managerial economics concepts can be used in the decision process. But in addition to this internal, transactional data there will be the necessity of inputting the appropriate environmental and competitive information. This can often be done adequately through the Step 6 dialog process, with this "external" information coming out of the knowledge and the experience of the individuals participating in the dialog/decision process. To assist in providing "external" information, key external measures may also be monitored to provide data and trend information. External measures commonly monitored include:

1. market size and growth (or change)
2. share of market
3. business conditions—seasonal, cyclical, and trend measures
4. competitors' prices, product offerings, and marketing programs
5. government regulatory actions, and prospective actions

Example 1. As is typical of periods of inflation and business upturn, fixed costs are rising and marginal income rate is declining as variable costs rise more rapidly than can be offset by price increases, mix, and productivity improvement. As a result of rising fixed costs with declining marginal income rate, the breakeven point has been rising sharply. Income, however, has remained high as volume has increased sharply. Those trends are illustrated in Figure 11-4. The conventional operating report shows income about on budget and sales volume above budget.

Everyone is happy except for us. We are looking at the same results by marginal income accounts and see trends that spell BIG TROUBLE when the rate of business expansion slows or turns downward. Sales volume may then decline while marginal income rate continues to decline and breakeven continues to rise. The result will be a sudden, sharp decline in operating income. Even the present performance looks poor when we apply the business economist's perspective of futurity and appropriately revalue assets and costs. By those calculations, or

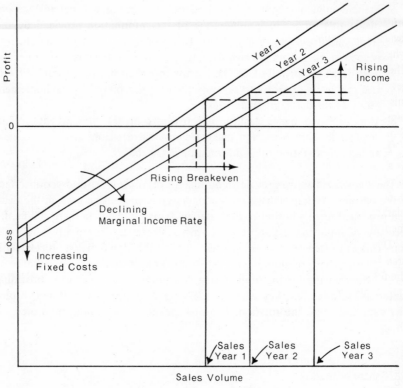

Figure 11-4. Trends typical of inflationary periods.

rather estimates, we find that much of what is being called current income is actually cost—if the enterprise is to remain successful in the future. In economics terms, much of the reported profit—or even all or more than all of it—can be a liquidation of assets.

Identifying the problem is the first step toward resolving it. The actions necessary are the kind more traditionally undertaken late in a business downturn, after poor income performance shows up in the operating report. Through marginal income analysis we see the problem from one to three years earlier. And with marginal income data we also have the elements to work with to find solutions. They are these fundamentals:

1. Reduce fixed costs.
2. Increase MI% by reduction in variable costs.
3. Increase MI% by increases in price.
4. Increase MI% by improvement in mix.
5. Increase sales volume.

For low marginal income rate businesses, major leverage is in variable costs, price, mix, and fixed costs. For high marginal income rate businesses, major leverage is in sales volume, mix, and price. The people in the organization know where actions can be taken to apply the five fundamentals most productively. Their participation, through dialog, will help identify what is to be done and will get those things done. Really, with that approach, we are using the concept of mission, managerial economics, and participation to avoid the fat-lean cycle in organization. Instead of getting fat when business is good and lean when business is bad, we remain lean and achieving always.

Example 2. Business area P showed an operating loss of $29,000 for August as shown in Figure 11-5. Historical data were not available by marginal income accounts, but it was felt that the illustrated results were typical. What should be done? It was found that the business area could best be segmented into seven market segments with, essentially, different products going to each market segment. Basic information estimated for the year is summarized in Table 11-1.

Dialoging the situation with management and professional people in business area P led to the conclusion that the business could be made profitable by taking the following actions:

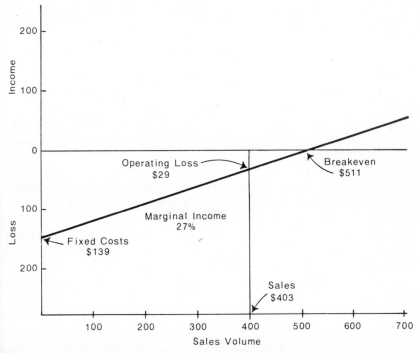

Figure 11-5. Business area P, August 19- ($ and 000).

Table 11-1. ($ in millions)

Segment	Market			Business Area P		
	Size	Growth Rate, %	Market Share, %	Sales	MI%	MI $
Market A	$12.5	8	20	$2.5	8	0.20
Market B	6.0	8	15	0.9	20	0.18
Market C	12.5	10	12	1.5	44	0.66
Market D	4.6	9	Minor	0.08	30	0.02
Market E	2.8	5	7	0.2	8	0.02
Market F	7.1	0	7	0.5	26	0.13
Market G	4.0	5	10	0.4	40	0.16
Total				$6.08	23	$1.37

1. Concentrate technical and sales development on Market C to obtain major share of market growth and to increase share with target accounts. Products are unique, so higher marginal income rate can be maintained and perhaps increased through improved mix.

2. Raise prices in market A, reduce technical service and development costs, and concentrate on reduction of variable costs.

3. Program improvement in mix in other markets.

4. Reduce certain fixed costs.

All those actions are consistent with the marginal income data shown in Table 11-1, but they could not have been based on those data only. They also required intimate knowledge of raw material sources, markets and individual accounts, competitors and probable competitive reactions, and product knowledge. The business area people had that knowledge among them, and the discipline of marginal income economics enabled them to apply their knowledge to resolve a very typical but very difficult business problem.

Example 3. For the first seven months of the year business area K showed average monthly breakeven performance by marginal income accounts as shown in Figure 11-6. In August a competitor announced a substantial price reduction. What should be the response of business area K? Several possible alternatives were explored by using marginal income economics. The effect of each alternative on sales volume, variable costs, marginal income, marginal income rate, fixed costs, and operating income was projected. The following were among the alternatives.

1. Continue present program and prices. That, it was projected, would lead to loss of one-third of the business and unprofitable operations.

2. New technology that was available could reduce variable costs 8 percent. At present levels of operation that would increase operating income by $20,000 per month. However, present levels of operation could not be maintained unless an adequate response to the competitive threat was found.

180

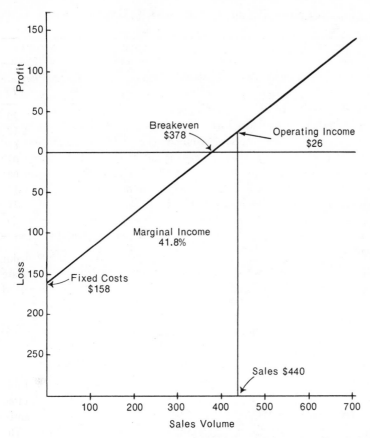

Figure 11-6. Business area K, average of seven months, 19- ($ add 000).

3. Reduce price 10 percent to maintain present volume. That would result in reducing income to a breakeven level.

4. Initiate a program to communicate product quality differences to business area K customers in target markets where the quality differences were most significant and to assist them in selling their products at the retail point of sale. A consumer value differential could be demonstrated. It was projected that such a program could increase sales at present prices but with an increase in programmed fixed expenses and an increase in breakeven point. Monthly operating income of $55,000 to $60,000 could probably be obtained.

5. Initiate the communication and point-of-sale marketing program and reduce prices 10 percent. That would result in operations below the increased breakeven point and monthly operating losses.

By dialoging the problem with the experts in the business, having reliable economic data by marginal income accounts with alternate courses of action, it was determined that the appropriate and most profitable action would be to maintain the price differential, install the process improvement, concentrate on target market segments, and increase programmed fixed costs by a point-of-sale marketing program. Developing the program in that way also made possible the setting of specific goals and the monitoring of progress so that appropriate changes in the programmed fixed expenses could be made as the plan was implemented.

Example 4. Should direct salesmen replace agents in certain key market areas? With operating data arranged by marginal income accounts, the probable effect on income can be determined. Elimination of agents' commissions will reduce variable costs and increase marginal income rate. The direct salesmen's salaries and expenses can be projected as an addition to fixed costs, and any commissions included as variable costs. The key determinant will be projected sales volume of direct salesmen versus that of agents. With these projections the marginal income accounts will provide the probable effect on income. Again, whatever the decision, the process will make possible the determination of sales program goals.

Example 5. What are my competitor's economics? Competitive assessment is an important input to business planning. We seek understanding in detail of the economics of our business enterprise. And we seek also to understand in a general way the economics and the strategy of significant competitors. If the competitor publishes quarterly financial statements, marginal income economics can help us develop that understanding. The procedure is simply to plot income (operating income, if available) versus sales volume for several reporting periods as shown in Figure 11-7. From the resulting scatter diagram we can calculate—or estimate—a least-squares regression line. Here we have an approximate marginal income breakeven chart for the competitor. By keeping the chart up to date and by analyzing the competitor's actions in relationship to it, we can improve our understanding of the competitor and the existing competitive relationships, important inputs to marketing and business strategy.

Example 6. Which plant should produce new contract requirements? A contract has been secured for 100,000 units as a selling price of $800 per hundred units, total contract value $800,000. Which of the two company plants should produce the new order? Both plants have the necessary capacity. Plant O is an old plant, largely depreciated. Plant N is a new plant, more efficient and more highly automated than plant O. The vice president decides to put the two plants in competition for the new contract, and he will schedule the order with the plant having the lowest cost. Each plant figures its costs to fill the new contract (see Table 11-2). Manufacturing the contract in the old plant, plant O, will result in a saving of $50,000.

That might be the end of the story: The contract could be produced in plant O, and management would be satisfied that the decision had resulted in $50,000 additional income for the company. There would be no data that refuted the "saving." But the vice president reflected. The new plant had been built to im-

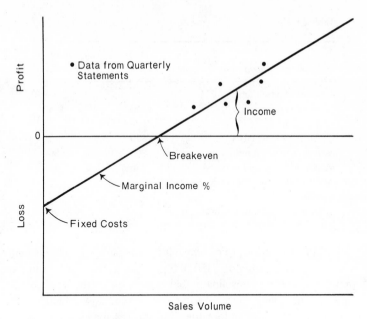

Figure 11-7. Competitor's estimated economics.

Table 11-2. Comparative manufacturing costs.

Cost or Saving	Old Plant O		New Plant N	
Cost per hundred units				
Materials		$350		$350
Direct labor		100		70
Overhead rate	200%		400%	
Plant overhead		200		280
Cost of sales		650		700
Savings per hundred		50		
Total saving		$50,000		

prove productivity and reduce costs. Why would it now prove to be higher cost? His controller then made a new calculation by marginal income accounts (see Table 11-3). Looking at the contract by marginal income accounts shows that producing the contract in the new plant, plant N, will contribute $30,000 more to company income. If the full-costing data were used and the contract produced in plant O, instead of a $50,000 saving the company would have $30,000 less income from the order.

Table 11-3.

Cost or Contribution	Old Plant O	New Plant N
Cost per hundred units		
Materials	$350	$350
Direct labor	100	70
Total variable costs	450	420
Selling price per hundred	800	800
Marginal income per hundred	350	380
Additional contribution per hundred		30
Total additional contribution		$30,000

Example 7. Plant location. Two companies in the same city had been merged. It was estimated that a saving of $350,000 per year in labor costs and fixed expenses would result from consolidating all operations in the larger of the two plant locations. The saving appeared to be one of the major benefits that could result from the merger. But before the decision was made, further studies by marginal income accounts were undertaken. Three basic alternatives, each in several variations, were considered: (1) consolidate all operations in plant A and sell plant B, (2) sell both plant A and plant B and consolidate all operations at a new and larger facility at a new location, and (3) continue with the two present plants and optimize operations in the two plants. Very quickly it became apparent that much more was involved in the decision than the calculated saving that would result from consolidation. Everything is related to everything else, and for each action all accounts on the input side and all accounts on the output side must be considered. All the basic questions on income effect must be considered:

What are the changes in fixed costs?
What are the changes in variable costs?
What are the changes in sales volume?
What are the changes in mix?
What are the changes in price?

The income statement by marginal income accounts and the income model can be used as a starting point, and all changes plus or minus can be identified and calculated. In this case, although there were no differences among the alternatives in mix and in price, it was found that there were many considerations in the other three areas in addition to the previously estimated saving. They substantially affected the determination of the most appropriate alternative.

1. The economy was at a turning point from recession, and there was oppor-

tunity for substantially increased sales volume. Production would be disrupted by a move and consolidation and sales volume would be lost. Probable lost volume would mean lost marginal income contribution of more than $1 million.

2. Not only would sales volume be lost but market share would be lost to competition. That would mean a continuing loss of future sales by amounts that could be estimated in both sales volume and marginal income contribution.

3. There was great variation in capital cost, moving cost, and optimization cost among the three alternatives. Some of it was obscured by book valuation of assets, but that was clarified by economic valuation of assets for all alternatives.

4. Costs and savings in addition to the projected $350,000 cost reduction were identified for all alternatives. They included costs in materials handling, shipping, pollution control, sale of assets, interest, services, communications, energy, and the cost of future expansion.

5. Benefits in labor management with two plant locations with smaller work groups were identified.

Decision was made to continue with the two plants and to optimize operations in the two plants. The apparent $350,000 cost saving from consolidation was ephemeral. The evaluation of all inputs and outputs by marginal income accounts clearly showed that the company would earn far greater income both in the current year and over time by operating two plants.

Example 8. Pricing products having discrete variable costs. In order to understand costs and to use cost information appropriately in the pricing decision for products having discrete variable costs it is important to know:

1. Variable costs, replenishment basis
   a. For current sales
   b. Recent trend and forecast, including supply/demand balance present and projected for key raw materials
   c. Comparison with competitors' variable costs
      (1) Domestic
      (2) Foreign
2. Fixed costs
   a. Total for the profit center having responsibility for the product
   b. Significant aggregates within the profit center

Variable costs should be monitored for each accounting period and related to marginal income as input to a continuing pricing and market planning review and decision process. Fixed costs must be monitored monthly and appropriate decisions made on a continuing basis. The profit center income model and the trends in the variables making up the model (volume, fixed cost, variable cost, mix, and price) provide the overall framework for monitoring cost and income performance. This information, combined with external information on market and competitive conditions, provide the information input for pricing decisions.

For the profit center business, for the range of probable sales volume and the existing and planned level of constant and programmed fixed costs, the marginal income rate required for achieving profitability objectives can be calculated. If this calculation should appear to be unreasonable or unattainable, adjustments elsewhere in the income model will have to be found—sales volume change or change in fixed costs. Through this kind of an interactive process a business unit can arrive at an overall marginal income objective. For each sales transaction, then, it can be determined what the amount of contribution is in relation to what is required for successful operations. With both cost and market information available, appropriate decisions can be made whenever a price quotation is made, or whenever changes in conditions require changes in prices. The marginal income objective will always be an important input to the pricing decision. The key variables to monitor for individual products are marginal income rate, sales volume, and where appropriate percent of capacity. For the overall profit center the key variables to monitor are marginal income rate, fixed costs, sales volume, breakeven, and operating income. In many instances it is also useful to monitor breakeven as a percent of capacity. The simplest and a very useful technique for this monitoring is three-month moving averages. Here is a summary format of a computer printout illustrating how one company monitors and reports marginal income performance by product:

PRODUCT SALES AND MARGINAL INCOME REPORT

Products	Last Yr. Actual Sales $'000	MI %	Current Yr. Objective Sales $'000	MI %	Current Month Sales $'000	MI %	Year-To-Date Sales $'000	MI %
All Products, Total								
Product Line A								
Product 1								
Product 2								
Product 3								
Product 4								
Product 5								
etc.								
Product Line B								
Product 1								
Product 2								
Product 3								
Product 4								
Product 5								
Product 6								
Product 7								
etc.								

PRODUCT SALES AND MARGINAL INCOME REPORT (cont.)

Product	Last Yr. Actual		Current Yr. Objective		Current Month		Year-To-Date	
	Sales $'000	MI %	Sales $'000	MI %	Sales $'000	MI %	Sales $'000	MI %
Product Line C								
Product 1								
Product 2								
Product 3								
etc.								
Etc.								

Figures 11-8 and 11-9 illustrate worksheet formats used by one company to evaluate its product lines and products using the principles and the techniques described in this chapter.

The first form, "Product Line Audit," summarizes basic cost and income data. A separate form is used for each product line. The period covered by the audit is shown at the top of the form, and should be the latest period for which data are available such as, "four months, 19___." Products comprising the product line are listed down the left-hand side, and available data is filled in. In columns 1 and 2 sales for the period are shown in units and in dollars. Column 3 shows marginal income percent for the period. Column 4, marginal income dollars per hour of equipment time, and column 5, marginal income dollars per unit of raw material, are filled in if these data are significant for the products being audited and if the data are available. To begin the audit, however, the marginal income percent will be the focus of attention, since for most situations this is the relevant optimizing principle. Column 6 shows average selling price per unit for the audit period, and column 7 the current selling price (which may be up or down from the average for the period). Totals for the product line are shown across the top of the form.

From the overall income model for the business it can be determined what average marginal income percent is required to achieve targeted profitability at anticipated levels of sales volume. This figure becomes a sort of "par" for assessing marginal income percent for individual products. If, for example, 42 percent marginal income rate is the objective for the overall business, an analysis of column 3 will quickly show where the strengths and the problems are, by product. Some may be in the 50's; some in the 20's. Often MI% figures for individual products will be found near zero, or even below, while others will be much higher than the targeted figure. The management job, then, is to "fix" the low ones by price increase, variable cost decrease, or by dropping or replacing the products or perhaps minimizing their sale. Marketing effort will be directed toward increasing sales in high MI% products in place of lower MI% products,

Prepared by ____________
Date ____________

PRODUCT LINE AUDIT

Period:

Units ____________
Product Line ____________
Market Growth Rate (1) ____________
Competitive Position (2) ____________

	Sales (add 000) Units	Sales (add 000) $	MI%	MI $/Hr.	MI $/RMU	AV SP/Unit	Current SP/Unit	Action
Product Line								
P1:								
P2:								
P3:								
P4:								
P5:								
P6:								
P7:								
P8:								
P9:								
P10:								
P11:								
P12:								
P13:								
P14:								

(1) Indicate: High--growth over 8% per year; Medium--growth of 3% to 8% per year; Low--growth less than 3% per year; Neg.--negative growth rate

Note: all growth rates are in real terms—units or deflated dollars.

(2) Indicate Company position among all competitors. Example: 2/10 = Company is number 2 of 10 competitors in sales volume for this product line.

Key: MI -- Marginal Income
RMU --Raw Material Unit
SP --Selling Price

Figure 11-8.

PRODUCT PRICING ANALYSIS

Product _____ Unit _____
Prepared by _____ Date _____

PERFORMANCE DATA:	Year-to-Date	Last Year	Previous Year
Sales: Units (add 000)			
$ (add 000)			
Average Selling Price			
Marginal Income $ (add 000)			
Marginal Income %			
MI $/Hour of Equipment Time			
MI $/Unit of Key Raw Material			

MARKET DATA:

Major Customers: Major Competitors:

Customer Values Offered by Company:

Projected Sales Volume This Year: Units (add 000)   _____
$ (add 000)   _____

ECONOMICS:
Current Selling Price per Unit: _____
Cost Structure:
Variable Costs (List below or attach cost sheet.)

Item	Replenishment Cost	Amt/Unit	Variable Cost/Unit
1.			
2.			
3.			
4.			
5.			
6.			

Total Variable Costs per Unit   _____
Marginal Income per Unit: _____   Marginal Income This
Maringal Income %:   _____   Year, Total: _____
Throughout per Hour: _____
MI $ per Hour of Equipment Time: _____
Units per Unit of Key Raw Material: _____
MI $ per Unit of Key Raw Material: _____
Fixed Costs Assigned to This Product: Estimated This Year
Constant Fixed Costs: _____
Programmed Fixed Costs: _____   Total: _____

ACTION TO BE TAKEN:

Figure 11-9.

and perhaps adding new, high MI% products to the line. In this way product line management can improve and manage profitability through improving and managing the marginal income rate by actions taken to: (1) increase price, (2) reduce variable cost, and (3) improve product mix.

When more detailed information is wanted on a specific product to aid in the pricing decision and in other product management decisions, the second form, Product Pricing Analysis," can be helpful. This form provides additional historical data, market information, and more detail on current economics. Summarizing both market and cost information in this way can help determine the most appropriate actions to be taken.

Example 9: Pricing products having common variable costs. In some cases it is not possible to identify variable costs for the individual product. This occurs when a common raw material input, usually processed by common direct labor, and production equipment, produces a variety of end products. Examples include the barrel of crude input to the refinery to produce a variety of refined products; the pig input to the meatpacking operation to produce a variety of meat products and by-products; the raw material input to a chemical process that produces more than one product. In some cases the range and the quantity of finished products may be varied to some extent; in other cases the output finished products are produced in a fixed relationship.

In such cases of common variable costs, instead of allocating these costs to each individual product the more useful approach is to manage the joint products as a group and to optimize group performance using the same considerations as discussed in example 8.

Because there are all degrees of discreteness and/or commonality in variable costs it becomes an important management decision to define the products and product groupings for pricing and cost management.

Example 10. Job order pricing. In order to understand costs and to use cost information appropriately in pricing (and for other management decisions) in a job shop equipment business the company identifies and controls:

1. Variable costs (replenishment basis) for each job order
2. Fixed costs
   a. Total for each profit center for each accounting period
   b. Significant aggregates within each profit center

For each job order, variable costs are estimated and then controlled to these estimates through production, with a post-audit following the completion of each production run, or production period. Fixed costs are monitored monthly and appropriate decisions made on a continuing basis. The income model provides the overall framework for monitoring cost and income performance.

For estimating and controlling variable costs for each job order the company uses the approach illustrated in Table 11-4. This is typical of a job order.

Table 11-4. Cost and Pricing Management, Equipment Manufacturer

			Direct	Comm-	Variable Cost		Selling Price		
Qty.	Set-Up	Materials	Labor	ission	Total	Unit	Total	Unit	MI%
100	840	8,750	9,465	1,588	20,643	206.43	31.758	317.58	35.0%
200	840	17,500	18,100	3,037	39,477	197.38	60,733	303.66	35.0%
500	4,200	41,000	34,200	6,617	86,017	172.03	132,333	264.66	35.0%

The selling prices shown in the table are prices calculated to result in a 35% marginal income, which in this case is the objective MI rate for the business. At this average MI rate, for the projected range of operations, adequate profitability and ROI objectives can be achieved. These calculated selling prices, however, will not normally be the prices quoted. They only provide information for the decision process. Actual prices quoted will be arrived at in consideration of variable costs estimated and the probability of making those costs in production, targeted marginal income, desirability of the job, and the projected competitive situation at the client account. The role of costs is not to determine the precise selling price, but rather to determine the profitability of the pricing decision. A few comments on the data shown in the table:

1. Focus is on costs and profitability of the job, not the unit piece. Some of the data will of course be estimated per unit as a starting point, but depending on quantity some of this unit data will change. It is the total job that must be estimated and controlled.
2. Set-up costs are shown to be the same for 100 and for 200 units. However a higher set-up cost is shown for 500 units to provide a set-up that will require less direct labor (and some reduction in scrap).
3. Materials in this case are shown to be the same for both 100 and 200 units (per unit). However, for 500 units a reduction in per unit materials cost is shown, resulting from better prices for the larger quantities purchased, and some reduction in scrap from the improved set-up.
4. Some improved efficiency is shown in direct labor for 200 units as compared with 100 units, accounted for by the greater amount of labor typically required for the first units of a production run. For 500 units a significant reduction in direct labor is shown to result from the improved set-up, and some modest benefits from the experience curve.
5. Commissions are figured at 5% of selling price in the following way: set-up, materials, and direct labor are totaled and divided by 0.60. This gives the total selling price to yield 35% MI at a 5% commission. The commission is then calculated at 5% of this sales total.

6. Total variable costs are now determined by adding set-up, materials, direct labor, and commission. Dividing by the quantity gives the unit variable cost.

When cost estimates, and cost performance in manufacturing can be summarized in a table as shown above, the business has the data base for controlling business operations using the managerial economics concepts discussed in this chapter.

Evaluation by Marginal Income Accounts
Evaluation by marginal income accounts can be an immense aid in all business decisions. The procedure is simple. First of all relate the decision to the company's concept of mission. Then examine, by using marginal income accounts and the income model, the economic changes that will result from the alternatives considered. Even when the economics cannot be accurately quantified, approximations or even rough ideas of direction and quantity can be helpful. Ten specific examples have been briefly summarized above; others would include whether or not, or how, to automate a plant for variable cost reduction and higher margin to offset the higher fixed costs and also expand capacity, using own or leased trucks versus shipping by common carrier, acquisition of a new facility or a company, establishing a sales incentive plan, reaching decision on a value analysis proposal, or any of the areas of business decision listed in Chapter 10.

One of the great advantages of marginal income economics is to point out the leverage points in each business situation. Businesses are different, and particular actions will differ greatly in their impact on income. For high marginal income businesses, by far the greatest leverage for improvement in income will come from increased volume. Secondary but important leverage will come from mix and price. Actions such as the following will be appropriate:

1. Add salesmen.
2. Increase promotional activities.
3. Offer sales contests and incentives.
4. Develop and introduce new products.
5. Extend geographical market.
6. Extend more liberal credit terms.
7. Increase service and other areas of non-price competition.
8. Expand into new markets or new market segments.
9. Increase advertising.
10. Improve mix.

For low marginal income businesses, on the other hand, the greatest leverage for improvement in income will come from cost reduction and price. Improvement in mix may offer opportunity, and increased volume can contribute additional income, depending on cost behavior. But for low marginal income businesses, cost control is the key. Actions such as the following will be appropriate:

1. Reduce cost of purchased raw materials. Low marginal income businesses are materials-intensive, and that may be the major leverage point for profit improvement.
2. Increase prices.
3. Reduce scrap, waste, and rework.
4. Reduce freight, distribution, and handling by such methods as centralization, simplification, small-order premiums, and large-order incentives.
5. Challenge all fixed costs to find reductions.
6. Control inventory closely for activity and high turnover.
7. Improve mix of products, customers, shipments, and markets.
8. Tighten credit and other sales terms.
9. Automate.

Both high and low marginal income businesses can be profitable, but they are different. For the high MI business, the key is volume; for the low MI business, the key is cost control. One of the management problems in many companies is a tendency to manage all businesses as if they were low MI businesses. The result is lost opportunity and lost income from mismanaged high MI businesses. No one notices because what is being practiced is tough management. Tough, good management is fine and promotes achievement, but tough mismanagement needs to be changed. It can be changed through managerial economics.

It is not easy to manage parts of the same company differently. One company I worked with had exactly that problem. The company comprised two businesses that were related technologically and served the same markets. But one was a low MI business and the other a high MI business. The high programmed fixed costs important for the high MI business tended to migrate over into the low MI business as well. The cost reduction requirements of the low MI busi-tended also to be extended into the high MI business. The result was confusion and less than satisfactory operations. Only after the discipline of managerial economics was applied did management and the entire organization fully realize its situation and take the appropriate steps to operate each business according to its unique requirements.

For both low and high marginal income businesses, mix is one of the important variables for income improvement. In analyzing product mix, however, it is not enough to base decisions and actions on marginal income rate alone. For manufacturing industry, throughput in terms of man-hours or machine-hours is also important. Two products might each have a 45 percent marginal income rate, sell at about the same price, and therefore produce about the same marginal income per unit. But if reactor time for one is six hours and for the other ten hours, the first has greater income potential than the second. To optimize plant operations, the appropriate focus is on marginal income dollars per hour of equipment time. That, of course, enables production to support a larger volume of sales from the same facilities and is one of the important routes to improved productivity. In times of raw materials shortages, marginal income per unit of the scarce material is the route to optimization. All optimization decisions must relate to company mission so that each action we take today will be good for today and will also move us toward the normative future we are creating.

Time Series Analysis—Identification
of Trends and Changes in Trends

Once the most fundamental measures of performance of an enterprise or a component of an enterprise are identified, it is important to know more than the measurements at any particular time. We must also understand the trends and any change in them that may be developing. A business enterprise grows and evolves and changes continuously. Nothing is static. We can think of the business enterprise as continually changing, growing, living, evolving in ways similar to those of biological evolution and perhaps also those of hierarchical change. Since growth and evolution and change are continuous, it is a gross distortion to describe business performance as aggregate measurements of an accounting period. Accounting measures were invented for paying taxes and writing annual reports. They cannot be used for measuring organizational performance. Instead, the performance measure must parallel the way in which the enterprise grows and evolves; that is, the measure must be a continuum. That kind of measure can be provided by trends and changes in trends; in statistical methodology, by time series analysis.

With such an approach to performance measurement, and by the thinking process of identifying the key performance measurements as discussed in Chapter 12, we free ourselves from the tyranny of the fiscal year, except for tax payment and a few other regulatory requirements. We can now manage and work and achieve in the way our enterprise grows and evolves—continuously. A December 31 measurement has no greater significance for those purposes than a measure on August 27 or March 26 or December 11. Useful measures will always be *now* and always oriented to the future. And from the measurements we will at all times have an understanding of what our performance is, its history, how it is developing, and what it is likely to be in the future. In measuring and understanding our enterprise as a continuum, we cannot only escape the tyranny of 12-month fiscal year leaps but also avoid any annual ordeal of budget making and any periodic task of 5-year planning. For when we think through our business to identify key performance area objectives and understand and measure them as trends and changes in trends, we do continuously everything we attempted to do intermittently in budgeting and 5-year planning, and we do it far better.

The time spans of our measures will vary with the key performance areas. Some will be months, some days or weeks, some years. Totals by fiscal years will not be significant, but such totals, past or future, will be a simple output from the measurement system when they are wanted. Performance area objectives will not be the same for all businesses, because each business situation is different. Nor will the performance objectives for an enterprise remain the same. Everything is related to everything else, and changes in achievement and the environment will result in changes in performance objectives. The following are some of the performance areas in which we typically find key objectives set and which can be understood and measured as trends and changes in trends:

Sales volume	Other factor productivity
Operating income	(raw materials, capital, energy)
Major market sales	Marginal income rate
Market share	Breakeven point
Major product sales	Fixed costs, total and
Prices	by category
Value added	Numbers of employees
Productivity in physical	Employment costs
units per man hour	Fixed and working capital

Performance areas that can be comprehended on the basis of trends and changes in trends but are difficult to measure quantitatively include:

Innovation	Management style
Motivation	Public responsibility
Organizational competence	

Figure 11-10 illustrates a time series chart of operating income and sales volume for a manufacturing company, Company L. The technique used in this case was the 12-month moving total. Since a 12-month moving total is, by its method of calculation, 6 months out of phase with current performance, a chart of monthly variations from the year-ago month is included for currency. The chart of variances shows direction and rate of change and also signals cyclical turning points. It is very useful for short-range forecasting. To smooth the curve of an erratic or noisy series, variances in 3-month moving averages may be plotted instead of individual months. I prefer the individual month variances as most current and as superior for dialoging current change and outlook. In Figure 11-10 and similar charts in this book, the 12-month period is always plotted at the midpoint of the 12 months totaled. Monthly variance from year-ago is plotted at the current month.

In Figure 11-10 the 12-month totals show sales on a slowly rising trend, with

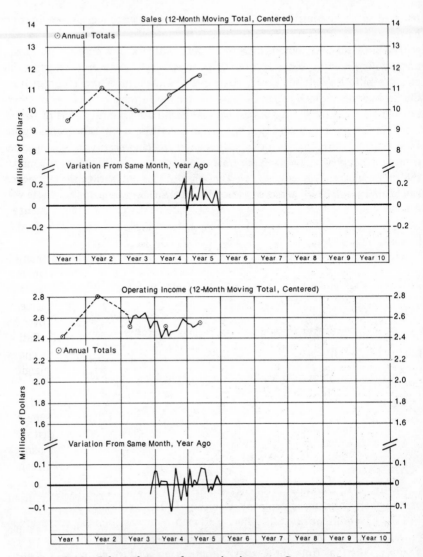

Figure 11-10. Sales volume and operating income, Company L.

the possibility that the cyclical expansion may be slowing. The trend of monthly variances indicates a cyclical turning point as probable, with, therefore, little likelihood of much further increase in sales. The moving total of operating income shows an increasingly deteriorating relationship between sales and income over the past two years. The slowdown or decline in sales that is indicated as probable by the sales trends would result in deterioration in income.

The two charts have been drawn on an arithmetic scale for simplicity and ease of understanding. The scales chosen are such that, in the range where data are recorded, a visual comparison of the two charts will reveal approximately comparable rates of change. Semilog charts could be used, but I find that people generally are more comfortable with arithmetic scales. If arithmetic scales are used, however, care must be taken in choosing them for charts that may be directly compared so that the visual comparison will show the real situation. Charts that are to be compared can be made into transparencies and superimposed one on the other for analysis.

The deteriorating income performance in relation to sales shown in Figure 11-10 and the projected decline in income anticipated with moderating (or declining) sales would be more specifically seen in the trend of the key marginal income accounts—marginal income rate, fixed costs, and breakeven. The trends and changes in trends in such key performance area measurements as those will provide clear comprehension of present and prospective future achievement in relation to company objectives. A system for that kind of achievement reporting is outlined in Chapter 13.

Figure 11-11 shows sales to customers and operating income for Company L over three more years. The sales volume time series curve shows the development of the cyclical downturn that had been indicated, with recovery after a year and a half. Total decline in sales volume from peak to trough was about 15 percent. Operating income, however, dropped off precipitously; it declined by over 50 percent. Here is illustrated the typical result of expansion with cost inflation followed by recession and continuing cost inflation. The two time-series charts show the problem developing over the three prior years, but data by marginal income accounts would show it even more clearly.

Company L was not using marginal income accounts in the prior period, but it began using them when well down the income slide. The marginal income discipline clarified key issues and made possible the decisions and actions that soon had the company's operations rapidly improving. The history for Company L over the eight-year period shown might be summarized about as follows: years 1 to 3, operations normal with no distortions apparent; years 4 and 5, sales rising and income remaining about constant. Over that period of time some significant distortions begin to develop:

1. Fixed costs rise. The fixed costs are for the most part additions of people and higher wage and salary costs per employee. The additional people appear needed for reason of functions to be performed more than for reason of outputs to be produced. But profits are good, outlook is favorable, and the business can afford it.

2. Marginal income rate declines. With inflation, variable costs (materials, direct labor, energy) increase faster than can be offset by increases in prices in what remains, for Company L's products, a competitive market.

3. Rising fixed costs and decreasing marginal income rate combine to increase the breakeven point. It increases steadily and substantially.

4. Value added increases only slightly over this period, just enough to offset rising wage and salary costs.

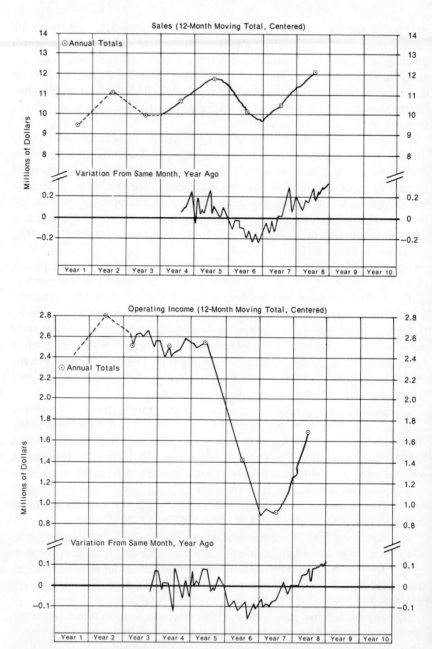

Figure 11-11. Sales volume and operating income, Company L, for an additional three years.

5. Higher sales volume offsets the deteriorating trends of the income dynamics to just maintain year 3 income level. But that is during a period of cyclical expansion that can't go on forever.

Year 6. The cyclical expansion did not go on forever. It turned down, and so did Company L sales. What happened to Company L income can be readily seen in marginal income accounts:

1. Fixed costs continued to rise for the same reasons they did in years 4 and 5.

2. Marginal income rate continued to decline. Variable costs continued to rise, and Company L's market became even more competitive as sales volume declined. That made price increases to offset higher variable costs even more difficult.

3. Breakeven point continued to rise.

4. Value added now declined rather sharply.

5. Sales volume declined. It moved down as breakeven moved up, and in one year's time almost half the operating margin over breakeven was lost.

Well past midyear in year 6, however, the conventional operating report for Company L signaled no great problem. It did not detect the sharp trend downward in income shown in the time series chart. Instead, it showed monthly and year-do-date variances from budget. Although they were negative, it was not at all clear that there really was a business downturn, and there were plenty of reasons to expect some recovery and better performance by year end. It was only very late in year 6 that the operating report was beginning to be aware of what the trend charts and marginal income accounts began to show in year 4.

Year 7. Turnaround from recession develops in year 7, and sales rise sharply during the latter part of the year. Income continues to decline. During year 7, Company L begins to apply marginal income economics to its business problems:

1. Fixed costs rise only slightly as jobs are related more to outputs than to function and there is reduction in number of employees.

2. Marginal income rate stabilizes by a combination of price increases, improvement in mix, and productivity improvement in plant operations that offsets the inflationary increase in variable costs.

3. Breakeven point rises only slightly.

4. Decline in value added is halted. Value added stabilizes.

5. Rising sales volume combined with actions taken as summarized above halts the decline in income over the last half of year 7. But recovery still lies ahead.

Year 8. Sales volume continues to rise, and income also now rises sharply. The actions taken in year 7 now pay off in rising income with rising volume.

Since inflation in costs continued, the year 8 achievement is significant. Company L applied the concepts recommended in this book. It found its identity, goals, and strategy through an articulated mission developed by broad dialog among its people. It formulated key performance area objectives. It worked hard to develop a more participative management style. It developed and applied PMBO concepts. And the result was a regeneration of the business—economically, organizationally, and motivationally. Marginal income economics was one of the disciplines that helped Company L accomplish its rejuvenation.

Company L's situation through year 6 is typical of the experience of many companies, but its experience and accomplishments in year 7 and 8 are less typical. Those too could be typical through application of the concepts described in this book. Important in the process are the identification of the key performance area objectives and their monitoring in a way that will identify trends and changes in trends. Marginal income economics provides a discipline for relating key performance area objectives to income performance. To identify trends in those key variables, I would recommend as a minimum time series tracking of sales, operating income, marginal income rate, fixed costs, and break-even. That, combined with monthly income reports by marginal income accounts as shown in Figure 11-12, will prove to be a useful and highly reliable instrument panel for piloting the economic course of what is always a very complex business operation. But we need no longer pilot by rote. We can now pilot by reason, and by purpose.

Productivity

Japan knows that productivity is important. A Japanese Productivity Center of labor, management, and government was established in 1955, and has operated to dramatically improve the productivity of Japan's industries. Our government also knows that productivity is important. Statistics and analyses on labor productivity for the overall economy are published by the Bureau of Labor Statistics. Economists know that productivity is important. They write about it in textbooks. Businessmen more or less know that productivity is important. They talk about it. But they seldom define it or measure it, and even less often do they record it in their operating reports. It is, of course, a GOOD THING. But it's not in the operating report, where the real guts of the business are found. Period. Or question mark?

Overseas it is not uncommon to find measures of productivity included in company annual reports and officially commented on. In the United States such reporting is quite unusual. Productivity can't very well be reported because it is not very much observed. It is not very much observed because it has not been very specifically defined for the individual enterprise. And so we advocate the generality without doing the homework necessary to define it for our particular enterprise. But that definition is now possible. Productivity need no longer be the product of technological change combined with out-of-phase management

Marginal Income Account	Three Years Ago Av. Mo.	Two Years Ago Av. Mo.	Last Year Av. Mo.	This Year's Budget Av. Mo.	This Year, Actual							
					Jan.	Feb.	Mar.	Apr.	May	June	July	Aug.
Gross sales												
Variable costs												
Materials												
Direct labor												
Energy												
Royalty paid to outsiders												
Other variable manu-facturing costs												
Commissions												
Freight												
Other variable non-manufacturing costs												
Marginal income												
Marginal income percent												
Fixed costs												
Manufacturing												
Marketing												
Distribution												
Research & development												
General & administrative												
Other												
Breakeven												
Sales above (below) breakeven												
Operating income												
Other income												
Other expenses												
Net income before taxes												

Figure 11-12. Income statement by marginal income accounts.

response to the vagaries of the business cycle and reported only for national income accounts. Instead, productivity objectives can be defined and programmed within the individual firm to contribute substantially to the achievement of short- and long-term company goals. The effort must begin with definition.

Productivity is the measure of output in relation to the inputs required to produce it. The most significant productivity measure is total factor productivity, which includes in its calculation all the factor inputs—labor, raw materials, energy, and capital. All interrelate and combine to produce the output, and are to some degree substitutable one for the other. A larger capital input, for example, may be substituted for some share of labor input. Total factor productivity provides us a measure of the efficiency of the combined inputs in the production of outputs, and can provide us this measure on a trend basis. Along with it we will want also to have partial productivity measures for each of the inputs—output related to man-hour inputs, output related to raw materials inputs, outputs related to energy inputs, and output related to capital inputs.

Productivity measurement begins at the job level, and feedback at the job level should provide information on output per man-hour, materials usage per unit of output, energy usage per unit of output, and the appropriate measure of capital inputs per job. Aggregates will show department, plant, profit center, and company performance and trends, but control must begin at the job level through feedback to the individual worker and supervisor.

Also important to the success of the enterprise is the concept of *economic* productivity. Economic productivity adds both a market and a futures perspective to productivity measurement by relating the economic value of the output of the enterprise (as measured by payments to the firm in exchange for its outputs) to the economic cost of the inputs to the firm (as measured by payments from the firm for the inputs to its operations). Here we sail a less-charted sea. But it is a dollars-and-cents sea, the kind of sea we say we sail best. Here is opportunity to apply our dollars-and-cents know-how to new horizons, to the immense benefit of the enterprise.

Productivity, both physical and economic, is one of the key performance areas that will determine the success of any business. I comment on it here briefly because it is one dimension of managerial economics. A more complete discussion, with recommendations, appears in Chapter 12.

Input—Output

Productivity is an input-output equation. Marginal income economics is an organization of the relationships between economic inputs and outputs. Time series analysis as recommended in this chapter is a methodology for identifying trends and changes in trends of the key inputs and outputs and their relationships. In business enterprises we create and live in an input-output world in which the primary input is people (who manage or create the other inputs) and the primary output is value to people—our client groups. Input-output provides a conceptual framework for managerial economics and the specific disciplines and techniques of managerial economics advocated in this chapter. Input-output can lead us to new modes of thinking and working and to new levels of achievement.

12

Key Performance Areas
That Determine Success

In Chapter 4 the seven key performance areas that determine the continuity and success of the business enterprise were described briefly. Objectives in the critical performance areas become the instrumental panel for guiding the destiny of the enterprise. The areas are:

Market standing.
Innovation.
Productivity.
Physical and financial resources.
Profitability.
Motivation and organization development.
Public and environmental responsibility.

Identifying and concentrating on a small number of fundamentals for the company and for each area of operations will make possible the integration of effort throughout the organization to fulfill the agreed-upon mission of the enterprise. In this chapter we will examine approaches that can be used to identify the fundamentals in each of the seven key performance areas. Each business enterprise is different, and so the fundamentals for each will be different. But the search—how to find the fundamentals—is common to all enterprises.

The search must be a creative one. New knowledge will bring new approaches. Ideas other than those presented in this chapter may be more useful for your particular situation. You may prefer approaches more creative or more conventional. Those presented here are not, for the most part, in widespread use today. But all are used and all have proved to be "practical" in terms of results achieved. In relating them to your business you may take ideas directly from this book and apply them or you may find concepts here that will help you improve what you are already doing.

Either way, there is more to what we are talking about here than technique alone. There is also a skill, a professionalism. An approach might be excellent but not immediately very helpful to us in improving operations. We need to experience it awhile and learn to use it. If we have developed our skills on the golf course, we can't expect to read a book and immediately ski the Nosedive or the National at Stowe. We'll need to practice the new techniques first and perhaps get a little coaching too. So if any of these approaches look useful to you in your situation, try them, experiment with them, develop them. Involve others in the process. When you find what you can do with them, use them. They have been very productive in organizations that have used them. Perhaps they can be for you.

Market Standing

All businesses have objectives for sales volume. In most companies, those objectives will be stated in many ways and in great detail. For an annual budget period, and for quarters and individual months as well, there may be objectives for sales volume in units and in dollars for totals, product lines, products, customer groups, customers, sales regions, sales territories, countries, and market areas and perhaps breakdowns of them, along with matrices and interrelations among them, such as territories by customer by product or product by market by customer.

The selling transactions of a large enterprise are vast and complex, and modern data processing makes possible the reporting of all of it in whatever arrangements may be wanted. In the midst of all that detail (1) we may never see the fundamentals or (2) we may overlook the fact that transaction data are only part of the picture. The rest of the picture, and the biggest part, is outside and not recorded in our transactions. It is out there in the markets that we deal with. Fundamentals will be identifiable in the analysis of transaction data, but alone they cannot be meaningful enough. They need to relate in some way to opportunity and "what is going on out there."

One way of relating company performance to opportunity is by analyzing and forecasting general business conditions. That is usual in the preparation of budget plans. Perhaps it is attempted more than it is carried out; for it is not easy to relate the two. Whatever the business forecast may be, there are likely to be strong internal pressures to show in budget objectives higher sales for the year ahead than are being realized in the current year. Those pressures can overstate sales objectives when the business outlook is unfavorable. On the other hand, when the business outlook is favorable, internal constraints may accept objectives that are lower than can be realized. In either case, subsequent comparisons with budget will not reflect achievement in relation to opportunity. They will only show achievement in relation to the budget objective.

As we have seen in Chapter 10, accounting is not economics, and business success depends on a capacity to realize present and future opportunity. From the viewpoint of the future the relevant measurement should be expressed in relation to opportunity. And the most direct way of so expressing it is in terms of market share. That measure takes into consideration size and growth characteristics of the market and our participation in it. In our sales and market share data we have the fundamentals of the sales opportunity. But there are two important questions to answer:

What is the market?
How can the market be measured?

It certainly is not enough to say that product equals market. The question is how narrow or how broad our definition should be. In regard to product, is the most realistic focus on individual product, product line, or product group? Should related products be included? Should substitute products be? In regard to market, is the best focus on total market or on market segments? What about international markets? Is the relevant consideration functional rather than product (transportation instead of railroad, energy instead of petroleum, entertainment instead of movies)? "What is the market?" is not a simple question. How the question is answered will have great impact on the future of the enterprise.

In the late 1940s General Electric's Ralph Cordiner found that the managers of the Telechron subsidiary were very pleased with their market share performance. They had over 90 percent of the electric clock market. The question was put in different terms, "What is your share of the clock market?" The answer to that question was, "Less than 5 percent." The question and the line of thinking that came from it opened whole new areas of opportunity for the company. What you do to maintain 90 percent of the electric clock market is very different from what you do to replace the wind-up clock.

There is no right answer to market definition; there are only different answers. And some answers are much better than others. The Telechron decision on market definition was made at a time when the company was very successful. Its performance record was good, and its income statement was good and improving steadily. It was the market leader. Motivation would not have developed from the accounting reports, but great motivation did develop from market share measurement when creatively used. Telechron made its own successful past obsolete and so became a different and even more successful enterprise. If it had not, it might well have been displaced.

"What is the market?" seems such a simple question that we usually give it the simple, obvious answer. Very often we do not even ask the question but instead go directly to the question of market share, unconcerned with the gut question of "share of what?" We look only at our product's share of some larger total. But it can often be very profitable to chew a little on the question of market definition. The chewing can be handled effectively as part of the dialog on the company's definition of its identity. Probing questions will lead to new understanding of opportunity. For example:

1. If we define our market this way, what other things could we be doing?
2. We have 25 percent of the market. Where do we stand in segment A? Segment B? Segment C? And what are the relative growth opportunities; what is the competition?
3. What would be a broader way to define the market?
4. What is the overseas market? In what major countries?
5. What would be a narrower way to define the market?
6. How can we apply systems marketing?
7. What functions do we serve in this market that we could serve in other markets?
8. What alternatives does the market have? What if they were part of our definition of our market?
9. How could we define the market in terms of function or service provided?
10. What would be a better way to define the market?

There is no right answer to the question of market definition; there are only different answers. And the different answers will greatly influence how we define our objectives and how we are motivated to achievement.

IBM sees its market in terms of problem solving. The company's operations focus on information-handling systems, equipment, and services to solve the increasingly complex problems of business, government, science, space exploration, defense, education, medicine, and other areas of human activity. Focusing on problem solving gives IBM a different scale of opportunity than would flow from a definition in terms of hardware alone. One of the greatest transformations in American industrial history was the $5 billion metamorphosis that IBM went through in developing and launching the 360 computer. It made itself into a new, much larger, and much more successful company. And its starting point was market definition. That starting point has continued to motivate company performance. The 360 was superceded by the more powerful 370. And as the large-scale integration of electronic circuitry dramatically reduced computing cost and equipment size the company offered small, low-cost computers for information-handling at local work centers. Market definition keeps IBM in tune with now and future opportunity.

Once we have settled on market definition, there remains the question of how to measure the market as defined. We may have statistical data from governments or trade associations. We may need market research investigation. Whatever is most available we will want to use, and that, plus an organized use of the intelligence available within our own organization, will usually be enough to provide guidance for decisions and feedback on performance. For example, in our sales activities we will have good contacts with many or most of the major customers in the market as we define it. Our people who know those customers have among them a great amount of intelligence on the market. By observing, asking questions, and listening, we can learn more. By monitoring a group of customers as a sample of the total market, we can identify and follow trends and hypothesize totals. For big areas of uncertainty we can use Delphi techniques.

Measurement adequate enough for planning can usually be accomplished, once we have made our decision on market definition. Usually we think of measurement as the problem and think of market definition hardly at all. We would do better, first of all, to dialog, hypothesize, study, and make a decision on market definition. If we are good enough to do that well, we will have little trouble in making measurements good enough to serve our needs.

One other consideration is important in market share measurement: the consideration of growth and rate of growth. Nothing is static. The market as defined will be new or old, growing rapidly, slowly, or perhaps not at all. A good way to think of it is in terms of the growth curve shown in Figure 12-1. In business planning the curve is described as the product growth curve cycle, but it applies also to the kind of market definition we will probably be using in our business. That definition will be expressed as some combination of products and services to some kind of market or market segments. So both our products and our markets, as defined, can be related to the kind of a growth curve shown in Figure 12-1. The curve may represent months, years, or decades; some cycles move

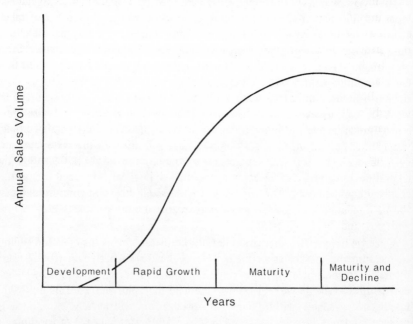

Figure 12-1. Product life cycle.

swiftly, others slowly. Commonly, four segments of the cycle are considered for planning and strategy purposes.

1. Developmental, including R&D, testing, and early commercialization.
2. Rapid growth. After the early introductory period, the product-market business, if successful, will enjoy a period of rapidly expanding sales. Over that period additional competition will appear and prices and costs will decrease in real terms.
3. Maturity. Growth eventually will slow. Competition will become more intense, and product differentiation will diminish.
4. Maturity and decline. Growth may cease or even decline. Competition will become very intense, and some suppliers will drop out of the market.

In terms of opportunity for income, stage 1 is all cost. Resources are put into the business, but very little comes back in sales and nothing in income. The objective at this stage is future income. In stage 2 there is profit opportunity for all, at least in the early stages of rapid growth. Much of that income, however, may be needed for reinvestment to keep up with the rate of growth. Stage 3 will be highly profitable for the leading suppliers, who will have scale and efficiency advantages, but less profitable for smaller suppliers. In stage 4 only the leaders can usually show satisfactory income.

Few product-market businesses will follow the neat growth curve of the theoretical model. A product-market business may go from introduction to failure. A mature or declining curve may suddenly take off on a new period of rapid growth as a result of some technical or market change. A rapidly growing business can suddenly change to maturity, decline, or failure ahead of its time.[1] Still, the growth curve idea is helpful as a guide to strategy thinking on the value and importance of market share objectives.

The Boston Consulting Group has split the product growth curve in two at the early maturity level and related the rapid- and slow-growth periods to market share. By relating market growth rate and market share in a matrix format, they have provided a useful way of applying growth curve concepts to business planning. The matrix, which can be used for developing resource strategy, is illustrated in Figure 12-2.

The resource strategy matrix can be used to plan resource commitment and develop long-range strategies by the following process.

1. Determine the most meaningful definition of the business by business area, major products, product lines or groupings, and markets. Assign each business as defined to one of the four cells in the resource strategy matrix.
2. Achieve a balanced portfolio for the overall business to provide both cur-

[1]Theodore Levitt, "Exploit the Product Life Cycle," *Harvard Business Review*, November-December 1965.

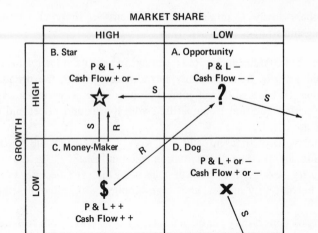

Figure 12-2. Resource strategy that can apply to business areas, product lines, products, or markets. Arrows labeled R indicate resource flow. Those labeled S indicate a possible strategy direction.

Source: The Boston Consulting Group, Inc. ©1968.

rent and longer-range profitability. A desired mix will include one or more money-makers, at least one star that can be a future money-maker, and an opportunity that will be developed into a future star and money-maker. A minimum proportion of sales should be in the dog classification.

3. Use cash flow from the established money-makers (a) to maintain high market share for stars and (b) to develop selected opportunities into stars.
4. As stars become money-makers, repeat the process.
5. Aggressively manage money-makers to maintain market position and optimize cash flow, but concentrate investment of resources in the stars and opportunities.
6. Maintain profitable dogs with minimum effort and resources. Drop unprofitable dogs.

In using the matrix there is, of course, the question of what is high and what is low. A high market share with twenty competitors is not the same as one with three competitors. And what is a high growth rate or a low one? Is everything really either high or low, or are there graduations? What about futures? Shouldn't we be thinking about future share and growth performance? Such questions can be resolved in a way that is helpful in formulating strategy decisions by diagramming the resource strategy matrix on a log-log grid. Required inputs are prepared in the form illustrated in Table 12-1. The log-log matrix is illustrated in Figure 12-3, which shows the product line businesses for Company J plotted for

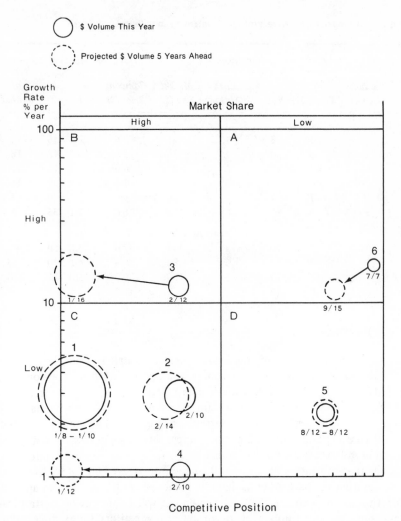

$\bigcirc$ $ Volume This Year

$\left(\begin{array}{c}\\\end{array}\right)$ Projected $ Volume 5 Years Ahead

Growth
Rate
% per
Year

Market Share

High | Low

100

B | A

High

6

3

7/7

1/16 | 2/12

9/15

10

C | D

1

Low

2

5

2/10

2/14

8/12 – 8/12

1/8 – 1/10

4

1

1/12 | 2/10

Competitive Position

Figure 12-3. Resource strategy matrix for Company J.

last year and for five years ahead. (For identification of product lines see Table 12-1.) Both the table and the matrix were developed by Company J people and dialoged in the search for strategy direction. The general approach used by Company J, and a good procedure for using the log-log matrix for developing resource strategy decisions, is on the following page:

1. Make the company business specific by defining it as one or more logical businesses selected by dialog and decision as the basis for running the company. Definition should be narrow enough to give direction but broad enough to give opportunity for growth.

Table 12-1. Company J resource strategy summary. ($ in millions)

No.	Product Group	Growth Rate Next 5 Years, %	Competitors No.	Competitors Company Position	Market Size ($)	Company Sales ($)	Marginal Income $	Marginal Income %	Percent of Market
				Last Year					
1	A	3	8	1	102	40.6	22.8	56	40
2	B	3	10	2	76	13.8	6.6	48	18
3	C	13	12	2	54	6.6	3.3	51	12
4	D	0	10	2	51	7.6	3.0	39	15
6	E	17	7	7	60	1.6	0.3	20	3
5	F	3	12	8	158	6.6	2.1	35	4
				5 Years Ahead					
1	A	3	10	1	117	47.0	23.6	50	40
3	B	3	14	2	88	20.4	8.1	40	23
2	C	15	16	1	100	30.3	15.8	52	30
4	D	0	12	1	51	12.3	4.5	36	24
5	E	12	15	9	132	8.2	3.3	40	6
6	F	3	12	8	183	7.2	2.1	30	4

2. For each of the company businesses, develop the data in Table 12-1.

3. Plot each business in the resource strategy log-log matrix as follows. (Table 12-1 examples are illustrated in Figure 12-3.)

a. For total market as defined use forecast annual growth rate for the next five years to locate position on the vertical axis log scale: one percent, bottom line; 10 percent, midpoint; 100 percent, upper line. Growth rate should be estimated in real, or constant dollar, terms.

b. On the horizontal axis, assume all competitors arrayed on the scale according to position in the market as defined, number 1 on the left to the smallest competitor at the extreme right. The midpoint will be the square root of the total number of competitors. If there are sixteen competitors, for example, number 1 will be at the left vertical axis, number 4 in the middle vertical axis, and number 16 at the right vertical axis. If there were nine, the respective positioning would be 1, 3, and 9; if four, it would be 1, 2, and 4; if fourteen, it would be 1, 3.74, and 14. Locate your competitive position on the horizontal axis ratio scale. It is not necessary to be precise—approximation is OK. Arraying competitors in that way emphasizes the importance and the value of market leadership.

c. At the intersection determined by the two points located as above, draw a circle approximately representing the relative size of your present sales volume for the business.

d. In a similar way locate your sales volume and market share as projected for five years ahead and draw a dashed circle at that point. If there is no projected change in market position, number of competitors, and growth rate, the dashed circle for five years ahead will be centered on the solid circle for present volume. If there is a projected change in position, connect the solid-line circle and the dashed circle with an arrow.

e. Under each circle indicate your competitive position and number of competitors; for example, 2/9 indicates number 2 of 9 competitors.

4. Number the circles by order of marginal income contribution. Use those numbers to identify the businesses on the data sheet.

5. Review the businesses as charted, the data sheet, marginal income analyses, business intelligence, and other relevant data and make your decisions on resource commitment.

Marginal income analysis of each of the businesses plotted on the log-log resource strategy matrix can be very helpful in developing sound strategy decisions. The following procedure is recommended:

1. For each of the businesses, summarize marginal income data for the past two years and the current year to date. Compare data for the average months of the periods to identify where changes have developed and what the changes are. Use the format of Table 12-2 for summarizing the data. For most businesses as defined for market share analysis the Table 12-2 data will be filled in only as far as marginal income percent. Only for profit center businesses separable by cost assignment rather than allocation will the complete operating data be filled in. For businesses having prime cost data, prime margin and prime margin percent may be used in place of marginal income and marginal income percent. Refer to Chapter 11 for a more detailed discussion of marginal income economics.

2. Plot the data for each business on an income model by using the format described in Chapter 11.

3. Compare the data and chart for each business with the position of the business in the resource strategy matrix. The typical characteristics of each group of businesses can be described as follows:

a. Group A businesses—opportunities (low share, high growth).
   High marginal income percent (or prime margin percent).
   Negative operating income.
   Strategy objective: increase market share or disengage.
b. Group B businesses—stars (high share, high growth).
   High marginal income percent (or prime margin percent).
   Positive operating income.
   Strategy objectives: (1) maintain or increase market share, (2) improve productivity by reductions in variable costs per unit of production, (3) price for market penetration, and (4) control fixed costs consistently with expansion and growth objectives.
c. Group C businesses—money makers (high share, low growth).
   Good marginal income percent (or prime margin percent).

Table 12-2. Format for summarizing marginal income data.

Marginal Income Account	Previous Year		Last Year		This Year to Date	
	Total	Avg. Mo.	Total	Avg. Mo.	Total	Avg. Mo.
Sales						
Variable costs						
Materials						
Labor						
Energy						
Commissions						
Transportation						
Other variable costs						
Marginal income						
Marginal income percent						
Fixed costs						
Manufacturing						
Sales						
General and administrative						
Other						
Breakeven						
Sales above (below) breakeven						
Operating income						
Other income						
Other expense						
Net Income						

High operating income.

Strategy objectives: (1) maintain market share, (2) optimize through (a) reductions in variable costs, (b) control (or reduction) of fixed expenses, (c) increase in prices if inflation of costs is greater than can be offset by experience curve cost reductions (a and b above).

d. Group D businesses—dogs (low share, low growth).

Poor to good marginal income percent (or prime margin percent).

Operating income may be positive or negative.

Strategy objectives: (1) disengage from businesses that are not profitable or adequately contributing or that cannot be made such with moderate effort, and (2) optimize profitable or adequately contributing businesses by using the same approaches as for group C businesses.

4. It will often be found that businesses classified in the preceding groups do not have the income characteristics described. In such cases determine the reason by using the following procedure:

a. Check your basic information to see that the business is correctly classi-fied.

b. Review your definition of the business. Perhaps in consideration of market and competitive factors you have not defined a viable business. Instead, you may have defined the business either too narrowly or too broadly.

c. Review the reliability of the marginal income (or prime margin) data.

d. If the preceding three steps check out and your operating performance is better than is described, look for uniquenesses in the situation that makes the superior performance possible. Look for ways to capitalize further on any uniqueness identified.

e. If the preceding three steps check out and your operating performance is worse than is described, consider the probability that you have not sufficiently developed an opportunity. The income characteristics described are usually attainable, but they are only opportunities. Good business management is needed to make them a reality. Check the marginal income data and ask yourself specific questions for the business on the three ways to improve income: (1) Can volume be increased? (2) Should fixed costs be reduced? (3) Can the marginal income (or prime margin) rate be increased by increasing prices, by reducing variable costs, or by improving mix?

Those are the only options. A general guide to probable answers is provided by the business strategy objectives summarized in step 3 for each group of busi-nesses.

You now have all the inputs required to determine your most important mar-ket share objectives:

1. You have your business defined in the form you believe best for you as the basis for running the business.
2. You have measurements of market share.
3. You have projections of future market growth rates.
4. You have identified and evaluated present and probable future com-petitors.
5. You have information on your own sales and income (or income contribu-tion) and estimates or projections for the future.
6. You have among your people good business intelligence on products, markets, competition, and trends to contribute to your determination of objectives.

In applying those inputs to the market share opportunities illustrated by the data in Table 12-1 and charted in Figure 12-3, the management group in Com-pany J established the following market share objectives:

Businesses 1, 2, and 4. Maintain market share. The objective to increase share for business 4 from second to first was concluded to be unrealistic. Without sig-nificant technical or market change an effort to increase share in a highly compe-titive, mature market would probably be unprofitable.

Business 3. Company J resources would be concentrated on this growth opportunity to achieve number 1 market position and the favorable economic performance projected to be attainable from that strong market position. This decision had not been made in earlier planning. It resulted from the work done in developing and dialoging the resource strategy matrix, marginal income data, and business intelligence.

Business 5. Maintain and optimize, since profit contribution is satisfactory. Otherwise, this business would be discontinued.

Business 6. Find a way to substantially increase share within two years by business program or—if viable—by a different definition of the business. Otherwise, discontinue the business and divert resources to other businesses or opportunities.

The thinking process done, the company then confronted the problem of significance. What out of all of that was most fundamental to the enterprise? As for a market share objective, three possibilities emerged as particularly fundamental to the continuing success of the enterprise.

1. Maintain market position in businesses 1, 2, and 4. Those three businesses accounted for most of the employment, three-fourths of the sales volume, and almost all of the income. That base of successful operations could be maintained only by maintaining market position in the major contributing businesses. To lose share would be costly. But to invest in gaining share would also be costly for those slower-growth businesses and would be less of an opportunity for the future than the same investment of resources in new opportunity would be.

2. Another major objective was found: a need to identify and support a major new high-growth opportunity. It was determined that business 3 could be that kind of opportunity, and resources were concentrated there to achieve market leadership and substantially increase income contribution.

3. In addition, an innovation objective was established to assure the continuing success of the company by identifying a further growth opportunity. That could be business 6 if a valid strategy approach could be found, or it could be a new and as yet unidentified opportunity. A development task force that included the president was named to find and formulate an additional high-growth, high-share business within five years time.

Market share objectives worked out in this way help us confirm our decisions on business definition (see Chapter 3, Defining the Identity). These objectives are also an important step in developing major business strategies (see Chapter 5, Penetration Versus Diversification). The product/market, penetration/diversification matrix described in those chapters can be used for each of the businesses identified and mapped in the resource strategy matrix to confirm decisions on business definition and to develop basic strategy.

To make resource strategy decisions effective an enterprise must be able to accommodate different approaches for different businesses. Strategies will be different, leadership will vary, organizational form will differ, and management control systems will be different for different businesses ... if the enterprise is to be successful in implementing its resource strategy. Figure 12-4 illustrates these differences. Thinking through the fundamentals summarized in Figure 12-4 we can see that:

- An enterprise must be big where it needs to be big, but it also must be small where it needs to be small. It must be both centralized and decentralized at the same time.

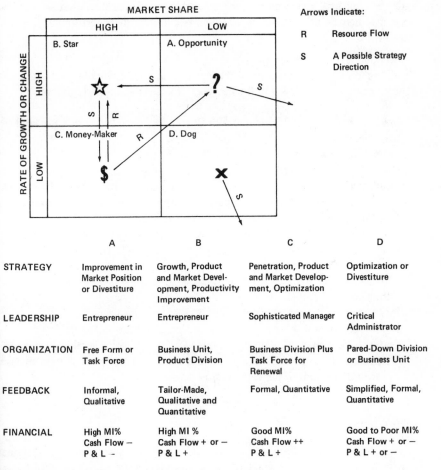

	A	B	C	D
STRATEGY	Improvement in Market Position or Divestiture	Growth, Product and Market Development, Productivity Improvement	Penetration, Product and Market Development, Optimization	Optimization or Divestiture
LEADERSHIP	Entrepreneur	Entrepreneur	Sophisticated Manager	Critical Administrator
ORGANIZATION	Free Form or Task Force	Business Unit, Product Division	Business Division Plus Task Force for Renewal	Pared-Down Division or Business Unit
FEEDBACK	Informal, Qualitative	Tailor-Made, Qualitative and Quantitative	Formal, Quantitative	Simplified, Formal, Quantitative
FINANCIAL	High MI% Cash Flow − P & L −	High MI % Cash Flow + or − P & L +	Good MI% Cash Flow ++ P & L +	Good to Poor MI% Cash Flow + or − P & L + or −

MI -- Marginal Income, MI% is gross sales minus variable costs divided by gross sales.

MATRIX FORMAT: Boston Consulting Group

Figure 12-4.

- Different styles of leadership must be accommodated.
- Differing organizational structures must thrive within any company large enough to establish the kind of resource strategy I have been describing.
- Management systems of reporting will be individually established for each business, and will differ substantially one from another.

An interesting observation is that successful, large companies do meet the requirements listed above. But sometimes their score is barely passing. And sometimes the requirement is met in "unofficial" ways. Knowing the requirements, and knowing how they can be met through the approaches described in this book may help companies to improve their resource strategy performance.

Market Share Objectives
From some of the companies and businesses that I have worked with, here are some examples of objectives in the key performance area of market share:

Increase market position in product line _____ from seventh to second in five years.

Achieve number 1 market position in PG machines by December 31.

Maintain number 1 market position in product line _____.

Concentrate development effort in market segment A to promote the growth of that segment and achieve 50 percent of that growth for the company.

Maintain or achieve a leading market share in the specific business areas and segments targeted for concentration of efforts and resources.

Concentrate target account sales on product lines U, S, and E to achieve market share objectives.

Increase market position from number 3 to number 2 in area 2 and from number 6 to number 4 in area 3 this year.

Increase market share to achieve sales of $_____ this year.

Regain lost market share in product line _____ by the end of the year.

Concentrate resources on market segment _____ to achieve sales this year of _____ pounds, thereby increasing our market share from 18 percent last year to 25 percent in this rapidly growing segment.

Innovation

For product and technology innovation the concepts and techniques of technological forecasting (TF) can be of immense help. TF helps us to understand and to apply in our businesses the process of technical innovation and provides us with techniques for measuring, monitoring, and forecasting technological change. A brief introduction to TF, and literature references, is provided in Chapter 9.

But the key performance area of innovation is concerned with more than new products; it is concerned with all areas of creative response to future change from the short-range "practical" change of the next one to five years to the longer-range "strategic" change that may be measured in decades. In each case the question is what, most fundamentally, we must do now so that we will be successfully applying the innovation by time X in the future. The scope for profitable innovation is unlimited; it includes:

Products	Performance reporting
Materials handling	Corporate structure
Manufacturing methods	Ownership
Measurement	Cash management
Standards	Customer relations
Reporting	Packaging
Process technology	Production scheduling
Services	Logistics
Systems	Advertising and promotion
Distribution	Employee education
Organization	Asset management
Communications	Product line management
Selling	Sales planning
Multinational operations	Government relations
Accounting systems	Environmental planning
Economics	Recruiting
Job enrichment	Team building
Management by objectives	

In short, every area of work and every arena of achievement offers opportunity for innovation. Some innovation objectives will also show up under another key performance area objective, such as an innovation in productivity. Change demands innovation as a requirement for our survival. In the midst of the discontinuous change around us, innovation becomes so important that it must become the orientation for all the talent of the enterprise if we are to find a successful pathway into the future.

Innovation is the kind of thing that everyone believes in but hardly anyone seems to want when it comes right down to cases. Innovation changes what we already know and are comfortable with. Organization constraints, especially in the more authoritative, bureaucratic, hierarchical structures, sharply limit innovation from within. Only an open, supportive, participative management will actively encourage innovation. Much is written about the need for an innovative climate. But creating such a climate is as hard and as easy as creating the participative management style described in Chapter 8. In such a climate the organization will find new ways and will support the search. Innovation does not come from wanting it; it comes only from a climate of working together that values innovation.

Another approach to specifically targeted innovation is to develop work groups that are separated from the operating culture of the enterprise to concentrate on identified areas of innovation. Such work groups can be established as part- or full-time assignments. They should be temporary rather than permanent or continuing. They should find their own way toward their own objectives and be limited only by whatever resources and time have been made available to them for their work. Four months, six months, a year or more might be provided; expenditures up to a certain maximum; objective: to formulate and develop the innovation. That approach has been used with great success by such companies as 3M and Xerox for new product development and commercialization. It can also be used for other areas of innovation.

To arrive at possible innovation objectives for an enterprise or a unit, the starting point, as for all of the key performance areas, is the concept of mission: what we are, what we intend to become, how we intend to get there. Dialog then confronts the question, "To realize our mission, what innovations requiring action now are most important to us?"

One important area of innovation may be identified from the resource strategy matrix used for examining market share objectives. If we find an unsatisfactory mix of businesses, there may be a very fundamental need for an innovative solution to the business mix problem. That was the case in the example used. For that business, one of the most important of the key performance area objectives was an innovation objective: to develop a new growth business opportunity for the company.

All areas of operations should be probed to find where innovation is needed. Dialog is the best method for the probing—not just in one group, but in many. Dialog searching for innovation can be conducted throughout the organization, always in consideration of the company mission statement and environmental change. All the possible areas of innovation can be examined. The examination will probably turn up one or two ideas that can be formulated into fundamental objectives for the enterprise. Certainly from such dialog there will derive ideas that will become objectives of components and of individuals in their areas of responsibility. So whether or not innovation fundamental to the enterprise will be found in such a search, the process of dialog will find inputs to an MBO style of management.

An often-cited restraint to innovation is the not-invented-here (NIH) syndrome. Research will develop little enthusiasm for someone else's invention. An idea from corporate planning may not be welcomed by operations. Market research findings may not be accepted by product management. A competitor's product change may be dismissed lightly by product engineering. The NIH factor is a common explanation of unconsummated change. It so clearly explains the failure in performance that it appears obviously to be the cause. But in that conclusion we may be the victims of a self-fulfilling assumption. We assume that people will be reluctant to accept ideas invented elsewhere; we organize our work on that assumption; and what do you know, they don't accept them.

We need to open our thinking and our ways of acting to new concepts of motivating and managing change as reviewed in Chapter 9. We can then focus on innovation, which is an organizational achievement, instead of on ideas. Ideas, both those invented here and those invented elsewhere, are inputs to organizational achievement. The NIH problem is solved by defining the innovation as the achievement. The innovation is what is aimed for, what is important, what is valued. The best ideas will be needed, whatever their source. All sources will be searched to find the way to make the innovation successful. Inventions and ideas may come from any of the sources. But only here, in our organization, can the innovation be created if it is to be our achievement. Like the process of hierarchical change described in Chapter 1, the NIH problem is resolved by integration at a new and higher level. NIH is a symptom of organizational old age and rigidity, resistance to change. It is a symptom not found in the organization that is continually renewed and continually motivated by a meaningful mission.

Examples of objectives in the key performance area of innovation are:

Introduce _____ equipment by July 19____.

By internal development or by acquisition commercialize by 19___ a new venture that will enable the company to achieve a leading position in a new growth segment of the plastics industry.

Diversify into significant new business opportunities depending for success more on mental than on capital resources.

Establish a target account selling program.

Initiate an export marketing program to country markets B, C, and D to achieve a sales volume of $_____ in two years time.

In Business R, discontinue the present annual financial budget plan and operate under an MBO achievement plan.

Productivity

Productivity is a key performance area of critical importance for business success. It is shown great respect and high esteem. But the recognition is more rhetorical than practical, for few firms today adequately develop their potential for productivity improvement. Although the individual firm is much concerned about outputs at the level of jobs and machines, it has little concept of productivity change over time for the company, for the significant aggregates within the company, and often for the job level as well. Two traditional views have perhaps obscured our understanding of the need for continuing productivity improvement within the firm: (1) concentration on production as the measurement without at the same time realizing that whatever the level of production, productivity—the output in relation to inputs—must steadily improve over time; (2) concentration on simplification and specialization as the route to increasing output without adequately taking into account the resources available to us in the man-hours of work to increase both production and productivity. (See Chapter 8, "Motivation.")

So while production certainly is important, we will not continue to produce successfully if we do not, while we are producing, constantly improve our productivity. Productivity improvement provides a route for both organizational and personal achievement. It is not a speed-up or working harder—it is working smarter by developing and applying knowledge to the materials and capital we work with, in all areas of business operations, not just on the factory floor.

Productivity is the relationship of output to the inputs required to product it. Changes in productivity measure changes in the efficiency with which inputs are converted to outputs. The achieving enterprise will show constantly improving productivity over time. It will set productivity objectives and regularly monitor productivity performance toward the achievement of those objectives.

Productivity goals and measures can be established for the work station, the department, the plant, the profit center, the total company. In the achieving enterprise productivity will be measured and monitored for each of these so that the appropriate decisions and actions can be taken at each level. Partial productivity measures will be followed at all levels. Total productivity measures will be followed from the plant level up. A few definitions . . .

$$Total\ Productivity = \frac{Total\ Output}{Total\ Inputs}$$

Total Output. Output expressed in physical terms, such as pounds, tons, gallons, cubic feet, square meters, yards, etc. When a mix of products is produced the commonly used measure is price adjusted to a selected base period price to keep all measurements on a constant basis.

Total Inputs. The physical measure of inputs used in the production of the total output. These are:

a. Labor—For labor the measure is man-hours. Since in many productivity calculations man-hour data is not available, or a mix of labor inputs in involved, total labor costs are often used, deflating the current period costs to the selected base period by an index of average hourly compensation. At the work station and department levels man-hours will normally be used. At the plant, profit center, and company levels labor costs deflated to the base period provides a convenient method of aggregation, and also provides for any shifting in mix among the kinds of labor used in the production of the outputs.

b. Materials—Here the measure is the quantity of materials and purchased services used in the production of the outputs. Since a number of different materials are typically used, the cost of materials and services used—the "intermediate inputs"—provides a suitable method of aggregation, with costs adjusted to base period costs.

c. Energy—Energy is a materials cost but because of its importance in many companies I find it useful to make a separate calculation for energy productivity.

d. Capital—Here the measure is the sum of the cost of capital used plus capital consumed in the production of the outputs. Included will be interest charges on capital employed, depreciation, depletion, and amortization. As for other inputs, all capital valuations will be adjusted to base period values.

Our total factor productivity equation can now be seen as:

$$P = \frac{O}{L + M + E + K}$$

Where: O = Output
L = Labor input
M = Materials input
E = Energy input
K = Capital input
P = Productivity

Output and inputs will be measured by base period valuations. Output will be measured as:

$$O = {}^{n}\Sigma Q_x P_O$$

Where: Q_x = the quantities of the various products produced in the current period
P_O = base period prices

Similarly, all input factors will be expressed in base period costs, so that our formula becomes:

$$P = \frac{{}^{n}\Sigma Q_x P_O}{{}^{n}\Sigma L_x P_O + {}^{n}\Sigma M_x P_O + {}^{n}\Sigma E_x P_O + {}^{n}\Sigma K_x P_O}$$

Partial productivity measures may be calculated for each of the inputs, such as for labor inputs:

$$P = \frac{{}^{n}\Sigma Q_x P_O}{{}^{n}\Sigma L_x P_O}$$

Such partial measures are inadequate as productivity measures because of distortions arising from factor substitution: substitution of capital for labor, substitution of energy for labor (or vice versa), and other substitutions among factors. I recommend following all four of the above partial measures plus the overall total factor productivity. The following charts, Figure 12-5, show such calculations for a commodity chemical plant. In this study 1972 was selected for the base year. To show changes and trends all productivity measures are indexed to the base year.

In Figure 12-5 total factor productivity is shown compared with total output. In this case there is a clear relationship. Among the factor inputs, relationship to output is most pronounced in the case of capital inputs—a reasonable expectation since capital inputs are difficult to vary with volume change, at least in the

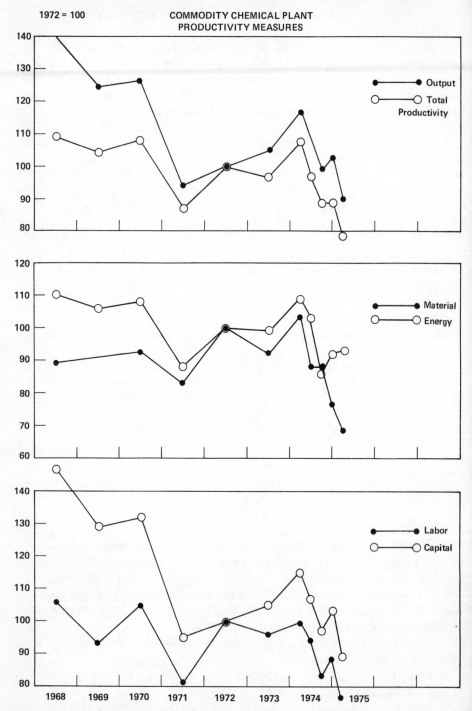

1972 = 100

COMMODITY CHEMICAL PLANT
PRODUCTIVITY MEASURES

Figure 12-5.

224

short run. Still the question must be posed on capital productivity trends, and an effort made toward improvement. In regard to materials, energy, and labor productivity, measures such as these can identify problem areas and focus attention on programs to achieve the essential productivity improvements. Productivity improvement does not just happen. It has to be made to happen. And the starting point must be an awareness of productivity achievement and trends.

In setting productivity objectives and monitoring performance, we should keep in mind two major aspects of productivity change. The first is the short range, which measures the efficiency of present technology and present levels of motivation and organization development. Both operating rates and efficiency of operations will be reflected in short range productivity measures, such as those shown in Figure 12-5. Longer range, productivity measures will be altered by changes in technology and changes in organizational competence, and such changes should become a part of the key performance area objectives of the achieving enterprise including:

Innovation based on new invention, new methods
R & D programs
Education and training
Motivational restructuring of work

The effect of such longer range productivity achievement is illustrated in Figure 12-6.

The new innovation may immediately improve productivity (D), may continue present trends (C), or may result in a temporary lowering of productivity (B),

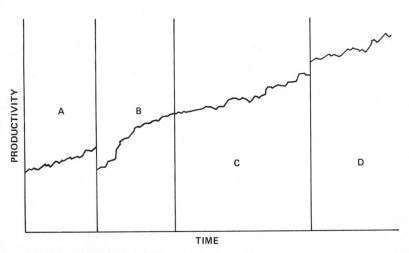

A, B, C, D - - Successive Innovations

Figure 12-6.

but the overall trend will be for improvement, as will the trend during the life-time of each innovation.

In developing productivity measures, many technical questions will arise. But these have been dealt with satisfactorily through approaches well documented in the literature. I recommend the following references for use in working through the details of a productivity measurement program:

John W. Kendrick, *Understanding Productivity*. Johns Hopkins University Press, 1977.

John W. Kendrick and Daniel Creamer, *Measuring Company Productivity*, Studies in Business Economics No. 89. The Conference Board. 1965.

Charles E. Craig and R. Clark Harris, "Total Productivity Measurement at the Firm Level," *Sloan Management Review*, Vol 14, 3, Spring 1973.

Douglas L. Cocks, "The Measurement of Total Factor Productivity for a Large U.S. Manufacturing Corporation," *Business Economics*, September 1974.

An organization established to develop and provide information and counsel on productivity measurement, and productivity improvement programs is:

American Productivity Center
1700 West Loop South, Suite 210
Houston, Texas 77027

The American Productivity Center is developing practical company-level methods for increasing productivity and bringing together both labor and management to solve productivity problems. It gathers and develops productivity measurement systems and provides this information and technical assistance in using the methods to interested firms. The Measurement Program covers a "family" of measures, ranging from simple single-input measures to more sophisticated approaches which relate the productivity of each resource element to total output, providing a total productivity measure. The most innovative system relates productivity to profitability, weights output to recognize quality differences, analyzes performance at various organizational levels, and isolates the effect of inflation on profits. The American Productivity Center also serves as a focal point for compiling information on productivity improvement approaches used in firms and organizations throughout the world and makes this experience available to American industry.

C. Jackson Grayson, chairman of the industry-supported American Productivity Center, writing in the March 25, 1978, issue of *National Journal* observed: "While many firms agree that productivity is important, most have no explicit program for improvement. Some give periodic pep speeches on productivity. Some initiate cost cutting drives. Most programs die as start-stop efforts. Firms need to create sustained, formal efforts toward productivity improvement with detailed goals, objectives, strategies, assignments, data gathering systems, monitoring, and follow up.

"Both labor and management gain from productivity improvement. Yet recent years have seen a growing adversary relationship detrimental to each. The relationship is often structured so that employees have the incentive *not* to cooperate—threatened job security, no gain sharing, poor management and poor working environment. Labor and management can work together on programs for improved productivity. Restraints can be reduced, and opportunities opened up. Some firms and industries are already doing this with productivity teams, quality of working life programs, and gain-sharing agreements.

"There are literally hundreds of ways to improve productivity, and new ones are created daily, in this country and abroad. The waste is that many firms know little about these techniques. Improvement occurs in another industry, in another country, and many firms have no way to share in the ideas. Ideas are sometimes not even transferred within the same firms. We need to have documented data on successes and failures, and to know who to contact for information and assistance.

"The American Productivity Center was brought into being one year ago to help industry and labor focus on these key areas that will make productivity improvement possible. We are all now paying the cost for having ignored productivity for too long."

One way to begin a productivity improvement program is to conduct a one-day lecture-discussion-dialog session of the individuals most concerned. The following objectives and agenda were used by one company for this kind of session:

OBJECTIVES

1. To: Define productivity
        Relate productivity to profitability
        Review causes of productivity change
        Study methods for productivity improvement
        Review techniques of productivity measurement
        Relate all of the above to company operations
2. To agree on a program for the development of productivity measures for:
   Division A
   Division B
   Division C
3. To develop an approach for monitoring productivity measures in these three divisions, and for separable business areas and components within each division

AGENDA

Opening remarks	Company President
Company situation	Internal expert
Measures currently used, and trends	
Division A	Division Manager
Division B	Division Manager
Division C	Division Manager
Critique	
A Short Course in Productivity	Outside expert
Problems and procedures in developing productivity measures	Dialog
Company experiences in productivity improvement	
Division A	Dialog
Division B	Dialog
Division C	Dialog
Plan of action	Discussion, led by internal expert

Productivity measures and productivity improvement is not something only for plant operations. All areas of the business must constantly and consistently improve productivity. They must steadily improve the ratio of outputs to inputs. In administrative functions the outputs may not be so clear as in the case of production. But they must become so. For in a firm's total factor productivity measures all inputs including administration go into the calculation. Functional and job outputs can be expressed in terms of objectives related to company mission. This becomes the starting point for productivity improvement in administrative departments, and for administrative jobs. I have used the worksheets illustrated in Figure 12-7 as a way of identifying and programming productivity improvement in administrative groups. The objectives and procedures for the use of these worksheets are as follows:

OBJECTIVES

1. To identify opportunity for productivity improvement in administrative departments
2. To develop productivity improvement programs

PROCEDURE

1. Use worksheet 1 to "brainstorm" possible areas for productivity improvement. List on easel pad.

228

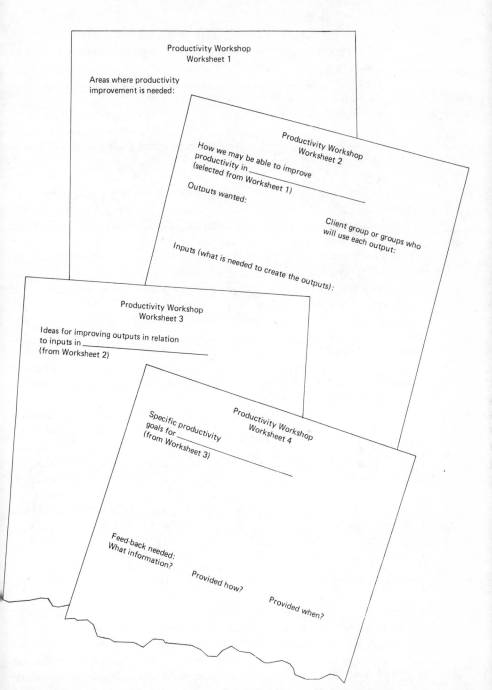

Productivity Workshop
Worksheet 1

Areas where productivity
improvement is needed:

Productivity Workshop
Worksheet 2

How we may be able to improve
productivity in _____
(selected from Worksheet 1)

Outputs wanted:

Client group or groups who
will use each output:

Inputs (what is needed to create the outputs):

Productivity Workshop
Worksheet 3

Ideas for improving outputs in relation
to inputs in _____
(from Worksheet 2)

Productivity Workshop
Worksheet 4

Specific productivity
goals for _____
(from Worksheet 3)

Feed-back needed:
What information?

Provided how?

Provided when?

Figure 12-7.

2. Select one area identified on Worksheet 1 and, using Worksheet 2:
   (a) Define the outputs from this area most important in contributing to Company mission achievement.
   (b) List the client group or groups that will use each of the outputs.
   (c) List the inputs used for creating the outputs.
3. Using Worksheet 3, dialog ideas for improving outputs in relation to inputs.
4. Using Worksheet 4, develop specific productivity goals and planned feedback reporting.

An excellent discipline for setting objectives and measuring productivity performance is provided by experience curve theory. The theory states very simply that the more we do something the better and more productive we can become in doing it. But not only can we become more productive, the typical experience is that we do become more productive at a constant rate in relation to our experience. The generalization of that phenomenon is seen in government data on productivity as measured by the total output of production in constant dollars in relation to the input of production man-hours.

In the United States the long-term trend for man-hour productivity improvement over the years 1948 to 1968 was 3.25 percent per year. Recent history has been as listed in Table 12-3.

Table 12-3. Output Per Man-Hour (Productivity) Change in Private Business in the United States

Year	Productivity Change, %	Year	Productivity Change, %
1966	3.2	1973	1.9
1967	2.3	1974	−2.8
1968	3.3	1975	2.0
1969	0.3	1976	3.7
1970	0.7	1977	1.8
1971	3.2	1978	1.0
1972	2.9		

Source: U.S. Bureau of Labor Statistics

There is, typically, significant short-run variation in the productivity rate change accounted for by the business cycle. As the economy slows and moves into recession, output slows or declines more rapidly than production man-hours or other factor inputs, and with recovery from recession output increases more rapidly than production man-hours or other factor inputs. Both capacity utilization and management decision response to business cycle change are involved in those short-run variations. The recession and recovery periods 1969-1971 and 1973-1974 illustrate that effect on output per man-hour (see Table 12-3.)

Productivity trends in the United States indicate a significant structural-type of change. From Table 12-3 it can be seen that only in our two best years since 1966 have we equalled the 3.259 average productivity improvement achieved during the twenty years 1948-1968. Some fundamental, structural kind of change developed in the mid-1960s reducing the rate of productivity improvement. Related effects included inflation, unemployment, falling profits, declining capital formation, and sluggish gains in real wages. In an important competitive measure, U.S. performance in productivity was poor in relation to other countries' performance. Figure 12-8 shows average productivity improvement for twelve industrialized countries for the period 1966 to 1976.

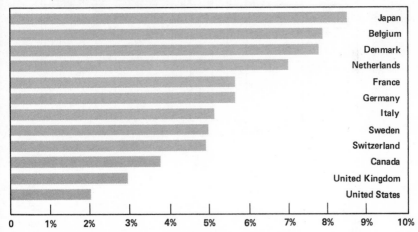

INTERNATIONAL COMPARISONS PRODUCTIVITY GROWTH—1966-1976
(OUTPUT PER MAN-HOUR)

Figure 12-8. International comparisons productivity growth—1966-1976 (output per man-hour)

Source: U.S. Department of Labor, Bureau of Labor Statistics.

We see the operation of experience curve theory in price behavior. With accumulating experience, as a product progresses along its growth curve, prices in constant dollars decline. Successful producers remain profitable, so it is reasonable to expect that there has also been declining cost as measured in constant dollars. There is now a considerable support for that hypothesized nature of cost behavior, and several firms have successfully used the concepts for planning future costs and present business strategy.[2] The implications of experience curve theory for corporate strategy also relate to growth curve concepts and market share, an interrelationship that has been investigated and reported by The Boston Consulting Group and applied in strategy formulation by many companies.

[2]Winifred B. Hirschmann, "Profit From the Learning Curve," *Harvard Business Review,* January-February 1964, pp. 125-139.

From its investigations, The Boston Consulting Group has concluded: "Costs appear to go down on value added at about 20 to 30% every time total product experience doubles for the industry as a whole, as well as for individual producers."[3] That relationship of cost to experience for a constant rate of growth over time is illustrated in Figure 12-9.

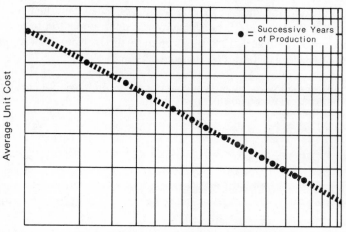

Year	Production (10% Growth)	Accumulated Experience	Percent Increase in Total Experience
1	1	1.00	
2	1.10	2.10	110.1%
3	1.21	3.31	57.6
4	1.33	4.64	40.2
5	1.46	6.11	31.5
6	1.61	7.81	26.4
7	1.77	9.58	22.7
8	1.95	11.53	20.4
9	2.14	13.67	18.6
10	2.35	16.02	17.2
11	2.59	18.61	16.2
12	2.85	21.46	15.3
13	3.14	24.60	14.6
14	3.45	28.05	14.0
15	3.80	31.85	13.5% (will approach 10%)

Figure 12-9. The effect of constant rate of growth in physical volume on rate of increase in accumulated experience.

Source: The Boston Consulting Group, Inc., *Perspectives on Experience,* 1970, p. 16.

The Boston Consulting Group has also studied industry prices over time and related price history to costs. It concluded: "Prices follow the same pattern as

[3] *Perspective on Experience,* 1970, p. 12.

costs if the relationship between competitors is stable. If they don't, the relationship between competitors becomes increasingly unstable."[4] Those relationships of industry price costs are illustrated in Figures 12-10 and 12-11.

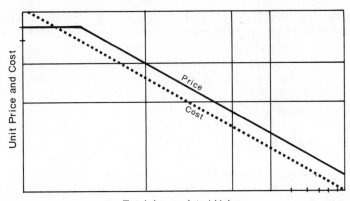

Figure 12-10. A typical stable pattern of industry prices and costs.

Source: The Boston Consulting Group, Inc., *Perspectives on Experience,* 1970, p. 19.

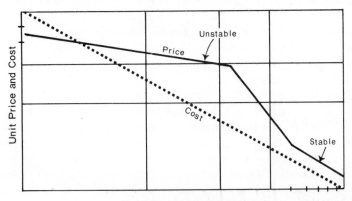

Figure 12-11. A typical unstable pattern of industry prices and costs.

Source: The Boston Consulting Group, Inc., *Perspectives on Experience,* 1970, p. 21.

Experience curve principles should be an input to strategy planning of resource allocation and to the determination of productivity objectives. Those principles provide a guide for areas of potential opportunity and a yardstick for

---

[4]Ibid., p. 19.

evaluating cost reduction achievement. Such a yardstick is a necessity; for while industry costs may behave as described by The Boston Consulting Group, such cost reductions may or may not actually be achieved by the individual company. The improvement in productivity is not an automatic result of accumulating experience; it is only a possible result. If a company does not have the internal discipline to achieve reductions, its costs may well drift upward. For the individual firm, the possibility for achieving experience curve cost reductions lies in the knowledge that reductions are possible and the organization's commitment to achieve them. Since all cost calculations must be expressed in constant dollars, and since high rates of inflation have persisted over a number of years, it is seldom clear whether or not experience curve cost reductions—or experience curve price reductions—have been achieved. As with all productivity measures we have to find ways of adjusting dollar data to a constant basis so that we are looking at what is real and undistorted by monetary change.

But experience curve theory is not the whole story. Or, stated somewhat differently, it may apply differently to primary aluminum, publishing, and ladies' fashions. Product differentiation, technology change, new products and styles or fashions of products, systems of services, and environmental change as well as physical products go into the equation. So we will have to think of and apply experience curve concepts not only to specific products but to broader concepts of products and to company operations as well. A company skilled in new product development, such as 3M, can acquire a competitive cost advantage in the process of developing and commercializing innovation. A company skilled in systems technology, such as the General Electric Aerospace Business Group, may have a competitive cost advantage in applying that technology to a new and different field of human need.

Needs change; opportunity changes; and the successful firm will not only do better what it has already done but will also do new things. Products with which it has achieved market leadership and superior exeprience curve costs may be phased out by replacements serving the need better or by products serving new needs that have become prevailing. A low-cost position in steam locomotives or vacuum tubes is not today a foundation for commercial success. Fashion value (swimsuits, Hula-Hoops) or service value (24-hour food store, contract maintenance) may be considerations as important as cost. All that may be involved in value *from the customer's point of view* can be summarized in an overall concept of economic productivity. How are we satisfying our customers, as measured by the ratio of economic inputs to economic outputs—costs to the firm for materials, energy, capital, and employees, in relation to what our customers pay us for the products and services we provide? Productivity measured in physical units is not enough. We also need some guiding concepts on the total economic productivity of the enterprise. And we must relate that concept not only to historical transactions and accounting records but also to probabilities for the future. How?

We can begin by looking at the accounting record of all input factors to the enterprise and all major outputs. I find it useful to do so by marginal income accounts:

INPUTS

Numbers of employees
Wages, salaries, and employment costs
Raw materials used
Other variable costs
Fixed assets at replacement cost
Working capital
Fixed costs

OUTPUTS

Sales
Value added
Production
In-process and finished goods inventory
Operating income

Other classifications of inputs and outputs may be used. The classifications are aggregated for simplicity, but even so they are useful for indicating the situation and trends. Much greater specificity is possible, but I find it wise to begin with the more general and work toward the more specific as may be indicated. We must find the fundamentals in shape before we can measure them in detail. The fundamentals are what we very much need to find; for then we will be able to make economic productivity an important theme in our objectives and our reporting systems, whereas it is now almost completely ignored.

So let's begin with the simplified listing of inputs and outputs by marginal income accounts. From the accounting record we can get annual data for each of the accounts over the past several years—a minimum of five if possible. At this point let's not be concerned with questions of historical or future valuation or changes in price level. We'll use what is most readily available: data in current dollars. Once the data are assembled, we consider the first year for which we have data—or some selected year—as 100 and convert all other years to an index number. We plot the indices on charts of the same scale and make transparencies of them. Now we superimpose the charts in pairs and groups and examine the changing relations of inputs and outputs.

Shown in Figure 12-12 are illustrations of charts prepared in that way. The charts were first developed in 1971 as a part of the company's efforts to cope

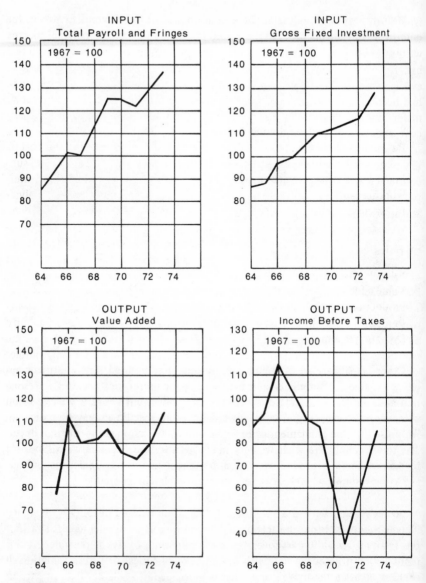

Figure 12-12. Input-output charts.

with its problem of seriously declining profitability. Through an examination of the trends of the major inputs and outputs, the problem was clearly defined. The largest dollar cost input to the business was raw materials. Raw materials tracked a little favorably in relation to production, which suggested some combination of improved productivity for that factor input and improved mix, or relatively favorable raw materials costs. In 1970 raw material use was down 7.9 percent from 1967, the base year, whereas production was down 5.7 percent. Except for raw materials, however, all other inputs had trended upward. In 1970, compared with the base year 1967, number of employees was up 8.1 percent, payroll and benefits were up 25.7 percent, gross fixed investment was up 11.6 percent, and average working capital was up 26.2 percent. On the output side, however, there had been no growth and 1970 was actually lower than the base year 1967 for all major outputs. Production was down 5.7 percent, total sales were down 1.1 percent, and value added was down 4.7 percent.

Value added—the difference between the value of shipments and the cost of raw materials, supplies, parts, fuel, energy, goods purchased for resale, and subcontracted work—is the best measure of the economic value of what the enterprise does. Data are easily obtained; they are essential to input-output analysis and an understanding of the economics of the firm.

Why does this essential measure continue to escape the scrutiny of businessmen? If we don't clearly understand our economic outputs and their trends and changes in trends, we might not notice when our economic inputs are getting out of balance. That is exactly what had happened in the company whose performance is charted in Figure 12-12.

With inputs up and outputs down, there had to be a balancing out somewhere, and the balancing came out of profitability. To restore profitability would require reducing inputs or increasing outputs or some combination of the two. Since 1970 was a recession year, there was prospect of an increase in sales and value-added output. But rising costs were continuing to pressure inputs upward. Here was a very complex but very typical business problem. Dialog among management and professional employees with frank and open communication among all employees resulted in a number of important action programs, including:

Price increases.
Plant productivity improvement.
Target market, target account, and target product sales programs.
Job enrichment.
A better methods program for cost reduction.
Product line audit to simplify and standardize.
Reporting operations by marginal income accounts as an aid to decision making (see Chapter 11).
Inventory reduction.
Improvement in collections.
Reduction in number of employees.
A diversification project.

It is interesting to note that if the work done in the company in 1971 and 1972 after the income problem showed up in the financial reports had been done in 1967 to 1969, the problem could have been seen developing. Then actions to cope with it could have been taken two to three years earlier. The achieving enterprise manages ahead and avoids or minimizes crisis recovery situations. The concepts recommended in this book provide a way for that kind of managing ahead. The reporting system needed for it is described in Chapter 13.

An examination of input-output charts and a dialog among knowledgeable people on what is happening and possible reasons for it will provide valuable insight into the economic productivity of the enterprise and the developing trends. From the examination and from the dialog, certain measures and certain relations will emerge as more significant and more useful than others. Some measures that were selected from the study illustrated in Figure 12-12 are listed in Table 12-3.

Table 12-3.

Input	Output	Measurement	Reporting Method
Total employment costs	Total sales	Sales per dollar of payroll and benefit costs	Monthly and 12-month moving average
Number of employees	Value added	Value added per employee	Monthly and 12-month moving total
Total employment costs	Value added	Value added per dollar of payroll and benefit costs	Monthly and 12-month moving average
Working capital	Total sales	Ratio of sales to working capital	Monthly and 3-month moving average
Fixed costs	Value added	Value added per dollar of fixed costs	Monthly and 12-month moving average
Costs of raw materials	Production at selling price	Ratio of raw materials to production	Monthly and 3-month moving average
Total direct labor costs	Production at selling price	Ratio of direct labor to production	Monthly and 3-month moving average

In addition to those specific measures, the index charts also were continued. In Figure 12-12 data through 1973 are shown.

The use of annual accounting data for investigating economic productivity is only a first screening approach, but it will provide a general picture of the developing trends that affect productiveness measured in economic terms rather than physical units. The most significant measurements once identified can then be reported on a regular, monthly basis in a way that will identify change, trends, and changes in trends. Annual data are not of much help. Regular, frequent feedback is needed. Reports and measures can be worked out in great detail. I prefer to adhere to fundamentals and keep them simple. We can start with monthly data from the accounting record and follow each measurement month by month in some kind of time series format. Mathematical time series analysis may be appropriate for some. Simple charting techniques such as 3-month (or other period) moving averages, 12-month moving totals, and trends of variance from data of an earlier period can be useful. I prefer the charting methods. They are easy to use, and the charts will be readily understood. They provide a very helpful focus for decision-making dialog.

The kind of approach I have outlined here, in which we are looking for an understanding of the economic productivity of the enterprise, can indeed help us confront real problems and real opportunities that we may never have seen or understood before. And when we have found relationships and measurements especially meaningful for us and our present situation, we may also have found one or more fundamental objectives essential to the future success of the enterprise. Without a dialog on productivity we probably would not have found them.

The more conventional measure of productivity—physical units of output in relation to direct labor, machine-hours, or other factor inputs—are also of major importance. Competitive levels of performance or experience curve theory can guide us to the establishment of productivity goals for manufacturing that are critically important to our continuing and future success. Experience curve theory tells us what kind of productivity improvements we should be able to achieve, and market share gives us a perspective on potential competitive costs. But we still need motivation and discipline to achieve such cost objectives. If we have been lax, we have probably floated off well above the demanding experience curve opportunity for continuing cost reduction. When that is found to be the situation for any products with which we hold strong market position, specific productivity improvement objectives for production can be of fundamental importance. Examples of objectives in the key performance area of productivity are:

Achieve and maintain unsurpassed competitive economics in all targeted business areas.

Target and achieve experience curve productivity improvements and thereby achieve favorable competitive costs in targeted business area segments.

Relate experience curve economics to pricing and develop pricing strategies to optimize income over time.

Establish a reporting system to report key productivity measurements on a trend basis.

Maintain fixed costs within 27 to 28 percent of net sales this year.

Achieve a ratio of net sales to net worth of three times.

Increase sales volume per salesman to $_____ through a target account selling program.

Physical and Financial Resources

In the key performance area of physical and financial resources we cope with asset management and capital budgeting problems. As in all the key performance areas, our search for fundamentals begins with the company's statement of mission. Our major questions will be:

1. How do our present physical resources relate to our mission? What do we have that we will not need? What that is new will we need? On what kind of time scale?
2. What are the alternatives for acquiring the needed new resources (purchase, lease, merger, financing, and so on)?
3. What is the availability of funds?
4. What is the best programming of the new resources?
5. What is most important to the achievement of our mission?

Capital-budgeting approaches and techniques are well known to all top managements. They are a major consumer of executive time and probably most often in disproportion, so that key performance areas of equal or greater importance suffer from comparative neglect. When that is so, the principles advocated in this book can help restore a more equitable balance by (1) emphasizing the importance of the six other key performance areas and (2) suggesting approaches to simplifying the capital-budgeting problem. Several such simplifications can be very helpful.

1. Relate the capital-budgeting process first of all to the company's statement of mission and to the supporting mission statements of divisions and units within the company. The mission provides us direction, and the major problem of capital budgeting is that it often starts without direction except for an accounting profitability objective such as a company standard for discounted cash flow rate of return. There is no direction to being in business to make money; every road is then the right road and the organization will be running down all of them. That is a poor way to find opportunity, a fact that will probably show up later in the operating statements.

The way to find opportunity is to develop a concept of mission—what we are, what we intend to become, and how we intend to get there. Dialog throughout the enterprise will identify specific opportunities from the statement of mission. New opportunities will be found as the dialog process continues. The strategy is to identify opportunity through mission and then pursue the opportunity through the capital-budgeting process. The capital-budgeting process itself should not be used as a hunting ground for opportunity. Such an approach could only lead to confusion, poor performance, poor morale in operations, and an almost impossible capital-budgeting job.

It is quite possible to have a company statement of mission and still use the capital-budgeting process as a hunting ground for opportunity rather than a part of the planning to carry out the mission. Such a mission is vestigial. We have it but we don't use it. I once discussed with a company president his capital-budgeting problem. He expected he would have about $10 million of investment funds available in the coming budget year, and he had requests from his operating managers for over $50 million. What should have priority? His company did have its counterpart of a mission statement. We looked at the mission in comparison with the capital requests, and in two hours time we could see how the requests and the availability could be brought together. Many requests were inconsistent with the mission; some others could be changed. Some could be phased differently over time. Examining the problem from a mission point of view made it manageable. That work, to be effective and to provide learning experience for all concerned, would have to be done through dialog and not by the decision of top management alone.

2. Translate accounting data that are customarily used in the capital-budgeting process into managerial economics terms. Consider opportunity costs and replacement or future valuation rather than historic. Capital-budgeting decisions are decisions for the future, and the most helpful inputs to wise decisions will be inputs by the measurement of economics. We will not have the security of precision, but the future is an approximation, change, and uncertainty. Let's deal with it on its own terms. Managerial economics can help us do that (see Chapters 10 and 11) by translating the precision of accounting to approximations more relative to our business future.

3. Carry out the capital-budgeting process through a program of dialog among all the people in the organizations whose work will be affected. That will be a lot of people, but we are talking about a process that goes on at all levels among many individuals and groups. The dialog will not be a lot of informational meetings. Dialog is work done by man and manager, man and work group. And with our point of view of capital budgeting implementing mission, that dialog contributes to other areas of operations as well. It becomes a part of a participative, MBO way of structuring work.

Relating the capital-budgeting problem to the company's statement of mission and resolving the problems through dialog can lead to such objectives as the following in the key performance area of physical and financial resources:

Concentrate expansion and diversification investment in plant location X so that by 19___ we will have a major integrated facility at that location.

Acquire a company in business U that in combination with our resources can earn a leading market share in that growth business area.

Sell business T when conditions are most favorable over next four-year period.

Construct new facility H to be on-stream by April 19___.

Install new effluent control system in all process Y operations by December.

Increase credit lines by $12 million at best timing prior to July.

Profitability

The key performance area of profitability is discussed in Chapters 10 and 11; it is too important and complex to be dealt with briefly. I have given it two chapters; perhaps it requires a book. It also requires learning—a very stimulating process that we now find must continue and even increase throughout a lifetime. The concepts described in Chapters 10 and 11, when dialoged and applied within the enterprise, will develop the most significant and the most appropriate objectives for the enterprise in the key performance area of profitability. The following are some examples of profitability objectives that have been developed in that way:

Reduce costs of materials and subcontracted assemblies by 4 percent this year. [Objective for a low-marginal-income, materials-intensive business.]

Price new formulations in business area G to upgrade marginal income rate.

Discontinue low-market-share, low-growth, low-marginal-income lines H, M, and AK and redeploy company assets to new opportunities R and T.

Increase average, realized prices 5 percent in product line C this year.

Increase marginal income rate from 36.7 to 40.0 percent by June.

Improve mix through programmed expense of $100,000 to increase sales of product 0 from $3.6 million to $4.2 million by September.

Achieve operating income of $7.6 million this year.

Reduce breakeven from $314,000 to $280,000 per month by May 1.

Motivation and Organization Development

The assets that we show on our balance sheet are capital assets, but the greatest asset of any business enterprise is its people. Business organizations concentrate great effort on making their capital assets productive. They are likely to leave people assets unmeasured, unmotivated, and underutilized. Yet everything the business is begins with people. J.-J. Servan-Schreiber stated it well in his book, *The American Challenge:*

> The wealth we seek does not lie in the earth or in numbers of men or in machines, but in the human spirit. And particularly in the ability of men to think and create. The training, development and exploitation of human intelligence—these are the real resources, and there are no others.[5]

Most of us agree with the theme of his statement, but few of us act that way in our business organizations.

[5] New York: Atheneum, 1968.

Even if we start with the economics, we might change our minds on what assets are most important. Here are data from a medium-size manufacturing company:

Annual interest cost of fixed assets at original cost	$4.0 million
Annual interest cost of fixed assets at replacement cost	6.3
Annual interest cost of working capital	0.9
Annual total payroll cost	15.7

For that business we estimated the present value of future payroll costs for present employees, assuming retirement at age 65 and 5 percent annual increase in payroll costs per person and discounting future payments to present value by a 7 percent interest rate. The present value worked out to be $268 million. That is one economic measure of input cost commitment to the most important asset of the enterprise, its people. When we talk about our businesses, we say that people are their greatest assets. If we were to make capital calculations of them, we would find our people assets to be the greatest also in terms of economic costs. But in daily operations we are likely to concentrate first on fixed asset management and the trend of costs and income. Why not on people asset development and the trend of talent and value added?

Several proposals have been developed for putting people on the balance sheet.[6] Such a valuation and management approach might be useful in calling attention to the importance of human assets. But it's not the capitalization of people assets that's important. What is important is the creativity and the output of the people assets as measured by achievement. People are the value-adding element in our enterprise, and value adding is where the emphasis belongs. Rensis Likert, in his work on management systems, recommends a behavior approach for human asset accounting[7] that measures the motivational variables and relates them to productivity and profitability.

People—all people—are the primary resource in any enterprise, but the resource can be both unrecognized and underutilized. People don't show up on the balance sheet—and increasingly they don't show up for work either. Perhaps we are not performing well enough in the key performance area of motivation and organization development.

People are the resource that uses natural and physical and financial resources

[6] James S. Hekimian and Curtis S. Jones, "Put People on Your Balance Sheet," *Harvard Business Review*, January-February 1967.

[7] *The Human Organization: Its Management and Value* (New York: McGraw-Hill, 1967), p. 146.

to create value. Employees are the action, the creation, the achievement. They require a very wise employment. The key performance areas of people performance, development, and attitude are so central to the success of the enterprise that two chapters of this book are written specifically on the subjects—8 and 9. A review of those chapters will provide perspective and guidelines. Examples of objectives in the key performance area of motivation and organization development are:

Initiate for product managers a compensation plan that relates incentive compensation directly to achievement.

Establish informational, dialog meetings of top management and all employees interested in participating.

Make available to all managers and professional employees at least one training or development session this year.

Establish a PMBO way of working throughout the three top management levels over the next 15-month period.

Set up temporary task forces outside the normal organization structure and constraints to cope with important problems and opportunities.

Over the next three months develop definitions of management jobs in terms of outputs and client groups to replace the present definition in terms of responsibility and function.

Conduct workshops, using outside professional help, on career development and motivation.

Bring new ideas, techniques, and concepts into the company through employment of consultants in selected problem areas, lectures and workshops with outside experts, sending managers to university-run management and professional courses, offering management awards for innovation, and bringing highly competent people into the company at management and professional levels.

Develop and apply job enrichment concepts to the organization of work in department G.

Conduct technical training programs as a route to job upgrading and promotion.

Conduct an employee attitude survey, analyze the feedback, and take action as indicated.

Schedule regular walk-through tours, with dialog.

Publish a company newspaper to report information of interest or concern to employees.

Introduce short-segment scheduling in plant T with direct feedback to employees.

Conduct training sessions in team building for supervisory personnel.

Public and Environmental Responsibility

The business enterprise is a part of, rather than separate from, the economic-social-natural environment in which it operates. Its continued viability will depend on its inputs from and outputs to all segments of that environment. Some of the segments are dealt with specifically in the discussion of the other six key performance areas. Those that are not can be dealt with under the broad key performance area of public and environmental responsibility. Here can be formulated the corporate citizenship responsibilities to our nation and all its people, to the communities in which we work, to public sector priorities, to the development of legislation and its implementing procedures, to our biosphere, and, in our overseas operations, to our host countries.

The businessman, in considering public responsibility, may often feel very much in an adversary role. Matters that are forced on his awareness by public policy usually are difficult to deal with, restrict his freedom of action, and cost money. Problems are what he has enough of already. And here come more. To the ramparts!

The adversary role is important. For in the forging of public policy, differing and conflicting views bring perspective more than pressure to the search for direction. Contention can lead more to creation than to crisis. It is only necessary that all who are contending listen as thoughtfully as they contend. In the process, then, we can all, collectively, find our way.

If he works with both an open ear and an open mouth, the businessman will become involved in a process in which he will be protagonist as well as adversary in founding constructive public policy. His interest can be as real as any other's; his contribution as substantial. And in his participation he may find new opportunity even more often than he finds new constraint.

Some typical examples of objectives in the key performance area of public responsibility are:

Cooperate with authorities to develop effective and sound pollution control regulations.

Increase minority group employment by _____ in plant B.

Establish and maintain a companywide environmental procedure to avoid or control activities that might adversely affect the environment.

Participate with government in community development programs.

Conduct operations to meet the company's responsibilities to the general public and the communities in which it operates and the requirements of applicable law.

Administer multinational operations to respect the national interests and characteristics of each operating unit.

13

Achievement Reporting— A New Management System

Look at the reporting system within any business organization and you will learn very quickly what is officially important. The examination should begin with the reports prepared regularly, usually monthly, for the highest management levels. They will be management or operating reports prepared by top management for the board of directors and similar reports prepared by divisional or subsidiary managements for company top management. Such an examination will usually show the following measurements to be the most important: sales, cost of sales, expenses by major category, net income, capital appropriations, cash flow, number of employees, fixed and working capital, equity, and, for all of them, variances from budget and from year-ago performance and selected ratios of one to another.

Monthly Control Reports
Monthly control reports for a component profit center operation might include such schedules as the following:

Operating highlights: current month versus plan and year ago.
Outlook for the quarter and year versus plan and year ago.
Income statement for the month and year to date versus plan and year ago.
Income statement by quarters: actual to date and forecast for remaining quarters and for total year versus plan and year ago.
Sales and income by product group: month and year to date versus plan and year ago.
Sales and income by product group projected for current quarter and year versus plan and year ago.
Sales, general, and administrative expenses by area and department: month, year to date, and forecast for the year versus plan and year ago.

Manpower by plant, area, and department: current month and forecast for year end versus plan and year ago.

Month and year to date: significant variances from plan in price, volume, costs, and mix by product group and major product.

Funds flow (income and uses): year to date and forecast for year versus plan.

Capital appropriations and expenditures: year to date and forecast for the year versus plan.

Balance sheet: this month, last month, and final month of preceding fiscal year.

Investment in noncash working capital: current month and forecast for year end versus plan and year ago.

A monthly control report of that kind can include from 15 to 25 separate exhibits and require more than 50 pages. Management comments in such reports are predominantly on sales volume, income, costs or margins, and variances from plan and year ago. Most measurements are financial and the purpose evaluative rather than informative: "How good was performance?" rather than "Considering the results of performance, what actions should now be taken?"

If further levels of reporting are analyzed, the substantiating detail will be found to accumulate through successive consolidations to become the documents described in the preceding paragraphs. Data are expressed in financial terms to consolidate into, at the major operating levels, an income statement, balance sheet, and flow of funds. That is what is important. Not found in the typical reporting system, but vital to the success of the enterprise, are measurements of market position, economic profit as distinct from accounting profit, productivity, motivation, organizational competence, innovation, public responsibility, mission and changes in mission being considered, and all of the preceding in relation to environment.

The Reporting System

It would seem that the time has come to think more creatively about our reporting systems. Whatever we may say about ourselves on the public podium, our system of measurement and reporting describes us as we really are and prescribes the orientation for our future. Most company measurement and reporting systems are at variance with the reporting requirements of the approach recommended by this book. They are also, I believe, rather at variance with what most business organizations today believe themselves to be. How could such a situation develop?

The answer may be the normal, evolutionary specialization of a good budgetary control idea. In the 1950s the financial type of budgetary control system, as then practiced, was well suited to businesses in the environment of the time. The basic idea, simply stated, was to create a financial model of the business by months for the year ahead. Actual performance would then be compared with the budget model, and variances would be analyzed. It was all quite straightforward, and even for a large business it was easily within quite ordinary comprehension. And the concept was progressive and forward-looking, since the budget model was always constructed for the future period. Futurism was beginning to become a dimension of business. The financial model was one measure, but it was not the only measure used.

But along came the process of specialization, and the model became more complex. Then someone invented the computer, and very quickly the budget process deserted the worksheets of accountants for the memories of computers. Other measures atrophied as attention concentrated on the financial one. The model became still more complex and the measured dimensions still more numerous—by orders of magnitude. Variance analysis was no longer arithmetic that each manager could readily understand and even calculate himself. It became a business science understood by mathematicians but growing less and less related to operations. As the budgetary control system grew increasingly specialized, the business environment for which it had been created continued to change. A technically better and better control system grew less and less relevant. We are now at the point at which hierarchical change is needed.

When in the evolution of human institutions and their systems the specializing process brings a system to a divergence from its environment, problems accumulate. The problems are dealt with one by one as they arise, and the specializing process continues. But problems arise faster than solutions can be found. Finally, the unresolved problems become so overwhelming that they simply cannot be managed or dealt with in the conventional way. It is then that hierarchical change can occur. Instead of the problems being solved one by one within the context of the old system, a completely new way of resolving them is invented or created. All of them are integrated into a new framework at a new and simplified level that resolves them because, at the new level, they do not exist. We have then achieved, by innovation, a level of hierarchical growth that resolves, at once, all the accumulating problems and starts us off again on the evolutionary process from a new level of simplification.

One of the frontiers in business management today, it seems to me, lies in the area of reporting systems. When a business enterprise conceptualizes its present and undertakes to invent its future along lines such as those recommended in this book, a fundamental change in its reporting system becomes possible and even required. Financial reporting systems simply cannot serve a company operating in the new way; for it is achievement that is fundamental. The achievement will include the financial and also the other key performance areas on which the success of the enterprise depends. And we become quite disinterested in evaluative reports. We become very interested in feedback that gives us the progress of our achievement in terms that help us accomplish our goals.

Professor John Dearden of the Harvard Business School, a keen student of and wise counselor on financial measurement and control systems, has written extensively on the limitations of present financial measurements. He writes:

> For a profit budget system to provide adequate control, it must be possible to set a financial objective that will represent a *fair standard* against which to measure performance, and it must be possible to measure financially the accomplishments of a divisional manager during the period being evaluated. In other words, it must be possible to *measure output* in financial terms. *Neither of these conditions is met in most decentralized companies.*[1]

On the surface, financial reporting is obviously right; for after all, the enterprise must be profitable to survive. A whole conventional wisdom has been erected on the idea of profitability, and like much conventional wisdom it is more a structure of words than of reality. Profit is essential but not fundamental. It results from other things that are fundamental, and those other things are the focus of this book. Profit motive will not be found in lists of human motivations. If not found within people, how can it be the core motivation of one of man's major institutions—business enterprise? Again, reality is different from appearances, and the explanation can be found among the motivations described in Chapter 8.

A major weakness of financial reporting systems is their dedication to annual data. A 12-month fiscal year is compared with a subsequent 12-month fiscal year. Ten such fiscal years are lined up side by side in the annual report. Any student of economics will quickly recognize the tyranny imposed by the fiscal year reporting period. Aggregates are not a mark of performance. Trends and changes in trends *are* marks of performance, and they are developing continuously. Business does not work by annual aggregates; it works by daily, weekly, monthly achievement and change. Reporting rules required by the Internal Revenue Service, state taxing authorities, and the Securities Exchange Commission need not prescribe the reporting system used to manage company operations. A different perspective and a different content will be required.

Achievement Reporting

Reporting systems reflect company values and focus attention on the important company objectives, so a reporting system needed for the implementation of the kind of operating system recommended in this book will begin with the fundamentals of what the enterprise is and what it intends to become. As developed in Chapters 3 to 7, that company concept is made real by articulation of goals, selection of strategies, and development and implementation of action programs. Our reporting system will be designed to provide performance feedback to all company people so they will see the results of their work and be able to take effective action to achieve goals. Or if the situation changes significantly enough, a change in goals as well as a change in or continuation of program may be the

[1]*European Business,* Summer 1971, p. 27.

appropriate move. In any case, the objective of the reporting system is to guide performance in the achievement of goals. That kind of reporting is sometimes called performance reporting, but I like to put a rather more positive label on it: achievement reporting. Some of the characteristics of an effective achievement reporting system are

1. Employees and work groups receive feedback on the results of their effort immediately or very shortly after the work is done.
2. Feedback is informative and in relation to goal achievement, not evaluative of personal performance.
3. Feedback goes to the individual or work group doing the job. It may or may not go to the manager.
4. If the report does go to the manager, the manager's use of the report is to support and assist the individual or work group in goal achievement.
5. Feedback relates to goal achievement. It is not an expository summary of activity.
6. Reports deal only with significant measurements, not with all the details.
7. Reports are not accumulated through many levels of management; each person receives directly the specific feedback on his and his group's goal achievement.

The framework of company identity, key performance area objectives, strategies, and action plans provides us with all the inputs we need for an effective achievement reporting system. In fact, if we do not establish such a reporting system, our achievement system will not function. It can't operate from a financial reporting system. The needed feedback just will not be supplied. The values are different. But I have found that the very performance measures emphasized in the financial reporting system—sales, profit, investment, and cash flow—will be much improved when operations are assisted by an achievement reporting system that includes but does not limit itself to those measures. What it does emphasize is the achievement measures that will determine company success, and that success will include good financial results.

Our achievement reporting system can be thought of in input-output terms. The input-output model can be elaborated in as much detail as desired. But essentially resources go in and production, sales to customers, value added, and income come out—not just today, but over time. The significant subsidiary inputs and outputs will be included in our achievement reporting system. We begin with the key performance area objectives developed throughout the organization as described in Chapters 4 and 12. Then the whole input-output system will be summarized in marginal income accounts with measurements over time to identify any significant trends and changes in trends. That kind of reporting system will help people throughout the enterprise achieve the objectives that collectively will carry the enterprise to its goals. It will also provide an effective early warning of developing problems while there is still time to do something about them, an early warning, also, of developing opportunity when additional resources might wisely be invested. For example, I have found declining profitability indicated by an achievement reporting system two to four years before it was identified in the financial control reports. And I have, on the other hand, found improving profitability indicated six months to a year before any such improvement could be anticipated from the financial control reports.

The exact form of the achievement reporting system will be determined by the key performance area objectives that are chosen and the action plans implemented to achieve them. Since the objectives and the action plans will be continually changing, the reporting too will continually change. But there will be some continuing common elements to allay the cultural shock of abandoning a prescribed set of schedules, filled out in a particular way, for a fiscal period. Keep in mind that we are talking about achievement reporting for business decisions and action planning, not about cash transactions, taxes, or reports required by government regulation. With an achievement reporting system we will do the accounting that is required; from it, and in addition to it, we will develop the feedback that will help us achieve the objective of our mission.

The achievement reporting system will begin with the key performance area objectives and provide feedback on their achievement. In my work I have found that there are always important objectives in the key performance areas of market standing and profitability. For objectives in the other key performance areas the required reporting feedback tends to be different in each operation because the situation and the objectives themselves are different for each operation. But for market standing and profitability there are some feedback measurements that seem to be useful in most of the business situations that I have worked with.

Market standing. It seems to me to be most important for any future-oriented, success-oriented top management to have a keen awareness of the significant measurements that show company performance in market standing, an important key performance area. Market standing objectives become specific goals for marketing, product management, and sales. But market standing achievement becomes an important input to resource strategy and resource commitment that is a major concern of top management. At the top management level, the following feedback on market standing is useful:

The definition of business areas, product groups, or other business segment definitions can be developed as recommended in Chapter 3 and in the discussion of market share in Chapter 12. Top management should be a participant in the dialog that develops those definitions, not merely a judge of someone else's work. So information here can come more from involvement than from a reporting procedure.

Sales to target accounts measure the achievement of the firm's most important objective: the creation and maintenance of customers. Income comes from

Report	Frequency
Definition of business areas, product groups, or other business segment definition, and market growth rate and competitive position for each. (The resource strategy matrix or its equivalent; see Chapter 12.)	Every two years plus whenever there is a change.
Sales to target accounts.	Monthly.
Total sales and sales of major profit center businesses or other major business segments.	Monthly plus time series trend and changes in trend.
Market share for major business segments.	Monthly or quarterly plus time series trend and changes in trend.

customers, not from plants. The lost or poorly served account hurts just as plant down time hurts only more so, because the lost customer is harder to start up again. The customer created and maintained is the firm's most important achievement. The target accounts are the firm's major opportunities for that achievement. They need the attention and the effort of everyone throughout the enterprise, including top management. To maintain that attention and to assist in that effort requires a reporting feedback. Depending on the size of the firm and the complexity of its operations, the report may include all target accounts or summarize performance by target account group with information on individual accounts going only to the management individuals personally involved in sales to the account. The reporting form used will vary, but it is vital to have top management involvement with customers and not merely with a total sales statistic.

Total sales, however, is an important measure. Also important for top management attention will probably be the sales of major profit center component businesses or other major business segments. They should be reported monthly. But it is not enough to have the monthly statistic. Nor is it enough to look at comparisons and variations from plan and from year-ago performance. Neither may be significant. What is significant is trend and changes in trend, direction in relation to short- and long-range objectives, and performance in relation to opportunity. That kind of understanding of the sales situation can be provided if the monthly results are reported in a way that shows not a snapshot of the month's performance, but a frame from a moving picture of sales performance. Time series methods provide a way to accomplish it. And I find the most simple of the available techniques is quite adequate—12-month moving totals. The charting is simple and is easily understood. If continued, it shows the developing trends, the business cycle changes, and unusual or random change visually. And it provides a very helpful assist for short-range forecasting.

The major technical criticism of 12-month moving totals is that they are always 6 months out of phase with current performance rates. Exponential smoothing and techniques for deseasonalization and annualization of current rates are advocated as ways of overcoming that weakness. I prefer, however, a simpler method. In addition to the 12-month moving total, the variations of each month's performance from the same month a year ago can be shown on the same chart. Those variations, for any but the most statistically noisy series, will indicate cyclical or other current changes as they are developing. For many series of business data, I find the charting of variances more useful than statistical methods for interpreting current performance. Figure 13-1 illustrates the recommended method for charting sales data. Other examples are shown in Figures 11-9 and 11-10.

To provide a measure of performance in relation to opportunity, total industry data and variances can be shown on the same chart with company sales performance. Or more simply, percent of market share can be followed monthly on a trend basis. A plot of three-month moving averages over several years provides a useful format for dialoging share-of-market data.

Market standing measures will be different for each management level and will provide the feedback needed at each level for achieving objectives at that level. This means transaction and client data at the individual level, and appropriately simplified aggregates at higher levels. For the key performance area of market standing, the feedback measures in one company look like Table 13-1.

Table 13-1. Feedback Measures on Market Standing.

	Market Share	Unit Sales	New Products
Individuals and First Line Supervision	Target clients Other clients	Transactions, by client Product totals monthly: By client By territory By district	Sales, by client
Business Unit Management	Product lines Market segments Target clients	Product totals monthly: By product group By market	Dollar sales Unit sales
Division Management	Product lines Target clients	Product totals by product group	Dollar sales Unit sales
Corporate Management	As listed on p. 252		

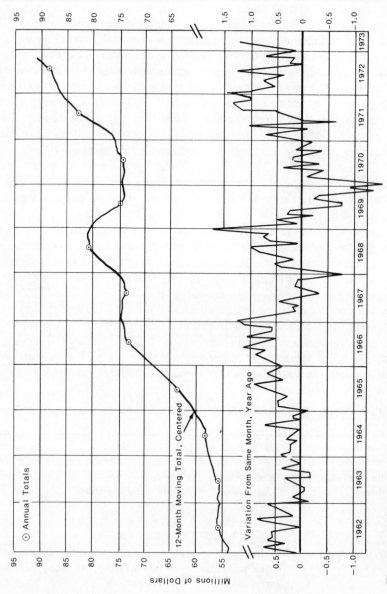

Figure 13-1. Recommended method for charting sales.

254

Let's look in more detail at some of the effective feedback measures referred to above for target client sales. Business success is achieved where the client is, more than in our plants. External returns from the market are more appropriate measures than internal returns on investment. Success is more in manufacturing satisfied, repeat customers than in manufacturing products. And the most important of these are our target clients in each market area. Figure 13-2 shows one example of feedback reporting on target client sales at the business unit level. Monthly feedback at the district and individual salesman levels shows data by individual target clients. The salesmen, in addition, receive individual transaction data, on a current basis.

DIVISION   INDUSTRIAL
CLIENTES   ESPECIALES
VENTAS   NETAS   (000)

RESUMEN

MES   ZONA

CLIENTES		Mes Act. 1.976	Mes Act. 1.975	Var. o/o	Acumul. 1.976	Acumul. 1.975	Var. o/o	Target. para 1.976
District 1	37	1.868.0	676.6	176	6.133.8	2.533.8	142	24.100.0
Clientes KTA	7	1.491.7	373.4	299	4.915.6	1.660.7	196	20.100.0
Otros	30	376.3	303.2	24	1.218.0	873.1	40	4.000.0
District 2	48	1.531.2	821.6	86	4.250.0	1.980.2	114	19.180.0
Clientes KTA	9	960.7	394.2	144	1.885.2	1.070.5	76	13.700.0
Otros	39	570.5	427.4	33	2.364.8	909.7	159	5.480.0
District 3	13	1.234.9	188.3	556	2.929.0	1.972.8	48	8.530.0
Clientes KTA	3	1.179.6	145.3	712	2.696.1	1.776.7	52	7.030.0
Otros	10	55.3	43.0	28	232.9	196.1	19	1.500.0
District 4	30	983.6	198.7	395	1.738.6	1.008.7	72	15.795.0
Clientes KTA	5	589.6	32.8	NS	673.4	533.1	26	11.700.0
Otros	25	394.0	165.9	137	1.065.2	475.6	124	4.095.0
District 5	8	114.6	54.6	109	276.6	101.7	174	1.800.0
Clientes KTA	3	103.0	35.3	191	255.9	57.4	346	1.500.0
Otros	5	11.6	19.3	(40)	20.7	44.3	(53)	300.0
District 6	7	76.9	97.9	(22)	200.8	127.3	58	1.073.0
Clientes KTA	3	69.6	12.7	448	188.1	12.7	NS	873.0
Otros	4	7.3	85.2	(92)	12.7	114.6	(89)	200.0
TOTAL	143	5.809.2	2.037.7	185	15.528.8	7.724.5	100	70.478.0
	30	4.394.2	993.7	342	10.614.3	5.111.1	108	54.903.0
	113	1.415.0	1.044.0	36	4.914.3	2.613.4	88	15.575.0

Tip. Ambar - 31-51-65

Figure 13-2.

Figure 13-3 shows an example of target client monthly feedback to salesmen and district managers. Here can be seen each month's sales and year-to-date sales,

always looked at in relation to objective. This kind of summary report, maintained over several years, helps us to think in terms of trends, direction, and goal
achievement. At the salesman level, customer sales planning provides target
client data on potential, and other situational intelligence that helps us to provide "superior customer value" in achieving sales objectives. Each transaction improves both the client's income model, and ours.

TERRITORY		1975 ACTUAL SALES	1976 SALES GOAL	JAN	FEB	MAR	APR	MAY	JUN	JUL
ACCOUNTS & PROSPECTS (M − MONTH) (Y − YEAR TO DATE)		1975 ACTUAL SALES	1976 SALES GOAL	JAN	FEB	MAR	APR	MAY	JUN	JUL
TOTAL TERRITORY	M									
	Y									
TOTAL TARGET ACCOUNTS	M									
	Y									
KTA 1	M									
	Y									
KTA 2	M									
	Y									
KTA 3	M									
	Y									
KTA 4	M									
	Y									
KTA 5	M									
	Y									

Figure 13-3.

Profitability. I have found two ways of reporting income to be very useful in
defining problems and opportunities and determining appropriate decision and
action programs. They are (1) time series and (2) income statement by marginal
income accounts. As with sales volume, it is important to see a moving picture,
not merely monthly snapshots, and we must see the picture in actionable terms.
The two reporting methods can help provide us that vision and understanding.

For time series, the same kind of charting by 12-month moving totals and
monthly variances as described for total sales can be useful. Figure 13-4 is a
chart of operating income for the same business as that for which sales are
charted in Figure 13-1. Both the sales volume and income charts can be drawn to
provide a comparison between the two series. Semilog scale could be used, but I
find communication easier if an arithmetic scale is used for both charts, with the
scales so chosen that the two are approximately comparable over the range
plotted.

For all such charting, selection of scale is important. Scales should be so
chosen that the visual impression and the statistical reality are comparable and
that one chart can be overlaid on the other to find any changing relationship be-

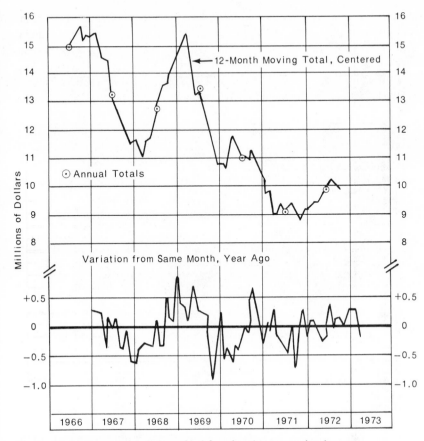

Figure 13-4. Recommended method for charting operating income.

tween the two. That kind of comparison helps to signal significant change and provides a very useful base for dialog on the current situation, outlook, and appropriate actions to be taken. It is especially useful when combined with the intelligence provided by marginal income accounts.

We are accustomed to income statements reported from a full-costing system. We are so accustomed to them that we may not realize there are other possibilities: conversion, prime, direct, and marginal costing. For the businesses that I have worked with, I find marginal costing far more useful than the others for providing the intelligence needed for sound business decision and action. That costing system and its use are described in Chapter 11. For top management reporting, a very useful monthly summary is provided by a monthly income statement by marginal income accounts. One format for that kind of income statement is shown in Figure 13-5. Average monthly performance for previous years is shown, along with each month's results for the current year.

Marginal Income Account	Average Month				This Year, Actual							
	3 Years Ago	2 Years Ago	Last Year	Budget This Year	Jan.	Feb.	Mar.	Apr.	May	June	July	Aug.
Sales	2,202	2,195	2,456	2,663	2,718	3,201						
Variable costs	1,054	1,175	1,312	1,423	1,362	1,632						
Materials			851	939	885	1,104						
Direct labor			283	304	286	312						
Energy			27	30	33	37						
Commissions			51	52	54	65						
Freight			80	88	96	104						
Other			20	10	8	10						
Marginal income	1,148	1,020	1,094	1,240	1,356	1,569						
Percent of sales	52.1	46.5	44.5	46.6	49.9	49.0						
Value added			1,578	1,694	1,800	2,060						
Percent of sales			64.3	63.6	66.2	64.4						
Fixed costs	935	963	1,008	1,086	1,112	1,130						
Manufacturing	691	638	627	654	684	709						
Selling	149	154	148	162	170	175						
G&A	95	112	173	203	189	184						
Distribution		59	60	67	69	62						
Breakeven	1,794	2,071	2,265	2,330	2,228	2,306						
Sales above (below) breakeven	408	124	191	333	490	895						
Operating income	213	58	85	155	245	439						
Other income		6	8	7	8	12						
Other expenses		2	2	16	12	14						
Net income before taxes	62	62	91	146	241	437						

Figure 13-5. Company G income statement by marginal income accounts.

That provides a visual check on changes and developing trends. For key accounts in the income statement it is also useful to maintain a time series chart over several years, tracking changes. Useful charts are:

Sales, 12-month moving totals.
Marginal income percent, 3-month moving average.
Fixed costs, 3-month moving average.
Breakeven, 3-month moving average.
Value-added percent, 3-month moving average.
Operating income, 12-month moving totals.

The income statement by marginal income accounts and the trend charts listed here are especially useful for problem-solving dialog because they summarize the measures that interrelate to determine operating income. Further, those measures correspond to operating areas of the company so that decisions reached are actionable. Goals can be set for the actions and performance can be measured—all by marginal income accounts. The methodology for that use of marginal income accounts is explained in Chapter 11.

Having the income statement by marginal income accounts helps us find opportunity for income improvement. There are three and only three possibilities: (1) increase sales volume, (2) reduce fixed costs, or (3) increase marginal income rate by increasing price, reducing variable costs, or improving mix. Full cost accounting does not provide us the information on the interacting determinants of income that we must have if we are to make wise decisions and implement effective business programs. Marginal income costing does. It helps us see through the mass of detail to find the fundamentals. And that search begins with the income statement by marginal income accounts.

While profitability objectives will typically be defined in terms of sales volume, marginal income, fixed costs, breakeven and operating income, the objectives and the feedback will differ at different management levels.

Let's look at profitability feedback controls in a typical company comprised of a corporate headquarters, divisions, and business units within the divisions. Within business units, sales and marketing individuals and operating supervision will be directly concerned with profitability goals and feedback by transaction and for individual clients, but will also be informed as to the business unit's total income model. (See the first chart on p. 260.)

Additional profitability measures may be included at the business unit, division, and corporate levels to relate profit to criteria established by management. Measures commonly used for this purpose are return on assets, return on investment, return on gross investment, return on sales, return on equity, and (at the corporate level) earnings per share. Criteria must be clearly defined, with procedures specified for calculating the measures.

Reporting Feedback on Profitability Lowest Management Level: Individuals and First Line Supervision

Sales volume	Transactions, by client
	Dollar totals monthly:
	By client
	By territory
	By district or region
Marginal income rate	By transaction
	Monthly:
	By product
	By client
	By territory
Fixed costs	By expenditure
	Account totals, monthly
Break-even	Business unit, monthly
Operating income	Business unit, monthly
Income model	Business unit, monthly

At the business unit management level, data is simplified into aggregates monthly to relate to business unit objectives:

Reporting Feedback on Profitability Next Management Level: Business Unit Management Monthly

Sales	Dollar totals:
	By product group
	By market
	By target client
	Total for business unit
Marginal income rate	By product line
	Total, business unit
Fixed costs	By organizational unit
Break-even	Business unit
Operating income	Business unit
Income model	Business unit

At the division level, data is further simplified to relate to division objectives:

Reporting Feedback on Profitability Next Management Level: Division Headquarters Monthly

Sales volume	Business units
	Total division
Marginal income rate	Business units
	Total division
Fixed costs	Major aggregates
	Total division
Break-even	Business units
	Total division
Operating income	Business units
	Total division
Net income	Total division
Income model	Business units
	Total division

At the corporate level, reporting feedback relates to corporate objectives:

Reporting Feedback on Profitability Highest Management Level: Corporate Headquarters Monthly

Sales volume	Division totals
	Corporate total
Operating income	Division totals
	Corporate total
Net income	Division totals
	Corporate total

Other key performance areas. For the other key performance areas, no generalized reporting system can be followed. Each enterprise will have unique needs, and its objectives will determine what reporting of achievement it will require. Some ideas will be found in the discussion of key performance areas in Chapter 12, but the specifics for each operation will have to be worked out for that operation. They will not remain the same; as objectives change, the needed feedback reporting will also change. Some of the concepts and techniques that I have used to develop goals and feedback measures in the seven key performance areas are:

Key Performance Area	Concepts and Techniques
Market Standing	Described above
Profitability	Described above

Innovation	Technology forecasting techniques especially:
	  Model of innovation process
	  Identification and measurement of key parameters
	  Substitution theory
	  Monitoring
	  Systems and information science

Productivity	Output related to factor and total factor inputs:
	  Raw materials
	  Energy
	  Person-hours
	  Capital consumption

Physical and Financial Resources	Plant audits:
	  Technology
	  Environmental standards
	  Productivity
	  Economics
	Balance sheet analysis (adjusting for inflation)
	Valuation at replacement cost of comparably productive facilities

Motivation and Organization Development	Measures of human resource development programs Attitude surveys Work structure surveys

Public and Environmental Responsibility	Environmental monitoring:
	  Economic
	  Political
	  Social
	  Ecological
	Audits of company programs responding to the needs of above environments

We do not want a procedural system of reports; we want feedback that will help us achieve our objectives. One way to keep those key objectives always in mind is to list them in a monthly operating report along with a one-sentence comment on recent achievement or current problems. The key performance area objectives listed on the report will not remain the same throughout a fiscal year. They will change continually as objectives are achieved, altered, or dropped because of environmental or other change. But whatever the major achievement objectives of the enterprise may be, they should always be in the view and conscience of top management. They are, after all, the statement of top management's current job. In addition to a summary report any specific feedback data important to the achievement of the objectives should be provided directly to those involved.

For top management, then, the most basic elements of the achievement reporting system can be summarized on five pieces of paper:

Page 1   Key performance area objectives of the company.

Page 2   Sales volume time series (Figure 13-3). Data can be included with the chart.

Page 3   Operating income time series (Figure 13-4). Data can be included with the chart.

Page 4   Target account sales summary. (Figure 13-2).

Page 5   Income statement by marginal income accounts (Figure 13-5).

Additional data may be desired, and some suggestions have been included in preceding comments, but the temptation to proliferate and specialize should be avoided. Concentration should be on finding the fundamentals. Once the fundamentals are found, adequate subsidiary data will be available to enable practical operating programs to be carried out.

Although the most fundamental feedback to top management from the kind of achievement system advocated in this book can be summarized in five pages, each enterprise will arive at its own conclusions on what is most important to include. One company that developed its plans and operating style as recommended in this book decided on a 12-exhibit monthly report for top management:

1. Key performance area objectives.
2. Income statement by prime margin accounts. (The company was using prime costing rather than marginal costing. Prime costs can be used in a similar way.)
3. Operating income: chart of 12-month moving total and monthly variances from year ago with data.
4. Prime margin percent: chart of 3-month moving average with data.
5. Total sales: chart of 12-month moving total and monthly variances from year ago with data.
6. Breakeven: chart of 3-month moving average with data.
7. Total fixed expense: chart of 3-month moving average with data.
8. Product group E: chart of 12-month moving total sales and variances with data and chart of 3-month moving average of prime margin percent with data.

9. Product group B: chart of 12-month moving total sales and variances with data and chart of 3-month moving average of prime margin percent with data.

10. Product group R: chart of 12-month moving total sales and variances with data and chart of 3-month moving average of prime margin percent with data.

11. Product group P: chart of 12-month moving total sales and variances with data and chart of 3-month moving average of prime margin percent with data.

12. Target account summary.

The company, which I shall call Company E, established objectives in all eight of the key performance areas. Achievement on these objectives is reported monthly, very briefly, in the first of the twelve exhibits. As objectives change or are achieved, the list of key performance objectives changes. There is not one list for a fiscal year. The list of key objectives keeps changing.

Company E had one year of experience with a new prime costing system, and it was using it in the way recommended in this book for marginal costing. Prime costs include only variable manufacturing costs in calculating prime margin, whereas marginal costs include all variable costs in calculating marginal income. Since business decisions and action planning involve approximation of many variables, either prime costing or marginal costing can be used in examining business economics. In Chapter 11, as a first step in changing from full costs to marginal costs, I suggest the relatively simple step of moving first to prime costs. From that point the further step to marginal costs may be taken if it seems desirable for the particular business.

Company E was well aware of the interaction of sales volume, prime margin, and fixed costs to determine operating income, and in its reporting system it followed those three measures on a trend basis. The 3-month moving average of prime margin percent was especially important to it, since one of its key performance area objectives for profitability was to increase prime margin from 32 to 38 percent within 15 months. That objective was not only a hope; it was supported by specific plans and programs. There were subsidiary objectives in pricing, costs, and mix calculated to achieve the prime margin objective, and the individuals and groups having responsibility for the subsidiary objectives had the encouragement and support of top management in their achievement and recognition for results obtained.

Few companies or profit center operations are aware of their breakeven point and whether it is changing and by how much. A common situation is for breakeven, unobserved and unmanaged, to rise and for the increase to be offset, if it is offset, by sales volume increase. Company E does not leave its breakeven point unmanaged; all its managers know what is happening to breakeven and use all available approaches to manage it constructively. That includes not only volume, as an offset, but also the management of fixed costs, prime costs, price, and mix, which are the determinants of breakeven. For Company E, four product groups offered the greatest opportunity for growth and income. For those target product groups, top management reports follow current sales and prime margin percent on a time series basis to see trends and changes in trends.

The 12 feedback measurements provide Company E top management with an understanding of trends and changes in trends important to the achievement of the key performance area objectives that they have selected. As objectives are changed, the measures too will change, but Company E will always have its future in view from its mission and key performance area objectives. And it will always be marking its achievement toward those objectives through an achievement reporting system that is specific to the objectives. The measures provide understanding as well as data, and through the process of dialog they make possible wise decisions and action planning.

Figure 13-6 illustrates the kind of feedback reporting system that I am recommending; and which was used in Company E. There is voluminous feedback from the work itself at the transaction level, but only a reasonable and a needed amount for each individual to achieve his objectives. At each higher level, simplified aggregates are reported as needed to achieve objectives at that level. Flows between levels are moderate. Work group efforts are coordinated through dialogue and are linked also through dialogue to other groups. All is focused on achieving objectives. This sort of control is less a system to help managers evaluate subordinates, and more a cybernetic feedback system to help each person and unit succeed in accomplishing intended objectives. And believe me, evaluation becomes simpler as we focus more on successful achievement.

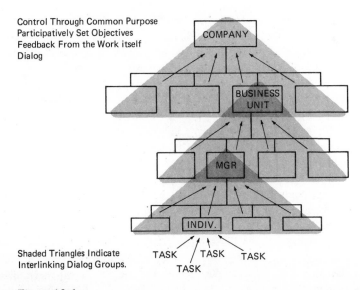

Figure 13-6.

One other, very important perspective, Feedback in this system is more than specific numbers for an accounting period. Each measure is seen in relation to trend and changes in trend. It is *direction*—trends and changes in trends—that matters. So each monthly figure is viewed, not as a variance from budget, but as one more measure of a trend: The management job then is not to explain the variance or to conform reported results to a budget, but to influence the trend in ways that enable us to achieve our mission.

This approach for developing an achievement reporting system can be followed for each unit of the company and each work group. As for the top management achievement reporting systems, the fundamentals will be:

1. Achievement feedback to each individual and work group on each of their objectives.
2. Time series measurement of critical performance variables to identify trends and changes in trends.
3. Where applicable and possible, the relationship of achievement to opportunity as well as to objectives.

The achievement reports in all the areas of company operations need not flow through organization channels to top levels of management. By the way objectives are developed, related management levels and work groups will have been involved. By the way the organization works together, the people who need to be informed will be informed. We will have achieved a PMBO style of management that can motivate exciting achievement. And our achievement reporting system will be simplified by orders of magnitude from the budgetary control systems now in vogue.

An achievement reporting system is not only simpler than the financial model kind of budgetary control system; it requires the enterprise to function in a different kind of way in two important respects: (1) Reports provide informational feedback needed for goal achievement. The enterprise acts on the basis of the reports. (2) Achievement reporting provides a time perspective—past, present, and future. The enterprise manages its affairs by predictive control rather than by after-the-fact management by exception. Those two concepts can lift organizational achievement spectacularly. As we saw in Chapter 8, informative feedback is essential to achievement motivation. It helps us find our way to the achievement of our objectives. Evaluative feedback that tells us only if we are good or bad provides no inputs for improvement, no measure of progress, and no motivation for achievement. Achievement reporting helps us find the way to our objectives by providing us the information we need for our next decisions and actions. And us is everyone—not just top management.

An Example

Let me illustrate with an example of how the methods I am recommending changed a struggling company into a highly successful, profitable enterprise. Satisfactory annual profitability for this company, which I will call Company S, would be in the range of $3 million. Results over several years up to the time of our rebuilding and achievement reporting program were as follows:

Year	Net Income ($ Thousands)
1969	$1020
1970	855
1971	1176
1972	1413
1973	2244
1974	1716
June, 1975 (6-months annualized)	(1572)

In July 1975, the management group of this company studied its situation, and determined where and how it could build its success:

1. Overall company objectives were developed in the framework of the seven key performance areas listed earlier.
2. The total business was defined into six business segments. This was the most difficult and time consuming part of the program, and required conceptual thinking more than analytical.
3. Income statements by marginal income accounts were prepared for each of the business segments, and for the total company, using the format shown in Figure 13-5. Statements were prepared from January, 1975, so that current trends of key measures could be identified.
4. 'Superior customer values' were identified for each of the business segments.
5. Business plans for each of the business segments were developed using a format similar to that shown in Figure 7-1, Chapter 7.
6. Sales personnel identified target accounts, developed situational data for each, and set sales objectives.
7. In each business segment, the management group dialoged their business plan and their monthly income models and developed specific objectives for:
   Market position:
     Total sales
     Target-client sales
   Profitability:
     Marginal income rate
     Fixed costs
   Other key performance area objectives as appropriate

8. An achievement reporting system was established:
   a. Salesmen and supervisors received:
      Transaction data, by account
      Monthly summaries by account with emphasis on the target accounts, using reports similar to those shown in Figure 13-2 and Figure 13-3.
9. Business managers and the company president together dialoged monthly results and trends in:
   Marginal income rate
   Fixed costs
   Breakeven
   Sales volume
   Target client sales
   Key action plans.
10. Decisions were made as necessary to keep the company, and each business segment 'on track' toward the achievement of its objectives. The achievement feedback not only indicated when and where decisions were needed; it also provided information needed for making the decision.

This program involved many individuals in a very responsible way in their unit and their company success. Both motivation and operating results improved. By year-end, 1975, the company had achieved break-even operations, and in 1976 the company had the highest income in its history, and for the first time, well above "satisfactory." Figure 13-7 shows the income trend chart for this company.

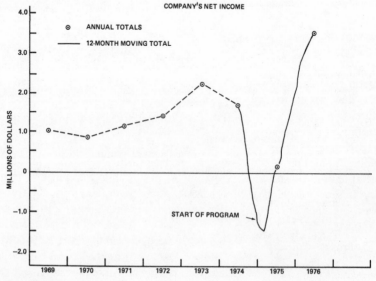

Figure 13-7.

This is only one of the many examples I have seen and worked with that demonstrates the effectiveness of an achievement reporting system. It combines general systems theory, behavioral science, and managerial economics into a new style of management and feedback control reporting that can define and achieve success in the complex environment we work in today.

Since achievement reporting provides us a moving picture of trends and changes in trends in all the key performance variables as they are defined by the enterprise, we now have a capability for the first time of managing our affairs in a predictive way. We can see the direction of the current trends in all the key variables and whether they are taking us in the direction of our goals. If they are not, we need not wait till poor results show up on the income statement to begin taking action. I have seen achievement reporting systems provide two to four years advance warning of developing problems. Those problems are less costly to prevent then they are to recover from once they are upon us, full blown. In today's world of fast-paced, discontinuous change, variance analysis and management by exception are not responsive enough. We can no longer watch operations to see when problems occur and then correct them. We must see problems coming and take action to prevent or minimize them.

On the positive side, there are successes as well as problems, and again predictive control is much superior to management by exception. Predictive control reveals opportunity developing and enables us to take early action to maximize it; management by exception reveals an opportunity already here. Very likely we will find ourselves trying, too late, to climb onto someone else's bandwagon. With an achievement reporting system we understand the past, comprehend the present, and see the developing trends and changes in trends relating to goal achievement. Our orientation is to the future. We look at where we are going, rather than at where we have been, and today we take the actions that can move us toward the objectives that we seek.

Predictive control, through achievement reporting, becomes an essential part of the way of life for the achieving enterprise. With achievement reporting we will still have all the financial measures we need but we will understand them better than we do from other systems; for we will at all times see the moving picture—past, present, and future—and not just snapshots in a frame of official expectations. In addition, we will have measures and understanding of all the key performance areas that determine the success of the enterprise: market standing, innovation, productivity, physical and financial resources, profitability, motivation and organization development, public and environmental responsibility. In short, we will have the feedback system we need to move the enterprise toward the achievement of its mission. There need no longer be an annual ordeal of budget planning. There need no longer be a periodic ordeal of official long-range business planning. The achieving enterprise can have the action-oriented equivalent at all times through mission, key performance area objectives, and achievement reporting. The system will be simpler. And the achievement will be greater.

A Structural Framework for Achievement Reporting[2]

From recent work in general systems theory applied to business operations there have developed some new concepts of structure that can be useful to us in applying the methods described in this book. In this approach, achievement reporting becomes the information flow and control function in a general systems structure of the organization.

By structure I do not mean the lines and boxes we draw on our organization charts. There is much more to structure than that. Structure combines the elements of the total business and its environment in a way that will achieve appropriately determined objectives. This kind of structure comprises both the elements and the functional way they are linked together. This kind of structure is a synthesis, a totality. It includes both what the business is and how it works. Included in structure are:

Business Units
  Strategic businesses
  Groups, divisions, business units
  Profit centers
  Projects
Resources
  People
  Information
  Capital
  Materials
  Energy
  ystem of Measures
  Relates to objectives
  Provides control feedback on what matters
Environment
Linkages, connectivities, relationships
Information flow

Figure 9-1, Chapter 9, shows the basic unit diagram that I have found most useful and practical in diagramming this kind of business structure. The unit diagram includes operations, management, management systems, environment, and the information flow that determines and controls performance. Looking at this form of a unit diagram we can visualize several important unit characteristics:

[2]This section describes a model and concepts developed by Stafford Beer and described in his book *The Heart of Enterprise* (New York: John Wiley & Sons, Inc., 1979). The systems concepts described come from Professor Beer and from the cybernetic services of Ernst & Whinney.

Unit Characteristics
1. Comprises operations or functions and the management of them
2. Relates to an external environment
3. Has a purpose and a structure to achieve its purpose
4. Is largely self-organizing and self-controlling
5. Is controlled through information flow relating to objectives
6. Provides information through a system of measures

Achievement reporting is an approach for achieving in an effective way the last three of these characteristics.

The unit diagram shown in Figure 9-1 can be the diagram of the total company, a division or subsidiary, a business within a division or subsidiary, a plant with a business, or a unit within a plant. The same unit concept and unit characteristics apply to each. Several units combine to form each higher level of organization and are appropriately linked together by communication channels so that each such combination, in turn, becomes a unit for the next higher level of organization. Each level of organization, as a unit, develops its objectives related to environment. With key performance area objectives and information flow through achievement reporting each unit, and the company collectively, can stay in tune with its environment and on course toward its objectives. Environmental change and operating performance become inputs to objectives and to action plans and operations on a continuing basis.

Figure 13-8 illustrates a combination of four Level 1 operating units into a

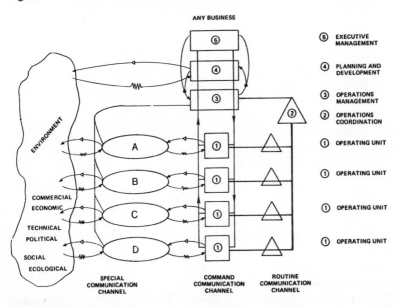

Figure 13-8.

higher level business unit. This could be a diagram of any business unit, such as:

Level 1 Operating Unit	Total Unit
Department or sections	Production unit
Production units	Profit center
Profit centers	Division
Divisions	Company or group
Companies or groups	Corporation

For the next higher level of organization the total of what is diagrammed in Figure 13-8 becomes a Level 1 operating unit. Or, going down one level, each Level 1 operating unit shown in Figure 13-8 can be diagrammed as five levels, with its subordinate Level 1 operating units. Such diagrams can be carried down to the level of the individual work station. Each level has its informational connectivities with its environment. The functions of the five levels shown are:

Level	Functions	Typical Business Organization Corporation	Typical Business Organization Division
5	Defines purpose expressed in objectives Establishes structure	Office of the CEO Board of directors	General manager
4	Monitors external environment Develops purpose and objectives Conducts R & D Plans and manages projects Designs system of measures Monitors organizational model Provides functional expertise	Corporate staff	Division staff
3	Monitors Level 2 Modifies Level 1 structures	VP, Operations	Manager, Operations
2	Coordinates Level 1 operating units Provides information to Level 3	VP, Operations Corporate staff	Manager, Operations Division staff
1	Produces an output Achieves objectives	Companies or divisions	Profit centers

The listing above identifies the functions of the five levels as they might be performed in a typical corporate organization and in a typical division organization. The important point is that all units can be described and managed in terms of these five levels and their functions.

With structure and information flow as illustrated in this model, we come now to the important matter of control. How are all the activities in all parts of the enterprise so conducted that in the planning function appropriate objectives are established and then in operations are achieved? Managing our businesses according to this model with its environmental connectivities, and using achievement reporting, helps make such performance possible.

Information flow determines the point at which decisions are made. Decisions are control actions. But if we attempt to exert control by making all decisions at a senior level we are as soon out of control as if we made no decisions. What decisions to make at what level is the key to control. And the criteria for this determination are two:

1. The manager makes operating decisions for the Level 1 unit he leads. Operating decisions apply resources to achieve intended results.
2. The manager makes structural decisions for subunits reporting to him. Structure provides the decision pattern for subunit managers, for—as we have seen—structure comprises business units, resources, relationships, systems of measures, and information flow. Achievement reporting provides the systems of measures and the information flow.

Both kinds of decisions are much improved and more effective when developed through the dialog process recommended in this book.

Control, then, is not something imposed from a higher center to make things work out right. Instead, control is an integral part of the unit being controlled. Once there is structure, as I am defining structure here, control becomes self-control and the unit more or less organizes itself to effect control through information flow and feedback mechanisms—that is, through achievement reporting.

Feedback as provided by achievement reporting is a very special kind of information. It is not simply data, not simply response, not simply a descriptive measure. It is, rather, a very specific measure from the output of a process which causes a change to be made in the input so that the output is kept within appropriate limits. Figure 13-9 illustrates this idea of feedback as it operates to control business units.

The operator at a machine, the salesman managing his territory, the engineer designing a process, the foreman supervising a shift, the manager running a business, the accountant preparing financial statements, and all others throughout the enterprise use feedback mechanisms to make decisions needed to accomplish their intended results which are all linked together in common purpose through the achievement reporting system of measures.

Figure 13-8 shows three communication channels. Each Level 1 operating unit controlling its performance through feedback mechanisms is part of a larger unit, and it contributes to the achievement of purpose of this larger unit. This contribution is controlled by information flow in the three channels of communication shown in the diagram:

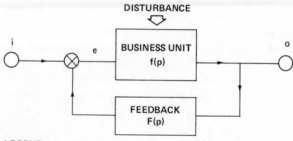

LEGEND:

⊗   :   Management decision (in the light of objectives and measures)
i   :   Resources
e   :   Modified resource allocation
$f(p)$:   Operations
$F(p)$:   Performance measures
o   :   Desired result

Figure 13-9.

Routine communication channel
Command communication channel
Special communication channel

In the routine channel flow all the data and all the information required by management systems and procedures:

1. Information required for coordination among the Level 1 operating units
2. Information required by the higher level unit for the achievement of its purpose and objectives
3. Information required for reporting to government and other outside entities

What actually flows in the routine channel in many businesses is a great deal more than this, much of it unused and unusable. Too often we find ourselves the victims of a new pollution—data pollution. In all companies there is an enormous amount of transactional data. And we record it, sort it, aggregate it, print it out, and circulate it with inadequate filters for finding in all this complexity of data the information that really matters. Data are raw material. Information is what changes us, and data are the raw material for information. Achievement reporting provides a well-designed system of measures to provide this information.

In the command channel most communications are very brief and often informal. Traveling up the command channel is information that tells higher management that the unit is or is not functioning within the desired levels determined by mission and objectives. This reporting is simply a brief statement of key measures and significant control actions. Traveling down the command channel is any change in structure (as I have defined structure) that may be required. When things are going badly in the lower level unit, the higher level manager does not go into the operating unit to make decisions at that level to correct matters. What he can most productively do is change the structure so that operating results will be different. What is changed in structure is some combination of business unit definition, resources, measures, relationships, and information flow. The dialog process can most effectively identify and implement such structural change. The command channel provides decision communications. The routine channel provides an information resource. Coming up the command channel when operations are satisfactory (as determined by mission and objectives) is the simple message "I'm OK, I'm OK" along with a few key performance measures.

The special communication channel carries nonroutine kinds of information needed for special purposes or for dealing with special problems or opportunities, such as audit reports, study teams, consultants, and technical seminars.

Companies that have used this model in structuring and managing business operations have often improved operating results substantially. It provides a useful framework for implementing the management approaches recommended in this book. And achievement reporting as recommended in this chapter provides the system of measures and the information flow that results in good decisions being made throughout the organization so that mission and objectives will be achieved.

14

Good Answers
Don't Last Forever

One of the reasons why good answers don't last forever is that, really, there are no answers. There are no destinations; there are only steps along the way. We like to think of answers and solutions because a world with which we can deal in terms of win or lose, right or wrong, and practical or impractical simplifies what could otherwise by very complicated indeed. One of the apparent benefits of such simplification is that it provides a solid base for answers and solutions. The answers and solutions may have a solid base in company policy, but their solidity in the real world may be another matter. Still, known answers confirmed in company policy give rise to a certain comfortable feeling, and we follow our past into the future.

Perhaps we would move faster into the future, and far more productively, if we thought less about answers and more about steps along the way in a continuing process. That, of course, is the whole theme of this book. Our whole business enterprise is a process, a contributing part of the overall environment in which it operates. And within our business itself there are many other processes. Everything is related to everything else in a network of systems all interacting and all evolving and changing. We cannot at any time blow a whistle and say: "Stop! This is it! We now have the right combination! This is the right answer for us!" However good it may be, it will not remain that way forever. It may not even remain that way next year. Business management does not prosper by instant freezing of success patterns. It prospers by creating better patterns of success from what has gone before. The guidance system and the accelerator are what's important, not the brake pedal.

But let's put the whole matter of change and decision making in perspective. For the long view, it is important to have developed a meaningful definition of our identity as an enterprise—what we are and what we intend to become. From that identity we establish the significant goals for our enterprise. For the identity and goals to be meaningful they must represent much more than studies and recommendations by professional planners. The management literature will remind all who read it that planning is not what the planners do; it is what the managers do. This book goes one step further and says it is what the organization does. And the best way to get organization performance is to have organization involvement in working out what that performance shall be.

As we have seen in earlier chapters, from our concept of identity and goals can come the development of strategies and action plans, all created through the same process of dialog. Through dialog we find our mission—identity, goals, and strategies—and the programs of action to achieve our goals. And we have as a result of the process a structure of objectives and action programs throughout the enterprise all coordinated to the achievement of common goals and all kept coordinated and current by the continuing dialog process.

Steps Along the Way

So at any time we have what could be called answers but might better be called steps along the way. The steps will, of course, be of quite different lengths. A decision on a major commitment of resources to a new business area or expansion of a present business might be a ten-year step or longer. If we have taken our step wisely, change will be measured over decades. On the other hand, change in a production schedule may be made twice in one day and might normally be made once a week or once a month. A change in design might be a 6-month step; a change in capacity, an 18-month one. A change in price may be a 6-week step; a change in vendors a 90-day one.

As we think of decisions and answers as steps along the way to the development and achievement of our concept of mission, a very interesting observation becomes apparent. Hardly any step at all is measured by a 12-month time span. And when we do find a 12-month step as logical, it can begin at any time. A facility expansion that requires 12 months can be initiated on May 15 or September 3 depending on its relation to our goals, strategies, and competence. Nothing in our journey into the future, none of the steps we take along the way, relates to fiscal years. Everything does relate to everything else in a continuing process. That is what we must manage. It's a creative, interacting, evolving process that we operate and participate in and occasionally restructure to achieve new levels of competence and performance.

That is the way we operate, however we may describe ourselves in our present budgetary control processes. However we recognize it and however we describe it, we pretty well know that, when we do achieve significant success, a lot has gone into the achievement. And now that we have the success we're going to keep it. We're going to do more of the same, only better! We sure are! We sure are?

We may very well succeed in doing more of the same. We may even develop a much greater competence and become better and better at what we understand as having brought us our success. With a systems management approach operated by dialog, we can use our success to create new successes by developing and responding to change along the way. With a good-answers approach we are likely to freeze on our successful strategy and become prisoners of our own success. Our response to problems will be to try harder instead of try differently. But dissonance increases and problems accumulate. Until we escape the prison of past practices, no solution will be found. The great success will have become an interlude in company history, perhaps the last chapter before Book II, "After the Merger."

Good answers don't last forever, but good business management can. If we operate in a systems way, with involvement throughout the enterprise, we can keep relevant to the world around us—both problems and opportunities—and keep achieving the identity and goals we choose for our future. With that kind of system and motivation we will not continue replaying the Hit Parade record of our current success. We will change the tune as may be needed as we go along, and we will find new tunes to play. New successes will be formulated while present success is at its peak. Success will become a launching pad, not a prison. The Ford Mustang was successful from the day it was announced, and it became a leader in its market segment. While still a leader in the market, it was joined by the Maverick. Then came the Fairmont; then a completely new Mustang. All were innovations, all successes.

A major plastics company developed and introduced a new thermoplastic material that would compete for markets already served by two of its other plastics. To avoid the competition and exploit different markets, it introduced the new material in a reinforced form only. Other competitors, however, quickly followed with similar materials of their own to challenge the company's existing materials directly. They offered the new material in a range of forms for many applications. The major company that had first introduced the new material lost its timing advantage to establish market leadership in the new class of plastic materials. It had tried to preserve a success instead of undertaking to create a new one by using past success as an input.

In Chapter 12, Company J was used as an example of resource strategy development. Its largest business segment was product group A, in which Company J had the leading market position and from which it had substantial income contribution in a market growing at 3 percent per year. The apparent strategy was optimization, but first and obvious conclusions are not always the best ones. Business area A management, in thinking through its mission, uncovered new opportunity and developed a different definition of identity. Market growth was no longer 3 percent per year; it was almost 10 percent per year. The competence from past achievement could develop for Company J a strong position in the differently defined business area. New strategies were developed to direct Company J achievement in the newly identified area of opportunity. Although product group A was still a strong and very successful business, it unfroze its success pattern to become a starting point for still greater achievement. Success became a new beginning instead of a destination.

The Dangers of Success

Often, however, success patterns will persist until they lead to ultimate decline and a crisis situation that demands change. The achieving organization will create new success from present success. The bureaucratic organization may follow historic success patterns to future failure. The secret is to prevent the achieving organization from becoming bureaucratic and to motivate the bureaucratic organization to becoming achieving. In the history of an enterprise, there can be periods of both eventualities.

Several years ago, as a part of an acquisition, my company acquired a business, Company P, that had a strong market position in its industry. For ten years the business had shown good and consistent profitability and an approximately level volume of sales. But management had a narrow view of its business and was oriented to current problems; it had no concept of future goals or strategies to achieve them. The organization, on the other hand, was skilled both technically and commercially. There was both a desire and a competence for greater achievement. Immediately after the merger, meetings were held to assist the organization to find better ways into the future. Alternate concepts of business definition, goals, and strategies were developed and dialoged; new opportunities were explored; new techniques of problem solving were studied. It was found that current practices followed into the future would almost certainly lead only downhill but that alternative courses offered great opportunity. Yesterday's practices and performance need not constrain tomorrow's achievement.

The management group developed a new and broader definition of its business, set goals, and developed strategies. Three major new areas of opportunity were defined, and organization and capital resources were committed to the development of the new opportunities. Other areas of the business were programmed as specific product-market segments with appropriate resource commitment to achieve the goals targeted for each and action programs implemented to reach the goals. The reporting system focused on goal achievement, and a more participative management style involved all employees directly in the progress of their company. Interest and commitment grew. The company became an exciting place to work; it became a winning team. Figure 14-1 shows the operating results. After ten years of no growth, sales increased 14 percent per year and doubled in the five-year period—all growth from within. Income, which had been declining slightly for ten years (3½ percent per year), over the next five years more than doubled, it increased 21 percent per year.

New patterns for success had been found, and they worked. At about that time, internal organization changes put the company into an operating group in which emphasis was on financial planning and efficiency. Cost reduction became more important than value added. Improvement in income was sought through

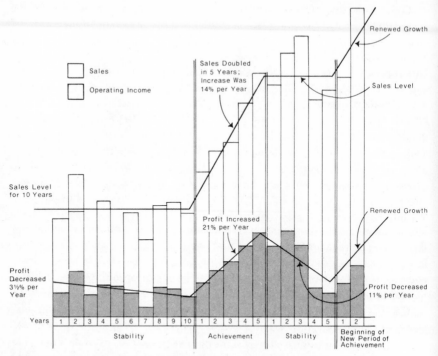

Figure 14-1. Company P operating results.

expense control rather than through achievement. An achieving organization became less motivated—and less achieving. Whereas sales volume had doubled in the preceding five years, over the next five years there was no additional increase in sales—they were up some when business conditions were good and down some when conditions were poor and showed no overall net gain. Income remained at a high level for about three years and then fell to lose almost all of its spectacular gain. The company had become a prisoner of its past success instead of continually and currently using success as a starting point for new achievement. Finally, the company recognized what was happening.

Explained as I have explained it here, what was happening may appear rather easy to see and understand, but in practice, in a real business situation, it is anything but obvious. For the company was following sound business principles in making its strategic mistakes. Roads into the future are not well-marked interstate highways. We can't get on them and just speed along and get there. Instead, we must constantly conceptualize both the route and the vehicle that will travel it and formulate and reformulate the journey. We can do that best from the strength and with the resources of each success achieved. Success is not a destination; it is a step along the way that makes further steps possible. That kind of journey requires the concepts and methods described in this book.

Company P, and higher company executive management, on recognizing that its great success had become a prison instead of a starting point for new achievement, began again to formulate a mission that could become the starting point for exciting achievement. And again the company began a new success story. But the base for new achievement was different, and the environment was different. The first great success story could not be recreated. A new one had to be found. Good answers don't remain good answers.

Finding New Answers: An Example
One of our country's largest and most diversified companies, the General Electric Co., has demonstrated over many years a remarkable ability to find new answers—to formulate new routes to success from past achievement and environmental change. Until the late 1940s GE was a highly centralized, hierarchical organization structure managed from the top with decisions reserved to top management. But growth to a sales volume approaching $2 billion and growing diversification required the development of new concepts if future opportunities were to be realized. Ralph Cordiner, then executive vice president, led the search for and the discovery of new ways. First of all, the company defined the businesses it was in; then it thought through the structure that could motivate achievement in each of those businesses. The result was a new concept of management—decentralization.

Under decentralization, each of GE's defined businesses became an operating department. The department was a complete business with a defined product scope and profit and loss responsibility. It also had responsibility for all business functions—marketing, manufacturing, engineering, employee relations, and finance. The department became a self-contained business operated entirely by its own management except for a very few reservations of authority necessarily applied on a corporatewide basis. At the same time there was established a corporate staff in marketing, manufacturing, employee relations, engineering, and finance to provide expert functional assistance to the operating deparments.

Decentralization was a revolutionary concept at the time. One large centralized company was made over into some 70 separately managed departments, each a complete business. A tree will not grow to the sky. To get more lumber, grow a forest, not a tree. Decentralization was a dramatic and effective restructuring of the General Electric Co. to prepare the company for its future. And while he was president, Ralph Cordiner saw the company more than double in size and the number of department businesses increase to over 100.

Growth continued; diversification increased; technology expanded; environment continued to change. By the mid-1960s General Electric was no longer a company concerned entirely with power generation, transmission, distribution, conversion, and consumption. It was also in the businesses of materials, aeronautics and space, engines, transportation, X-ray and medical technology, and defense. Some individual departments had become very large businesses involving risks of substantial magnitude; others had become only fragments of larger businesses at division or group level. Consumerism, minority group needs, the physical environment, and government controls and regulations had an increasing impact on operations and required management attention.

To cope with those growing business and social problems successfully and to motivate continuing General Electric success, new patterns would have to be found. A first step was another GE innovation: the establishment of a five-man president's office, or corporate executive office as it was later called. Five top executive officers instead of one would handle the increasing complexity of top management responsibilities. To strengthen departmental operations, the then 110 departments were reorganized into 170 departments aggregated into 50 divisions (there had been 29) and the 50 divisions were organized into 10 groups (there had been 5). The whole idea was to establish operating components of such size and complexity that each could be effectively led to the achievement of future goals.

But the increasing number of profit centers was developing certain conceptual problems. In the decentralization concept, the department was both the profit center and the business; with growth of the departments and with changes in the environment, the logically defined business was now frequently becoming more than one department. A new identity crisis was developing. A highly motivating concept of decentralization that had successfully built a $2 billion business into a $10 billion business through growth from within might not be adequate to continue General Electric's record of success. President Fred Borch determined that new concepts would be needed, and he committed his efforts and his organization's talents to finding what they should be. Two outside consulting organizations—The Boston Consulting Group and McKinsey & Co.—also participated in the search. In the late 1970s, as General Electric surged past the $18 billion mark it was motivated and directed by uniquely new concepts that were right for the company and right for the times. These were General Electric's new concepts:

1. Separation of strategic planning, operational planning, and strategy review functions, along with provision for careful integration of these functions.
2. Monitoring and projection of environmental change as an input to strategic planning at both corporate and business levels.
3. Definition of the component parts of the company that can most appropriately become the focus for strategic planning and strategic decision making.
4. Resource allocation decisions at corporate level to support a portfolio of businesses that can assure both present and future success for the company.

As has been noted throughout this book, mission and business planning is an iterative process. Everything is related to everything else. What is done now may alter what was done before. Although the process seems sequential, it is really concurrent; and there is a continuing exchange of inputs and outputs among the various elements of the system. In the new GE concept, the fundamental building block for present success and future achievement is the definition of strategic planning components of the company. That is the answer to the question of identity for a very large, very diverse, and very successful company. Whereas decentralization answered the question of identity in a way that motivated remarkable achievement for a quarter of a century, new answers were needed. The 70 strategically separate departmental businesses of 1950 had grown to 170 separate profit center departments. No longer was each of them a strategically separate business. The businesses had grown and changed; the environment was different. Although each department functioned effectively as a profit center, what was the appropriate strategic focus? For planning and motivating company success, what were the appropriate businesses? GE answered the question by defining about forty strategic business units (SBU's). Each was identified as the point in the organization at which the strategic decisions for the business can really be made. About half of the SBU's were departments; about half were divisions consisting of several departments; and the remaining few were groups of several divisions. But each was a strategic business defined in the following terms:

1. A business mission unique from the mission of any other SBU. Mission in this case defined what the SBU is, why it exists, and the contribution it can make to the company.
2. Specified markets and competitors.
3. Strategic planning objectives with respect to products, markets, facilities, and organization relatively independent of those of other company SBU's.
4. Identified critical areas of success in terms of technology, marketing, and physical and financial resources.

For each SBU, the critical areas for success, once identified, provided a basis for evaluating both the industry and the business to determine appropriate resource strategy decisions. That was done in a grid system somewhat similar to the resource strategy grid described in Chapter 12. GE identified the critical areas for industry attractiveness and the SBU position in those critical areas. The results could be plotted on a grid, as illustrated in Figure 14-2. Included among the criteria were market growth prospects, GE present and prospective competitive position and market share, profitability, technology, and significant economic, social, and environmental factors. As shown on the business screen diagram, businesses A, B, and C were in very attractive industries. SBU's A and B had strong positions in attractive, fast-growing industries and would have priority for commitment of resources.

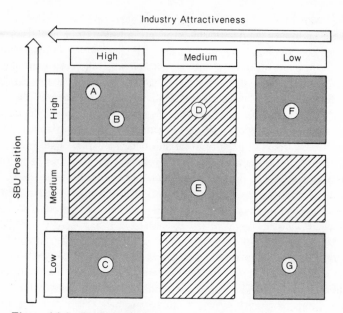

Figure 14-2. Business screen.

Business C was in an attractive, fast-growing industry also, but the SBU position was weak. Here, the decision might be to commit resources to improve company position. If the cost would be too high or the goal of strong position would be unattainable, the business itself could be marketed and the assets redeployed. That was the case with the GE computer business. After working for several years to gain adequate position, it was concluded that the best course was to combine the GE and Honeywell computer businesses into one new business that would have position, opportunity, and an adequate customer and technical base for success. For businesses like F, Figure 14-2, with a leadership position in a mature industry, the strategy is most often to optimize results by maintaining market position, quality, service, and value to customers and generating cash flow for investment in growth SBU's. Businesses like G, with weak position in an unattractive industry, would probably be inappropriate for General Electric from both a business and a social point of view.

From the strategic review of each SBU, the company can formulate its resource strategy to provide a balanced portfolio of businesses. Some SBU's will be contributing strongly to current income; some will be growing and developing to become the strong contributors of the future; some will be the source of future growth. Through the portfolio concept the company builds on its past achievement, relates to the environment in which it operates, and achieves a continuing renewal and success. Through the SBU concept General Electric makes possible both the wise strategic management of each business and the successful management of the total company.

As the company gained experience with strategic management of its business through SBU's, and as the number of SBU's grew, a new sector structure was put in place, with each SBU assigned to a sector. These broad sectors were: consumer, products and services, industrial, technical systems and materials, international, resources, and power systems. The sector represents the first level of segmentation of overall corporate strategy and has as its purpose the development of the company's overall mission within that sector. The SBU's in the consumer products and services sector, for example, develop strategic plans to optimize their competitive positions and use of resources within their served markets. The sector focuses on the higher level strategic issue of developing GE's total consumer thrust.

To insure continuing success, awareness of environment, awareness of change, and a kind of kinesthetic sense of the company's own development and achievement must be a continuing input to strategic planning. A corporate staff develops that awareness through expertise in critical areas: environmental, legal and political environment, human resources, financial resources, production resources, and technology. Through that expertise, there can be an appraisal of trends in the overall environment in which the company operates and their effect on and opportunities for the company. The study of changing values described in Chapter 1 is one example of that kind of appraisal. The staff also reviews SBU strategic plans, relates them to overall corporate strategy, and so develops and recommends courses of action to the corporate executive office on issues of strategic importance to the company.

Corporate level administrative work related to current operations that should be done at the corporate level because the company is a single entity or for reasons of economy or uniformity is also done at corporate staff level. Seven operations included in this administrative type work are: accounting, treasury, trust investment, legal, public relations, employee relations, and management personnel relations. There are also two components that assist and support operating units on a cost-liquidating fee basis: a corporate consulting service, including marketing, engineering, and manufacturing, and a corporate education service. General Electric for many years has emphasized continuing training and education and has maintained a major educational center for that purpose and included outstanding people from universities, public life, the professions, other institutions, and the company among its faculty. That orientation to learning and new knowledge is perhaps one of the important motive forces that has made General Electric an organization that continually develops and renews itself and a business enterprise that builds from success rather than rests on it.

General Electric intends to be an enterprise that's always good for its people, its customers, its suppliers, its owners, and all the communities in which it works. At all times it intends to have a meaningful identity, motivating goals, and constructive strategies. In its new concepts of organization and strategic planning it intends that the company shall follow a way of working together that will make the mission and the company way of operating always current. In this way, General Electric can continue to be an achieving enterprise.

Good answers don't last forever, but the achieving enterprise can forever continue to find a meaningful future and achieve it. From each success, new successes will be created. Progress will be more than the product of strong leadership; it will be the product of a strong organization. And it will begin—for the leaders throughout the organization and for the whole organization—with an awareness and an understanding of what's new—what's new technically, economically, socially, politically, organizationally, and environmentally that affects and will affect the mission of the enterprise.

Change today is rapid and even discontinuous from past experience. The achieving enterprise will operate in that kind of environment both to succeed today and to understand and develop the actions that will bring success in a changed and different tomorrow. The approach will be both pragmatic and creative so that the enterprise may operate effectively and efficiently today and have a strong and vital orientation to new conditions and the particular future that the enterprise has chosen for itself in its mission.

The Conceptual Approach

The foundation for the achieving enterprise is the conceptual approach—an organized search for the fundamentals, expressed as ideas, on which the success of the enterprise will be built. Much long-range planning that is done today involves monumental detal in numbers, a great amount of research, and voluminous documentary support. Often missing are the fundamentals. Unfound and unexpressed is a common understanding of the past, the present, and the future. A vast amount of work has been done, but too much time has been spent in the brickyard and not enough at the construction site. All the elements have been analyzed, but there emerges no design for the structure. The conceptual approach focuses on the structure. It emphasizes the fundamentals, takes more thinking, requires much less time and many fewer man-hours of work, and creates a successful future—this year, next year, and for the years ahead.

The conceptual approach begins with a definition of identity. First of all, there must be articulated a clear concept of what the enterprise is and what it intends to become. Present and future identity may be found and formulated and announced from the office of the chief executive, but then it may be too much the executive's and not enough the organization's. Identity is found best if there is participation by many in the important search for it. A better one will be found, and the prospects of its achievement will be much improved. The concept of our identity is more than what the leader says; it is what the organization does. Through dialog, the organization can find and formulate a clear and motivating concept of what the enterprise is and what it shall become. Finding its identity is the first task of the achieving organization.

When we know what our enterprise is and what it is striving to become, we can develop the goals most important to our present and future success. In addition to sales volume and profitability there will be goals in the key performance areas of market standing, innovation, productivity, physical and financial resources, motivation and organization development and public and environmental responsibility. By having a concept of our identity, present and future, we can establish the goals most important for us in each of the key performance areas. The goals become the control panel for guiding the enterprise to the future it has chosen. The concept of identity and the key performance area goals become both a long-range plan and a short-range operating plan in actionable form. Supportive goals will be established in divisions, departments, subunits, and individual jobs. The network of goals, in their achievement, carries the enterprise to its goals and the future it has defined for itself. Extended through the organization, the approach becomes a participative management by objectives way of achieving individual and company goals.

Not only is it important to have goals, it is equally important to have clearly thought out strategy approaches to how the goals will be achieved. Strategy answers the how question; it provides the way in which resources will be used to achieve goals. Such strategy approaches can be developed from a thorough knowledge of the business, the changing competitive situation, and the social-economic environment as it is related to the firm's own competences and limitations. From such knowledge and introspection, validated by objective measurement and experience in the environment, each successful firm will develop valid strategies that provide it with unique advantages in the achievement of its goals.

The Function of Mission
The enterprise as it is defined, the goals it seeks, and the strategy approaches it selects for achieving its goals become its mission. Because there has been participation throughout the organization in developing it, the mission not only stretches the organization to high levels of achievement but also coordinates all the related work of the organization that must be done to accomplish the goals. A business organization can be excitingly successful when led by a strong leader and management group that, with the entire organization, conceptualizes a mission and then guides all actions, decisions, and programs by that fundamental concept. But the development of such a mission is an iterative process—each new development, each company achievement, each environmental change has an impact on what has gone before so that the mission itself constantly evolves and changes. In this way it keeps up to date with the changing situation. When so developed and followed, it can remain fresh and alive and not become stale, procedural, and bureaucratic.

The mission itself is made reality through a large number of interrelated, very specific action plans carried out by individuals and work groups throughout the enterprise. Mission provides the integrating force that keeps all the plans related and coordinated to the achievement of the overall enterprise goals. And mission also provides the starting point for personal and organizational motivation.

The basic resource of any business enterprise is the people who make it up. How they work together to solve problems and achieve results provides the major leverage for outstanding success. In most organizations today there is tremendous opportunity for improving the motivation of employees and increasing the capability of the organization to achieve goals. Through motivation, the organization will not only respond effectively to change but also anticipate and make constructive use of change that occurs, or can occur, to move the enterprise toward the achievement of its goals. The creation of a successful future becomes the creation of successful people and successful groups. Developing successful people and groups is the subject of motivation, described in Chapters 8 and 9. Mission, if participatively developed, becomes the starting point for motivation.

Managerial Economics

The achievement of mission will require many skills. Important among them is an ability throughout the enterprise to use the discipline of managerial economics. In important ways, economics is different from accounting and the financial management methods now commonly used in the budgetary control of business enterprise. It is future-oriented and conceptual. It is quantitative but not necessarily precise. It uses accounting data but is not accounting. It can, through the methods described in Chapters 10 and 11, be of immense value to all members of the enterprise in developing decisions and programs to achieve company goals. Managerial economics and the other methods and skills described in this book can be used by enterprise to achieve objectives in all the key performance areas that determine the success of the enterprise.

Reporting Systems

Fundamental to the successful achievement of objectives for any organization are the measurements and the reporting systems used. For the kind of planning operations system described in this book, financially oriented control reports are inadequate. A new kind of reporting is required—one that measures performance in all the key performance areas over past, present, and future. Feedback does not go to managers for the evaluation of subordinates; it goes to everyone to help them get their jobs done and their goals achieved. The system is conceptually different from traditional financial control reporting, in which a financial model of the enterprise is projected for the budget period. The model is described in perhaps thousands of measurements. Then, for each monthly or other reporting period, the actual measurements achieved are compared with the measurements in the budget model and the variances are analyzed.

All that makes for a great deal of work but relatively little understanding. Much superior is the conceptually different system of achievement reporting described in Chapter 13. Achievement reporting first of all determines what is important in consideration of what the enterprise is striving to become. What is important becomes the major objectives in the key performance areas that determine the success of the enterprise. For each of the objectives the significant measurements will be followed to determine trends and changes in trends and whether they are moving toward the objectives set by the enterprise for its future. By looking ahead as we monitor current achievement, we are able to take action now to resolve problems and develop opportunities that by other methods of measurement would not yet be discernible. We become able to manage predictively and ahead of the need rather than by exception and after the fact. Achievement reporting provides feedback and guidance to all, not just to management.

There are no good answers from our past that can insure our future. The achieving enterprise is not successful because of yesterday's success or because it happens to be in a growth industry or is the beneficiary of some other favorable circumstance. It is excitingly successful because of what it has made itself. It uses each success to create new success and each achievement to create new achievement.

The achieving enterprise is an enterprise with a mission and a very special competence not only to achieve that mission but to change it as is appropriate to changing circumstance. It is a value system with goals that belongs to all the members and to the enterprise too. Skills and competences we must have, and continually develop in abundance. Having them, participation and dialog will help us find our way toward tomorrow by such methods as those described in this book. Good answers don't last forever. But the achieving enterprise can.

Index

59085

DATE DUE